Home Staging for Profit!

How to Start a Six Figure

Home Staging Business and

Begin in 7 Days or Less

Barbara Jennings, CSS/CRS

Original Copyright © 2006 by Barbara Jennings
12th Revised Edition © 2008 Barbara Jennings
Published by Ahava Enterprises, Inc. | Ahava Press

All rights reserved under International and Pan-American Copyright Conventions.

Library of Congress Catalog Card Number:TX 6-428-351
ISBN: 978-0-9618026-2-2

Cover Design by Eurie Jennings

Printed in the United States of America

15 14 13 12 11 10 9 8 7 6 5 4 3 2 1

Table of Contents

Chapter Four (129)

Chapter Five (157)

Chapter Six (204)

Additional Resources to Consider (Courses, Books, Visual Aids, Action Tools, CDs, Slideshows, Directory, Certification, Members Only Site, Free Forum, Free Newsletters)

Bonus Section (211)

Chapter One

Introduction

Background of Home Staging

The concept of "home staging" or "staged homes" or "home enhancement" has been around for many years, though it has never been as popular and recognized as it is today. But as popular and well known as it is, offering this type of service to real estate agents and home sellers is still a ground floor business opportunity. While you may encounter competition in your area, rest assured that there is plenty of work for everyone. When you consider that the average person in

the United States changes residence 10-15 times in a lifetime, you begin to understand just how huge the opportunity is. Of course, not all of these people own homes, not all of them are open to hiring a home enhancement "stager", but the vast majority of them need help, whether they realize it or not.

So it is merely your task to get the word out to them. As you begin studying this tutorial, you will learn just how to go about doing that. You will learn how to contact real estate agents and homeowners alike. Once you get into the business and get some projects under your belt, you will be in a position to gain more work as word of mouth, referrals and experience are on your side. The toughest time is in the beginning. If you follow the steps I outline for you, and you give it your earnest devotion and allow yourself time to learn, grow and develop, there is no reason why you cannot be as successful as you want to be in this business.

To help you further, we sponsor the largest online directory for home stagers and interior re-designers called **The International Staging and Redesign Directory**. It is not uncommon for members to receive phone calls or email from prospective clients in their local community seeking help. Since most people search for products and services over the internet these days, it would behoove you to list your business as soon as possible. A listing in the directory will also provide you with a monthly business building newsletter and notification of special discounts and sales of all our other resources itemized for you in Chapter Six – Exclusive Resources. We offer many resources to help you build your business, including certification courses, books, sales aids, management aids, promotional tools, newsletters and hundreds of free tips pages, a members only website and a free discussion forum for the exchange of ideas and tips.

Since the field of home staging and interior redesign are so closely related, you might also consider training yourself in the very creative redesign business. I have additional training tutorials and manuals that fully cover that business as well. You will see plenty of opportunities through your study of these materials to get more information on redesign, not only in the training aspects, but all of the fantastic tools of the trade that I also offer to help you in your business. Be sure to check these out as they can really help you achieve all your business goals and do so much faster as well.

Real Estate Agents and Home Sellers

Real estate agents and brokers can be a great asset to you and your business. Not only do they know people who are buying and selling homes and who may have the greatest potential of becoming your clients, they will probably be people who recognize an immediate need for a home to look attractive in order to sell.

Let's face it. There are hundreds and hundreds of homes on the market that look pretty horrible inside. Not because of the home itself. But because of the way the owner has decorated or their failure to keep the home repaired and up-to-date. Some homes are sold empty, some are foreclosures, and some are sold with the owners still living on the premises. Whenever there is furniture present, one of the easiest solutions, of course, is the proper arrangement of furniture and accessories in the home. But even more crucial is the need for de-cluttering, organization and minor repairs.

One thing I can guarantee! There are many, many sellers who need help to make their homes instantly look more inviting to a potential buyer. Sellers tend to look at the home as an owner with emotional attachments, not as a buyer. This is a virtually untapped goldmine if you can get some agents and brokers seriously pushing your service to sellers they represent whose homes are unappealing. It is particularly essential if there is a housing glut where there are more homes for sale than there are buyers looking to buy. Most sellers are eager to get offers as soon as possible. Many of them do not know that they are defeating themselves right from the start because their home is just a "turn off" to potential buyers.

There are many ways to go about contacting agents and brokers. You can personally visit their offices, you can write letters and send cards, or you can telephone them. You should spend quality time each week getting the word out about your services and getting agents to look at your web site, where you have, hopefully, addressed all these issues in living color. More about all of this later.

You can even drive through the residential sections near you and look for the signage in front of the homes up for sale. Then contact the homeowners, either in person or by leaving them a flyer or business card. Whatever you do, don't try to sell them at this stage on hiring you. Just sell them on the idea of talking to you. At the same time, write down the name and phone number of their agent. Offer the agent a deal on providing the service to their client as a free marketing strategy. Visit the web sites of real estate offices near you. Most of them list the names and email address of all their agents.

Send them a personalized email telling them about your services. Direct them to your web site for more information. Be sure to contact them periodically to remind them of your service. Let them know of homeowners whom you have aided in getting a quick sale. One of the best aspects about working and developing a relationship with real estate agents is that they can be an on-going source of referrals for you.

Both the real estate agent and the seller are highly motivated to close the sale as soon as possible, in most cases, so they are both ripe prospects for your specialized home enhancement service.

Before   After

Home Enhancement Services

Home Enhancement, otherwise known as "home staging, staged homes, ready to sell services", is the process of getting a house ready to be sold. It can be as simple as moving the furniture around that already exists, or as elaborate as hiring a wide variety of people to come in and "transform" the home. While the scale of the job will vary, the whole goal always is to sell the house. You can learn how to do this as my student, Barb Coombs, so beautifully did here.

One should always keep in mind that there is a big difference between preparing a home to live in and preparing a home to be sold. I will be discussing the differences between the two goals as you proceed further into this material.

This process began as early as 1976 in the state of Washington when a real estate professional named Barb Schwarz began to help agents help their sellers better prepare their homes for sale. The idea was to help the sellers move the property in a shorter amount of time and at a higher price.

It can simply be a matter of removing clutter and rearranging furniture to totally redecorating and re-furnishing all the rooms in a home - generally through the use of rented furniture and accessories, which you or the seller arrange for. You might even decide to stock some "props" yourself in your garage or a storage container.

Costs will naturally vary depending on the scope of the project. Some home sellers will simply want advice and will pay you an hourly fee. Other sellers and realtors prefer to have a professional stager do all the work and arrange for all necessary furniture rentals and repair services. So the average fee could be from a few hundred dollars to $15,000-25,000 depending on the size, condition, number of services you provide and the asking price for the home and the time it has been on the market.

Under no circumstances should you guarantee that the home will sell by a specified time. You can only promise that your services should spark more interest and likely increase the dollar amount a buyer will be willing to spend. While it is not at all uncommon for homes that have been on the market 2-3-4 or more months without offers to sell within 24 hours or within days, this is not something you should ever promise anyone specifically.

Tips on Home Enhancement Services

Bear in mind that Home Enhancement Services are different from redesign services. The goal of "redesign" or "one day decorating" is to bring out the personality of the homeowner and make their home more functional and more attractive. However, the goal of "home staging" or "home enhancement" is to feature the home, not the occupants. You never want potential buyers to get caught up looking at the furnishings, or photographs, or personal items. You want them to solely concentrate on the home and helping them to see themselves living happily in such a home. These are distinctly two very, very different goals.

In Home Enhancement, the idea is to **de-personalize** the home. By eliminating all furniture and accessories that are not needed or that make the room look cluttered, you will make the home seem larger. This will be far more appealing to prospective buyers.

When selling a home, it has become a *product* and you want to emphasize its good features, while de-emphasizing or eliminating it's less than ideal features. How well you do this for your client can make a significant difference. To compete with the competition, your seller must have the home priced right and it must look better than the other *products* in its price range. You must help the homeowner present it to prospective buyers in the best possible light.

Most buyers set out looking for a home with a special criteria list. It is often quite impersonal. The better you "show off" the features of your client's home, the better chance you'll have of exciting a buyer. In staged homes, as opposed to un-staged homes, it is not uncommon for buyers to so fall in love with the home that they let go of their criteria list altogether. That is the power of making a home stand out from the competing homes on the market at that time in that price range.

When a home is up for sale, the goal is to sizzle the HOME not the PERSONALITY of the present owner. This is a very different concept so be sure to keep it in mind. When done right, it will have a positive effect on buyer prospects. You see, they walk into a house carrying with them all their hopes and dreams for a new life in a new environment. How they are made to feel in the home of your client will be directly reflected in the sales price and the number of offers your home seller receives.

We all have the same common desires: prestige, love, dreams, hopes, goals. You will be helping your home seller to maximize on all of these inherent feelings by intensifying them when prospects walk through the door.

The higher the asking price, the more excitement you need to generate in a buyer. The higher the price, the more you need a buyer to be overwhelmed with the "Wow!" factor. You need to help the home seller inspire their prospects. You want the prospect to walk in and say, "This is where I'll curl up with my favorite book." Or "This is where I'll entertain the boss, or the relatives for Thanksgiving!" Or "This is where the kids will play and that is where we will relax and watch TV!"

The whole goal, boiled down to one statement is, you want to create for the home seller an atmosphere of spaciousness and homey-ness all at the same time. When you achieve this, the final sales price will surely be higher. Making the inside and outside of the home attractive, organized and yes, even neutralized, will be a very important part of your job as a home staging specialist.

The best situation in the world for your home seller is to have 10-15 prospects all bidding against each other for that home. This is called a "bidding war". In a competitive market, some homeowners will be willing to pay some pretty substantial fees for someone to transform their humdrum rooms into scrumptious interiors. The talented person who gets that assignment -

hopefully you - will not only get the opportunity to help someone else achieve their goals and dreams but make some handsome profit in the process.

I've worked professionally in the redesign/home staging profession since 1986 in Southern California. But it doesn't matter where you live. You will always be surrounded by people who are buying and selling houses, either to live in or to rent out. The opportunities are enormous!

You see, a lot of people don't know how to properly prepare a home to put it on the market and many, even if they did know, just don't want to take the time to do it properly or don't have the time. The mistakes they make are very common. But everyone knows what they like *when they see it*. So you need to listen very carefully during the interview portion which you will learn how to do. You'll need to ask the right questions and then utilize all that information when you plan out the new Enhancement Plan.

Benefits You Can Expect

I don't know about you, but I love a business idea that has minimal overhead and minimal risk. That couldn't be truer of the home enhancement consulting business. You are providing a valuable service. You get paid instantly: a deposit in advance and the balance upon completion of the service. The costs to generate business and maintain it are quite low compared to most businesses.

You can do it part time or full time. You can work from your home. You work strictly by appointment, so you have the luxury of working when you want to. You can have another career at the same time - or even an interior redesign business simultaneously. You can coordinate your work schedule with your family-time schedule

The career is fresh and innovative. It's prestigious. It's very creative and challenging and no two projects are ever alike. You have no boss except yourself. You can choose your clients and don't have to choose to work with any prospective client whom you feel uncomfortable with.

You can work as much as you want or as little as you want. What more could you desire from a career or profession?

What You Should Know About My Unorthodox Style

As you read this book, you'll probably notice there may be a big difference between my writing style and that of other authors. To understand me, you need to understand a few things about my philosophy of business, the tactics I use and the reasons behind them. Here are five issues that sometimes surface:

1) Self Promotion. The truth of the matter is that I fully believe in myself and I make no bones about it. I believe in me. I know where my strengths lie and where my weaknesses lie too. I promote my strengths so that you will do the same for yourself. Just as you will learn to promote the assets of your client's home and furnishings, diminishing its flaws, so too I promote my assets and diminish my flaws. No one ever became successful who did not believe in themselves. Donald Trump and Mohammed Ali are two of the most obvious advocates of the concept of "self promotion" in our generation, in my humble opinion, but because they had the audacity to proclaim themselves to be "the greatest" in their fields, and they backed up their claims, they went on to build massive empires in their respective fields. Listen and learn.

Every time you have applied for a job, you have been put in a position to "sell yourself" to the prospective employer. You've had to brag about yourself to an extent. If you did not, you probably were not hired. No one wants to hire someone with a poor self image – not by choice, anyway. Every employer – every potential client you visit or contact – only wants to hire those with a strong, positive opinion about themselves. That is a given.

When you're starting out, you've got to create your own sense of expertise. If you don't, you'll never reach first base in your business. So you've got to toot your own horn big and loud in the beginning. As your business grows and your reputation with it, you will find plenty of people willing to extol your virtues for you, but that takes time.

One visit to my website, to my testimonial page will show you I have plenty of people singing the praises of my programs. I don't need to do it for myself, but I write with the conviction of someone who believes in my self. And when you write your promotional materials in the near future, you need to write with the same kind of gusto and enthusiasm and confidence. So as you read this book, read it also with the mindset of learning from me the kind of attitude that creates leaders, experts, strong marketing copy, and profitable salesmanship. Take on for yourself a bit of attitude like Trump or Ali. It will help you build a business that lasts.

2) I do proclaim myself to be an expert and I've got the bumps and bruises, the failures and the successes to prove it. I've paid my dues. I've hung in there when it was rough. I've overcome obstacles. I've studied. I've worked. I've studied some more. I've worked some more. I've built my business into a mini empire. But significantly more than that I've become a mentor and teacher to thousands who depend on me every week and every month to be there for them, I've helped them grow, answered their questions, praised them when they did great, empathized with them when they faltered, and picked them up and cheered them on when they needed it. So, yeah, that makes me an expert in their minds. I've been there for them. I'll be here for you too.

3) You should know that I never ever push a product unless I know for a certainty it will help you build and grow your business. That's not my style at all. I plug products that will help you. I plug because I know how important they are to long term success. You don't have to buy any of them. Really you don't. But before you can make an intelligent decision on whether they are right for you or not, you first have to know they exist and you have to know where to find them if you decide you want them. So as you go through this manual, remember that I've pre-designed and pre-ordered and pre-created for you. I'll tell you what they are, how they will help you and why I think you should consider getting them in Chapter Six. I'm not going to encourage you to purchase something you don't need.

We're on a journey together. Your success is my success. I take that very seriously. So should you. I ask you, as you go through this manual, to think carefully about investing in your future. You're worth it. No business is built over night (certainly not a six figure income) and usually costs a whole lot more to start and nurture than everything I offer put together. So please read with an open mind and see my heart. If you don't need something, I'll tell you. But if you read about something several times, that should give you an idea of its importance for your future success.

4) I'm the first to admit I'm <u>not</u> a professional writer. I write the way I talk so I guess that's why I often receive mail saying it seems like I am sitting across the table from my readers, training them personally. Each time we update this manual, we try to catch pesky typos, woeful syntax and the like, but some are probably hiding still. My apologies in advance to you English majors and journalists if that is still the case. I am working on it bit by bit.

5) This manual was originally self-published by choice and by design. It is not true that self-published works are void of worth as some would have you believe. This choice is for your benefit, not mine. This way you can be sure you've purchased the latest edition currently available and not a book created some years go and never updated at all.

Major publishing houses print hundreds of thousands of copies in the first run to make it profitable for them. Since it could take a very, very long time before that many could be sold in a small niche market like staging, there would be no reprints or updates for some lengthy time period. But by publishing in small quantities, I update this book often. This is not the first edition, and it certainly won't be the last one either. But with being a small press publication, there are some inherent problems you should know about.

First, digital press is the only economical route for short run books. And while this type of media has its advantages, reproduction of photos does not seem to be one of them. It is very difficult to get the pictures reproduced properly. They either come out a bit too dark or a bit too light, especially when they are actual candid, un-doctored project pictures like the ones I'll be showing you. These are actual staging pictures. They are NOT taken by professional photographers with a multitude of photographic lights and high powered cameras and later "fixed up" in studios. No, these are real world photos – the kind you'll be taking for yourself for your own portfolio. To show you any other type would be misleading to you of the true nature of the business as you will experience it. If you want to see some of the photos in color, there is a link in the bonus section where you can go online and download a report with lots of color photos.

You might also, at first glance, think the pictures are dated. **They are not.** As a matter of fact, the pictures are quite recent. It is the homes that are older or the furnishings owned by the homeowner that may be dated. This is par for the course. You will be working in older homes as well as newer homes and, in time, your own pictures may take on a "dated feeling" because of the housing tract you may be working with. If your projects are in newly developed tracts, your pictures will look more up-to-date but that's just the way home staging goes. The furniture can be anything from Grandma's hand-me-downs to newly acquired modern furniture and everything in between. Just so you know.

Ken Kobayashi, author of the National Bestseller "Rich Dad - Poor Dad", was a self-published author. He might not be now, but the book was originally a self-published work. Corey Rudl, who has sold more copies of his insightful book "Car Secrets Revealed" than any other internet marketer, was a self-published author - his book is reported to be the all time most successful book on the internet. Corey died in a tragic car accident unfortunately, but left behind a wealth of helpful guides and training for the world to enjoy. Thank goodness there are self-publishers around like Corey and Ken and a host of other knowledgeable, talented experts who chose self-publishing over 3rd party publishing houses. I count myself privileged to join my mentor's in self-publishing.

If you want to seriously build a business (and I mean a six or even a seven figure business), you've got to be aggressive in marketing it. That's why I'm modeling strong promotional copy within these pages. Learn from my example. Be free and write strong sales copy for yourself.

Cultivate a positive attitude about everything. Express your gratitude to people willing to help you along the way. Look for ways to be complimentary to others, even if you disagree with them. You've no doubt heard the saying, "What goes around, comes around." It is really true in business. Those that give always receive back in like kind. It is called "The Law of Attraction". If you give, life will give back to you. If you complain, life will give you more to complain about.

A Bit About Me

I am a Southern California interior re-designer/home stager/graphic artist/artist/consultant/author and mentor to thousands. My career in design began in 1972 when I started my own graphic arts and printing business. I staged my first home in 1975, only back then no one called it home staging. In 1983, having tired of the graphic arts business, I began a successful corporate art consulting career offering decorating advice here and there for my corporate clients, providing services in their homes that was separate from my art consulting services. During those years I designed and implemented hundreds of art collections for small, medium, and large businesses, including several Fortune 1000 and 500 companies. I also wrote and self published the popular book of 101 wall grouping designs called, <u>Where There's a Wall -- There's a Way.</u>

Not being challenged enough, I began to market my rearrangement and staging talents and services in the residential market. My concept was simply to work with clients on a smaller scale than full service designers. I had discovered by that time that the average American homeowner has a pretty good sense of what furnishings and accessories to acquire, but where they struggle most is in the area of furniture and accessory **placement**. Without good placement, the most beautiful furnishings fall flat and homes won't sell very well. Whether a home is staged or redesigned, the furniture needs to be in the right place for it to look attractive and be functional.

Since 1986, I have simultaneously served both corporate and residential clients with art and interior design services. I have trained thousands of people in the process to start their own businesses and currently host one of the largest directories of stagers and re-designers on the internet. Almost all of them look to me as a personal mentor to help them grow their businesses. In addition to that, I have become a published artist. My work has been published in the form of decorative art prints by The McGaw Group of New York and Galaxy of Graphics of New York though they have sold out now and are harder to find.

You need to get the proper instruction, if you want to succeed, so I've itemized plenty of additional training and helpful aids for you in Chapter Six. Please take the time to peruse it.

Now that you know a bit about me and what makes me tick, let's get to work to make your dreams come true whatever they may be. You might just be looking for extra income – or you may be desirous of a six figure income (or even larger). The opportunity before you is endless and there is no ceiling on the amount of money you could earn. But you've got to have a firm goal in mind that is specific, and you've got to be willing to do whatever it takes to achieve your goals. If you have the passion, and you work hard, there is no reason why you cannot follow in the footsteps of those that have gone before you.

The Essence of Home Staging

Examples of Home Enhancement

The house was a nondescript three-bedroom, one-and-a-half bath split level in Illinois. It had tiny bedrooms and a one-car garage. Even its owner admitted that no buyer was going to find it very exciting.

That is, until home enhancement services were brought in. In just a few days, the house was cleaned, items were boxed up to remove clutter and furniture was relocated to better enhance the home, traffic flow was improved. Accessories were removed or strategically placed to liven and brighten.

The home was made to look like a model home, so people could visualize themselves living there.

The strategy worked. The house sold in three weeks for just $1,600 less than the listing price—in a market where listings in its price range were taking 79 days on average to sell.

Another charming home in the mountains had been on the market for 3 months with only one offer, which had fallen through because of financing issues. The home enhancement specialist arrived and worked on the home for just one day. Before the open house day arrived, the homeowner had an offer and a second offer came in the day of the open house. Now there was a bidding war.

But Does it Really Work?

Real estate professionals who use staging swear by it, no matter what part of the country they work in or the price range of the houses they sell.

The average real estate agent has five seconds to sell a home—five seconds to make an impact on the buyers when they first walk in the door. Staging ensures that that impact is a good and lasting one.

You can get staging ideas by looking at design magazines. Plus, you could go view several homes a week and learn what features interest buyers and what turns them off based on how you react yourself.

One house listed was decked out in colors from the 1970s, with avocado green and heavy gold decor and a seller who didn't want to put much money into the house. The house had already languished on the market for three months, but when the home enhancement specialist took over, the agent removed it from the market for a week so it could be prepared. She took out the old-looking lamps and furnishings and stowed them in the garage. Then she added subtle earth tone accessories in order to play down the greens and gold in the house. She removed the homeowner's artwork from the walls, replaced his outdated accessories with candleholders and plants, covered his shabby bedspread with one of her own and added mounds of pillows to create a cozy look. She even had her own gardener plant flowers for added curb appeal.

A sales associate with Coldwell Banker has been using professional stagers for about 10 years. "I believe that my homes sell quicker and for more money as a result of staging," he says.

He enhances even his moderately priced listings. He recently hired a home enhancer to work on a condominium he listed at $184,900. The unit was vacant, and he knew that vacant homes are difficult to sell because buyers have trouble visualizing what they'll look like furnished. So he paid the enhancer $1,000 to furnish the bedroom, the baths, and the dining room, using props from her inventory. The result? The seller received multiple offers on the unit, and it sold within a week—for more than the listing price.

Some agents whose clients live in swank areas usually have impeccably decorated homes that need little styling. But when agents list a home, they rely on staging to give it lived-in appeal.

One agent hired an enhancer to fill a 7,000-square-foot house with furniture, draperies, and accessories. Although he had not used the firm before, he was impressed that the company was able to stage the house within a week. The agent paid between $15,000 and $20,000 to stage the house, absorbing the expense himself and treating it as part of his marketing plan.

The payoff? The house, originally listed at $3.995 million and on the market for six months, sold within three weeks, for $3.75 million. "That house actually had very lovely architectural features but it was empty, and a lot of times buyers just don't have any vision. Once it's enhanced with furniture, however, they can see themselves sitting by the fire."

Selling Home Enhancement Services to Clients

Empty homes just aren't going to be capable of helping a buyer visualize their family living in the home. Yes, you can see the architecture easily, but even the nicest home falls a bit flat when it is empty.

Although the subliminal effects of enhancement can't be ignored, that doesn't mean that all clients will be sold on the idea — especially when they realize that you're planning to hide their favorite plaid recliner in the basement or stow all of the adorable family portraits in a box. It takes finesse to avoid insulting or offending a seller. You've got to make them start seeing the home as a "product" and no longer their treasured and prized dwelling place.

Agents will have to convince their sellers by emphasizing that their homes will sell faster or for more money if they make a few changes. But they have to do it with the utmost caution and care. "You could really put a seller off because it is still their home after all".

Therefore agents understand that the best way to make home enhancement acceptable is to get homeowners to separate their emotions from the sales process, to convert the image of "This is my family's home" into "This is a house, a commodity that I need to sell."

If the agent gets sellers focused on the house they're purchasing, it helps make home enhancement go easier. "If they invest their emotions in their new place, it helps make "letting go of their precious home a little easier", one agent said.

Using as much of the seller's own furnishings as possible and just rearranging and eliminating one or two pieces is a good way to both hold down costs and make the process less threatening to sellers, suggests one agent. However, it is quite common to need to delete a good half to 2/3rds of the furniture and accessories, depending on how fully furnished the home is. "I always tell them that if they were taking their car to trade in, they'd get all the junk out of the back seat and get it washed and waxed, maybe even detailed," the agent said. "All we're really doing with staging is detailing the house."

Have the agent suggest to reluctant sellers that it's their policy to stage every home they list. "I believe real estate salespeople are doing a disservice to their clients if they don't introduce the concept and ask the seller to get it done," this agent added.

How Staging Makes a Difference

The staging of these houses show what an impact the practice can have on a home's appeal to buyers. Some of these examples were projects done by trainees, people just like you, who in many cases had absolutely no prior experience in design or staging. With the right kind of training and utilizing just good common sense, great results can be achieved for clients, even if the changes are minor.

Guest Room: Before

Guest Room: After

Family Room: Before

Family Room: After

Balcony: Before

Balcony: After

Empty Bedroom: Before   Bedroom: After

Dining Room : Before and After

Bathroom: Before and After

Dining Room: Before   Dining Room: After

Bedroom: Before   Bedroom: After

Kitchen: Before   Kitchen: After

Bed Room: Before
Bed Room: After

Empty Living Room: Before Staging
Living Room: After Staging

Kitchen: Before Staging

Kitchen: After Staging

As you can see from these few examples, little changes can have a very positive impact on the reception a home gets from prospective buyers. While the condition of the home can involve a huge amount of work, including removal of furniture and debris, cosmetic repairs and such, even homes that are in excellent condition but without a charming ambience need the services of home staging experts – you could be that individual helping to sell that home more profitably while making a nice profit for yourself.

Be aware, however, this manual may not be sufficient to give you all of the training you should have, and you should know that when you are being paid to do a project, answers to questions that are posed to you should be answers with authoritative training behind them. That's why you should consider getting additional design training, management tools and even advanced training if you're really serious about building a career for yourself.

Top 10 Mistakes Sellers Make

Even under the best of circumstances, selling a home can be difficult - and most certainly time consuming. While you're not the seller and probably not the agent, you should know the top mistakes that sellers tend to make. This will not only help you as an enhancer/stager, but will help you help the agent and home seller.

- **As a Stager, You Must Know "Why" the Seller is Selling** – There's a difference between sellers selling because they "want" to and selling because they "need" to. The difference can color how the seller views the property and the stress they will feel. Sellers who just want to sell the property can take less aggressive means, list at a higher price and wait it out until they get what they want. Those that need to sell tend to be more aggressive and might even be desperate to sell in a hurry for a lower price.
- **Under-preparation Before Putting Home on Market** - A seller won't get as much for the property if they sell it in an "as is" condition. It will also take longer to sell unless it is enhanced. They tend not to keep it as clean as they should as well. Most buyers want a "plug and play" type home - one where all they have to do is move in. They don't want to have to repair and replace.
- **Some Sellers Choose the Wrong Agent or Sell "By Owner"** - It's a myth to believe that because you are selling it yourself that you are saving money. All too often the house sits on the market for months, even years. It's important to pick an aggressive agent - one who is highly motivated to help you get the property sold. The longer a house sits on the market, the more wary potential buyers become, wondering what's wrong with the house from the outset.
- **Stale Listings** - That bears repeating. The longer a house sits on the market, the more wary potential buyers become. Even other agents start focusing on what's wrong with the property instead of what's right. If a house sits on the market for 3 months or longer, there is a significant problem that needs to be quickly rectified. If a home sits on the market for 6 months without offers, it needs to be pulled from the market, the price lowered or some significant work done to it by a home enhancer.
- **The Overpriced Home** - It's natural to want to sell a home for top dollar. But arriving at the correct figure will depend on several factors, not the least of which is condition, location and the current market. Failing to price a home correctly can be a deadly mistake.
- **Being in the Home During a Presentation** - Think about it. I hate to shop in stores where clerks follow me around, no matter how well meaning they might be. I'll walk out every time without buying anything. The same is true for selling a home. Sometimes sellers hang around trying to influence a buyer's decisions. Unless they are acting as their own agent, this can kill a sale instantly.
- **Showing a House That Smells** - The most common odor problems come from pets, cigarette smoke, strong foods and, yes, baby diapers. Homes should be thoroughly monitored by people who don't live there. They will be more likely to pick up on a bad scent than people who live there daily.
- **Failure to Make Final Mortgage Payment Before Closing** - Even if a contract has been signed by the buyer, it's vital that the home seller continues to make timely house

payments on the mortgage. Most house payments are due on the first of the month. Final figures are calculated based on the number of payments the owner has actually made. Some get huge surprises, hit with late fees and have their credit dinged for failing to make that last payment on time. They don't realize that if there is any over payment, they will get refunded by the escrow company.

- **Not Recognizing a Good Offer** - Typically the first offer a seller gets is the best one. But it's common for them to refuse the first offer, believing that a better one will follow. If the offer is close to the seller's minimum sales price, the owner should attempt to make the deal happen.
- **Setting a Poor Closing Date** - There are substantial tax savings for sellers who have lived in their home for twenty-four months or longer out of the last 5 years. the IRS allows a single person $250,000 of tax free profits and a married couple $500,000 of tax free profit if they have lived in the home for 24 months or longer. If a home is closed in 23 months instead of 24, the seller will owe tax on all of the capital gains from the house, not just the excess over and above the figures stated above.

Don't assume that the agents or home sellers know these facts. A wise home enhancer will use these typical mistakes to help sell their services.

Top 10 Most Common Problems

Before you start talking to a home seller about the cosmetic things you want to do, it might behoove you to at least check into the top 10 most common problems that are universally identified as ranking high in occurrence rankings.

- **Structural Problems** - Obviously you're not going to have expertise in this area. But at least try to look over the property with an eye open to this possibility. Structural problems can show up in the foundation, walls, the floor joists, the rafters, the windows and door headers. Look to see if there are any cracks in those areas.
- **Environmental Problems** - Here is a brief list of some of the issues a home could have: radon gas, lead-based paint, contaminated drinking water, leaking underground oil tanks, asbestos, formaldehyde, carbon monoxide, pesticides. Many of these issues are not visible to the naked eye. You might want to ask the seller if any studies have been done on the property for structural and/environmental problems.
- **Drainage or Grading Problems** - If the property has improper drainage or grading, water can collect and lead to problems that produce mold. Look for damp basements or crawl spaces. The seller might need to have the exterior re-graded or have new roof gutters and downspouts installed. These types of things tend to be addressed by property inspectors, but it can't hurt you to be aware of these types of issues.
- **Electrical Wiring That is Dangerous** - It's a common problem to find DIY sellers with improper electrical wiring. Many homes just don't have adequate outlets for today's lifestyle, especially since the home computer came along. Poorly installed electrical wiring can cause electrical fires putting every member of the family in serious danger.
- **Poor Ventilation** - Look for damage to plaster, wallboard and windows which can cause poor ventilation. A home shouldn't be drafty, but it should also not be over-sealed. This can lead to rot and mold issues. Look for vents and fans in bathrooms with no windows. Check out the cooking areas as well.
- **Roof Problems** - I don't recommend going up on the roof. It's dangerous and not your expertise anyway, but look from below to see if there are any obvious signs of roof damage, such as missing tiles or shingles, rotted wood, termite damage. Look for brown spots on the ceilings of the interior rooms.
- **Heating/Cooling Problems** - Look briefly at the water heater, and the heating/cooling units, usually placed in the garage. Blocked chimneys, leaking water heaters and the like are indications of neglect. Ask how often these systems have been serviced by a

professional. Most of the time home owners ignore these systems until one day one of them stops working.

- **Exterior Problems** - Look over the exterior windows, doors and walls where water and drafts can enter the home. Whatever the seller can do to eliminate discomfort and lower the utility bills would benefit and bring about a better deal. Look for adequate caulking and weather-stripping.
- **Poor Plumbing** - Look for annoying things like dripping faucets, leaky pipes and toilets, toilets that make noise when not in use, clogged drains. Plumbing is more likely to be a major problem in older homes where one can encounter leaky gas pipes, sprinkler systems that leak and so forth.
- **Overall Poor Maintenance Signals** - It's not hard to spot poor maintenance issues such as peeling paint, jammed garbage disposals, rotting decks, light fixtures that are broken, holes in the walls. If you see any of this type of problem it is a strong indication of much more to follow. There will no doubt be many things that you as a home enhancer cannot and will not attempt to fix. But noting these things on your paperwork and having a brief discussion with the seller about their plans to correct these issues will only serve to present you in a more professional light.

Identifying the Do-It-Yourselfers

Don't expect that every home seller will be interested in your services, no matter how affordable you might make them. Some people are just "dyed in the wool" DIY - "do it yourself" people. I tend to be one of them, even though I fully recognize that there are many situations where I would be further ahead to pay someone. Let's face it. There are just some things I'd rather do myself, no matter how much time they take.

But for every person who wants to do it themselves or who just can't see past the cost of hiring you, there will be plenty of others that will see the value and not want to do what's necessary themselves. They will gladly pay someone to come in and handle the time-consuming details for them. That's where you come in.

So here is a nifty list of how to know, in advance, whether you're dealing with a do-it-yourselfer. You'll want to casually pose some of these questions, either to the agent (who already knows the client) or to the home seller directly.

- Do you enjoy doing physical work yourself?
- What is your level of patience and persistence?
- What are your work habits? Do you have good follow through?
- What is the time factor? Will you have adequate time to complete the tasks? (Note: The estimated time should always be doubled or tripled.)
- What kinds of tools do you have? Are they the kind of tools you'll need?
- What kind of expertise do you have in making repairs and other home improvements?
- What is your level of tolerating unfinished projects for a period of time?
- How much stress can you manage before it negatively impacts your family?
- How familiar are you with the necessary steps involved in each project?
- What manufacturer instructions do you have on hand? Have you looked through them to understand the scope of the project?
- Will you need assistance to complete the job or can you manage it by yourself?
- Have you checked with your city for local building codes and permit requirements?
- Have you thought about what you would do if you are unable to complete the project?
- Is it safe for you to handle the project? What is the state of your health? (Some projects, such as putting on a new roof, rewiring, and so forth are much better handled by professionals. One's health and safety should be priority ONE!)

- How about procurement of materials? Who will supply materials? Do they deliver?
- What are the real reasons you would do things yourself? Financial? Other? Have you considered the costs of materials, your time and necessary tools into the equation?

What a Home Stager Must Do

So to recap briefly, let's break it down into its component parts and discuss the issues thoroughly. We'll also be discussing the proper attitude of the enhancer, typical tasks, goals and expectations and why and how all of these aspects come into play. If you are also an interior designer or re-designer, you're going to have to put yourself into a different mindset for home staging. You're going to have to let go of your innermost desire to make a room look and feel complete. Because in selling a property successfully, you do not want to fill the room up. You want to leave just enough to make the rooms feel warm and inviting, but keep it sparse enough to make the room look as big and spacious as possible.

See Homes Through "Buyer's Eyes"

Since the home seller is emotionally attached to the home, the way it looks, the way it feels to them, they are quite literally unable to disassociate their feelings about the home in the way they should. Buyers arrive at a property with no invested feelings. They are, therefore, far more objective about the house than the seller can ever be.

First impressions are formed instantly. The buyer arrives at the property and gets an impression from the curb. They get another impression right at the front door. Another impression is created upon opening the door. Those are the strongest impressions they will receive. They will spend the rest of the time in the home seeking to validate their first impression - whether it is a good one or a poor one. So you definitely want to have strong first impressions.

Develop Buyer's Eyes

So what can you do to hone your ability to use buyer's eyes? You might start with first referring to the dwelling as a "house", not a "home". The word "house" carries little emotional attachment to it. Whenever you're with the seller, refer to the dwelling as their "house" and not their "home". This will assist them in detaching their feelings from the structure as well.

Here are some quick tips on things you can do to strengthen your ability to relate to buyers.

- Visit Model Homes - Model home designers are fantastic at making spaces appeal to buyers. The homes are completely clean. There are no fingerprints anywhere. No scuff marks. No grease stains. The toiletries are fresh. The windows are crystal clean. Nothing is broken. All the walls are beautiful. Nothing needs paint. All the doorknobs work. They know how to create the right ambience to make visitors feel comfortable and visualize living in the home.
- Visit Open Houses - It's always a good idea to check out the local competition your seller is up against. Watch buyers going through those houses. Listen to their conversations. Watch what they are looking at and what seems to attract the most attention, whether negative or positive. Write down your first impressions and the reasons you reacted as you did. Write down the questions you hear yourself asking as you walk through the homes. Think about why you do or don't respond favorably to the home. Think about the natural progression of your viewing the home - which rooms were you most curious about?

- Subscribe to several decorating magazines. Study the pictures. Professional photographers and designers work very closely together to get precisely the right kind of picture to put in the magazine that highlights the space in the best manner. Think about your reactions to the arrangements. The accessories. The impact of the background (walls, windows).
- Keep a Notebook - There will usually be so many things that affect you from one open house or model home to another that it will be wise to keep a notebook. Write down all of the things that affected you positively. Write down all of the typical things that affected you negatively. Most of us react to the same kinds of stimuli, both positive and negative. Understanding what affects you will also help you key into the aspects that will most likely affect other people.

Use Objectivity

So it becomes crucial for you, the home enhancer, to view the house inside and out in the same manner that a prospective buyer would view it. You have to put yourself in the shoes of the buyer. Developing "buyer's eyes" will help you look at the home realistically. You should ask yourself upon arrival at every home you stage the following questions:

- Do I want buyers to see this?
- Do I want buyers to feel this?

By seeking to always answer these too questions with a positive response, you will help the seller make a strong impact on every potential buyer. You will help the agent encourage a sale. If the home is immediately crossed off the buyer's list, there isn't a prayer of selling the home.

Identify the Home's Faults

Home sellers tend to have "blinders" on. They can't get past the remembrances associated with the home. It is usually hard for them to give up the home in the first place as they will never be able to revisit the memories stored and preserved there. It's amazing how they stop seeing the flaws: the chipped paint on the window sill, the crack in the window, the missing door stops, the stain on the ceiling. But, believe me, the buyers see all of these flaws.

Some years ago, my husband (who is handy with home improvement) decided to build a storage room off the master bedroom and above the kitchen. He did a great job. But guess what? He didn't get any permits. If ever we decide to put the house up for sale, we will either have to get compliant or restore it to the original condition. While at first glance the room seems to be an asset, it is actually a negative.

You will have to play "devil's advocate" and look for everything you can possibly find that might turn a buyer off. Whether you get paid to fix the problems or not, you will want to make sure you point out these problem areas to the seller who can decide if they want to pay to fix the problems or not.

Believe me, if you don't address the issues as soon as you find them, eventually the property will be inspected officially and that's not the best time for the seller to be confronted with a host of faults - especially if they are minor and could have been easily addressed and resolved in advance.

To give you a hint of the types of things to be looking for, here is a really brief list:

- Chipped paint and other surfaces
- Scratches and scuff marks
- Tears and rips
- Cracks
- Dirt and stains
- Broken fixtures
- Overgrowth
- Poor traffic lanes
- Over decorating
- Chaos and clutter

Because buyers are prone to focus on the negatives first, they will invariably exaggerate them in their mind after leaving the premises. They will tend to calculate repair costs too high and assign more required to fix them than would be necessary. It doesn't even matter if they thought the kitchen was too small and it isn't. Perception reigns, not reality. So if the buyer thinks the kitchen is too small, you're not likely to convince them that it isn't, even with measurements.

Identify the Home's Assets

Conversely, your goal is to accentuate any possible natural assets the home has, and then even create the impression of other assets by the colors you use, the placement of furniture and accessories and the de-emphasis of the faults.

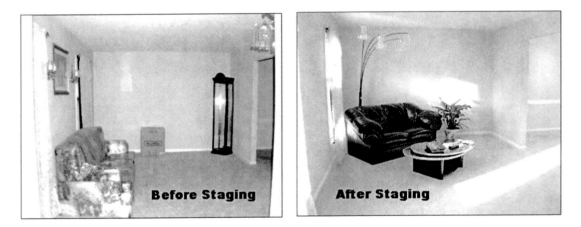

Some of the assets you might want to be focusing on might be things like:

- The phenomenal fireplace
- The view
- The flow of the rooms
- The large bay window
- The vintage bathtub
- The abundance of storage
- The cozy nook in the family room
- The two way fireplace
- The built in entertainment center
- The security fence around the pool
- The spacious living room, great for large parties

Whatever you decide the dwelling's best assets are, these are the areas you especially want to concentrate on. These are the areas which you will absolutely **NOT** compromise on as you enhance the house.

Seek to Portray Home's Potentials and Options

Not all assets are instantly recognizable. For instance, perhaps a bedroom can double as a den or office - or vice versa. Perhaps the family room could be converted into a library. Overly large rooms can be arranged to show two smaller rooms within the room, adding more flexibility. That recreation room could become an extra bedroom for a teenage son who likes loud music. You'll want to be looking for ways to bring out a home's flexibility as well.

As I mentioned earlier, buyers will enter with a preconceived list of what they're looking for. But if you can show them more than one logical usage for a particular space, you might discover that becomes the sole reason they purchased the home, even if this aspect of the home wasn't on their list. Buyers will make sacrifices once in a while to get something else in return. But for them to sacrifice something on their list, like a home being closer to work or school, they must get something of equal or greater value in return. As a home enhancer, you can help facilitate this process.

Assess First Impressions

You only get one chance to make a first impression. I'm sure you've heard that expression before. In a relationship, the average time it takes to form a lasting impression is 4 minutes. But when looking at a product, like a house, the time is shortened down to a few seconds - 15 to be exact. Buyers may not form sentences about their feelings right away, but their instincts are sharp and instantaneous.

They will get first impressions about:

- The view of the house and neighborhood when they drive up
- The view of the front door as they approach
- What they see when standing in the entry
- An impression of the current occupants
- A strong impression in the kitchen
- Another strong impression in the bathrooms
- An impression when opening some closets and looking for storage options
- An impression looking at the yards
- And a final impression when departing

Each time they get a negative impression, your home seller's fate is sealed. They might overcome one negative impression, but it's doubtful they will be able to overcome three or more. Would you? Of course not.

Have you ever pulled into a gas station that was unkempt outside and in the office/food mart? Would you ever in a million years consider using the bathroom in such a place? Well, sometimes you're desperate. But normally you'd leave and go to a competing gas station that is noticeably clean. Right? Well, another famous quote is "Cleanliness is next to Godliness". So it behooves the seller to present a house that is spick and span, white glove clean.

This is good for you, because often times they don't have the time or the incentive to really bring the house into that kind of condition. But that is what you do and you can make a lot of money offering a "white glove squeaky clean environment".

Turn Negatives Into Positives

So let's say you have a seller with a house full of little negatives, nothing hugely serious, but lots of little problems that need correcting or, at the minimum, need to be de-emphasized. Recognize that buyers just seem to have a knack for noticing every piece of lint, every little smudge. They seem to make it their mission in life to find every little flaw. Don't be too hard on them. We would be exactly like them - and have been already, right?

If a buyer sees clutter, they will invariably think the house is too small and not well maintained. They will be looking for other signs that support their impression - and chances are they will find the verification they seek. It won't matter one iota whether the impression is true or not. It's true for **them** and that ends the discussion.

Swimming pools may be a positive to some people and a huge negative to other people. High vaulted ceilings may be loved by one buyer but the next one only thinks about the expense of heating those huge rooms. The trick here is to make the house appeal to the greatest number of people while recognizing that it just isn't going to be loved by everyone no matter how great it is.

Some negatives you won't be able to do anything about. Like you can't go dig up the pool and dispose of it. But there are other areas where you can draw attention away from the negative "flaw" and push the buyer's attention in the direction you want it to go. You just have to focus on the home's attributes while de-emphasizing the flaws.

It only takes one person to purchase the home. You're just not going to know which person that will be. You won't know when they will show up. So to better your odds in finding him/her right away, you'll be assisting the seller to put the house's "best foot" forward at all times.

Ask yourself (or have the seller ask themselves) this question: **Does this room look brand new?** If the answer isn't "yes", then it needs work. You might not be able to make it look *as good as new*, but anything you do will help.

If a buyer drives up and sees weeds, peeling paint and such, they will immediately say to themselves, "This is a fixer-upper. I'll have to do a lot of work here. Not sure I'm interested." Some might even tell the agent to just keep driving. The seller is "dead" before getting a chance. And there are practically no second chances in selling a home. You either hit on the first preview or you're generally out of luck. People buy primarily based on emotional responses. This explains why, when they fall in love with a house and can visualize living there, that the buying decision comes rapidly. The less work they see they have to invest to make the house fit their lifestyle, the quicker the sale and the higher the offer. Simple as that.

How to Create the "Wow" Effect

Attack the Marketing Challenge

Many sellers never really stop to think that selling a home really comes down to a *marketing challenge*. At any given time there are likely to be other properties on the market that will meet the needs of many buyers. So there is usually competition for the same buyer. The person who does the best job of "presenting" the "product" in the most appealing manner is the person who will get the "sale". Having the right house, with the right number of bedrooms, the right location, the right neighborhood, the right size at the right price - well, there are so many variables, aren't there. So meeting all the criteria is a challenge, even without competition.

Now when you add competition to the mix, you're in for a real marketing challenge. These are all selling points you can make to the seller and to the agent, by the way. It's interesting. You want the seller to view the "home" as a "house" - an impersonal product. However, you want the buyer to see the "house" as their future "home".

This is where the home enhancement specialist (home stager) will shine. This is why your talents are so desperately needed. Even if the seller recognizes the importance, they often lack the skill or time to make it happen. Don't you just love it?

From Home to House And Back Again

Rather than letting a buyer walk through your client's house staring at their possessions and the way the client has lived in the house (which tends to feel like an invasion of privacy anyway), it's actually unfair to both parties. Buyers should not be expected to have to wade thru the owner's possessions to try to see the home's potential assets (or current faults).

You know when they are making the transition when they start saying things like, "This bedroom would be the perfect bedroom for Anna" or "We could turn this room into a den" or "I could host the next family dinner in this yard". Once a buyer starts thinking or making these types of comments, they have made the mental and emotional shift needed to close a deal.

A lounge chair placed next to a table with a lamp, an open book and reading glasses will subtly convey a message that it would be a perfect place to relax and read. It's a conveyed "feeling" as much as anything else. It's all about making the slightest suggestion in the mind of the buyer as to how the space might be used by them or their family. Done right, the agent hardly has to say anything. The home speaks for itself - and be assured - the home **will** speak for itself whether the seller wants it to or not.

As a home enhancement specialist, you are in a unique position to really make a positive difference, not only in how the home speaks to the buyer, but in how lasting that message is. You want to make positive strong first impressions, followed by strong supportive impressions as they progress through the house. Here are just a few simple ways to create a longer-lasting impression.

- fresh paint
- beautiful scents in the kitchen
- fresh cut flowers in a vase by a window
- a crackling fire in the fireplace

- scented soaps in the bathroom
- elegant towels tied fashionably
- a large artistic floral on the dining room table
- a large thank you wreath on the back of the front door, which they see when leaving
- a fresh cut rose and a book on a tray on the bed

The longer a buyer stays in a house, walking around, the more likely a sale will result. If they are in and out quickly the sale has been lost for sure. So a wise home enhancer will pull out every trick in the book to put little "finishing touches" around the house that generate warm, fuzzy feelings in their own quiet, unspoken way.

The senses trigger emotional connections that words cannot convey. Stimulating a buyer's feelings in this way is far more powerful, effective and longer lasting than an agent simply saying, "Hey, you'll be able to relax and read here."

Hopefully the other homes the buyer may visit that day will not induce these types of feelings. Chances are a good share of them will not have been enhanced by someone like you. When you can reach someone's emotions, you will have tapped into the real secret of selling, whether it's a home or a gadget. When you reach buyers on an emotional level, the home will stand out from the rest. You will even see some buyers changing their criteria for what they are looking for. It's fascinating.

How Long Will It Take Usually?

Well, of course, this is different for every home. Some homes have been enhanced in a single day and some have taken upwards of 10 days to get ready to go on the market. So it all depends on the condition of the home and the amount of tasks that are needed.

For the more complex projects, it is wise to have a check list of tasks and methodically go through the check list, noting the tasks and assigning a time frame for completion of each task. When the entire check list is filled out, the total time is added up. A buffer needs to be added, because nothing will ever go as planned. Tasks should be divided according to similarities or by rooms. Some tasks will need outside sourcing; some will be done by you; some will be done by the seller.

The downside of longer periods of transformation is the risk of damage or a loss of cleanliness that can occur with time. But for the most part, whether the home is enhanced in a single day or spread out over several days, the results will far outweigh the effort.

Lastly, there is a logical sequence of preparing a house for market.

1. De-clutter It
2. Clean It Up
3. Repair It
4. Neutralize It
5. Enhance It

Within that sequence, try to group like kinds of tasks together to streamline the effort and make life simple. There's little point in arranging the furniture and accessories first, then having to move them again to clean. Make daily to-do lists, crossing out each item as it is accomplished. You'll find this helps keep you focused, organized and motivated. By checking off items that have been completed, you will enjoy how much has been accomplished rather than worry about how much needs to be done.

That's exactly how I have written this book. I created the main headings first. I then listed under each heading the sub-heading topics I wanted to cover in the sequence that seemed most natural. Then I proceeded to sort of "fill in the blanks". As I scroll through the material, it's easy to get overwhelmed with how much I need to write. But as I move through the listed topics, it's also gratifying to see how much has been accomplished each day. That keeps me encouraged, because it's a long road for a writer, staring at an empty page and seeing a very long list of topics yet to be completed.

So it's disheartening when I get that occasional person who attacks me personally or how I write. I would hope readers would see beyond my flaws and appreciate the massive effort and genuine spirit of this manual. **NOTE**: Honey will bring sweetness to your life; thorns will draw blood and hurt you. Develop a habit of giving praise and compliments to others and life will reward you.

Your Expertise

If you have a degree in interior design or have taken any classes in the subject, then you're already ahead of the game. But for those who have not, don't worry. You do not need a degree in interior design to be successful as a home enhancement specialist.

What you do need, however, in addition to this business training, is some specific training in arrangement design so that you can walk in to any situation and feel confident and competent to improve the situation.

With that said, here is a brief list of the educational and business skills you should have (or be prepared to acquire) if you want to be good at your profession and gain the respect you will need to continue as a successful consultant and business person.

- a working knowledge of arrangement design that includes furniture and accessories
- a working knowledge of all other aspects of design, such as color, carpeting, wall treatments, window treatments, paint, design styles, terminology
- knowledge of good sources in your area for furnishings, accessories and labor
- personal integrity and ethical working procedures
- knowledge of practical business procedures, taxes and such
- an entrepreneurial spirit
- an ability to interact gracefully with people, to suggest changes without offending
- knowledge of and a good working relationship with other suppliers of goods and services: painters, paint suppliers, wallpaper hangers, wallpaper suppliers, woodworkers, art companies, framers, furniture rental companies, and so forth. You don't need to delve into other aspects of interior design if you don't want to, but if you do, you'll be offering a more complete service and it will add additional revenue to your business from time to time.

Remember, you need to perform with solid professionalism in order to be taken seriously by your clients and get the testimonials and referrals you're going to want to get to sustain your business.

Effective Communication

A good home enhancement specialist will have excellent communication skills. You'll have to explore the agent's goals and/or the seller's goals by asking the right questions and listening actively for the answers. If you ask the right questions, they will tell you what you need to know. After you have specified the project, completed your tour of the home and have made some design decisions, you'll have to communicate to your client what you propose doing and it's good to include the reasons why. This is particularly helpful to them if you are proposing some major changes in the way the home now presents itself.

You need to gently move them in the direction you want to take them, without using intimidating jargon. You need to know what aspects of the project to emphasize so that the client knows what to appreciate about the direction you are suggesting.

After I leave a client (if I was hired just to consult and not to perform), I always send a thank you note, and in that note I always re-emphasize the design concepts, the repairs needed or already done, the labor hired (if any) - an overview of the major details used to make the necessary changes. If I have thought of anything else that would be helpful to the client, I always put additional suggestions in that note. I want my clients to know that I didn't stop working for them just because I left the scene.

Being Service Oriented

Always refer to your clients as "clients" and not "customers". Consider the two definitions below:
Customer: a person who purchases a commodity or service
Client: a person who is under the protection of another

When you start to *serve* clients rather than *sell* clients, the limits to your business success will disappear. Don't take the attitude that you are going to sell them a product or service just so you can make the largest one-time profit possible. Take the time to discover and appreciate exactly what they *need*. Once you know the final outcome they need, you lead them to that outcome - in the process you will become their **trusted adviser** who protects them. This will give them reasons to remain your client for a lifetime. Clients who trust you will gladly recommend you to others.

I always tell my clients that I am there to "enhance" what they have already begun - or simplify what they have created so that it speaks to their basic talents. Your clients need to know that you are on their "side", that you are really a "team" for the day or time period. You are there to help them solve a problem and you are not there in any judgmental way.

I'm always checking with my client as I move along to make sure they are comfortable with the adjustments I am making. If they are starting to get unhappy or uncomfortable, the sooner you spot it and address it the better off everyone will be.

You don't want to get the whole project completed and then find out that your client just doesn't like the changes. Focus on how you can "serve" them and what additional ways there might be to make life more enjoyable for them or ways you can speed up the process if they are under pressure. Give more than you said you would give. When a client believes that you have their best interest at heart, that you are their ally, you will find it extremely easy to service them in the ways you feel most appropriate.

Knowledge of Interior Design

Just a word about having a thorough knowledge of the mainstream interior design concepts most professionals use. The client is hiring you for your knowledge - not just in design, but in organizational matters, in repair/replacement categories. She expects you to help her make decisions and sometimes the decisions you make for her will be emotionally painful for her to experience. She expects you to know what you're doing. She expects you to do enough but not to overdo it.

The agent has the same expectations from you, particularly if the agent is paying for the enhancement service. Some will consider it a business expense and absorb the cost themselves. Some will insist that the seller pay for the service. Some will pay for a portion of the enhancement, but if it rises higher than the prearranged figure, will want the seller to pay the difference. So your true client can be just one person or both the agent and the seller.

A firm grounding in interior design concepts will help you develop a neutral plan for the house that will appeal to the broadest segment of society. Strong design knowledge will make the rearrangement of furniture and accessories a cinch for you. Sometimes you will not have enough furnishings to work with. Strong design training will help you overcome that and still achieve the right end result. At the very least, you'll know what else needs to be brought in to complete the enhancement.

It's not necessary to go back to college full time to get sufficient knowledge to function well as a home enhancement specialist, but some independent study is absolutely essential.

It's important to stay abreast of what's happening in design too. Make sure you are subscribing to a couple of good decorating magazines that cater to your part of the country, if possible. If you have some design centers locally that are just for the "trade", visit them periodically. If not, walk around furniture stores, wallpaper and fabric stores in your area and check out what's currently popular and available. You just don't know when that information will provide you with the perfect answer to a client's question or help you resolve some dilemma the agent was concerned about.

Having said that, however, don't get overly caught up in trends. Trends come and go. The furnishings you have to work with, the style already present in the home - these are the things that will directly affect what you do, whether in redesign or staging. Trends are useless if the client doesn't like them or their furnishings don't lend themselves to the trend. You have to work with what the client has, whether you like it or not - or whether you feel it fits into the current style you happen to like.

Personal Attitudes

Keep a positive attitude. Confidence in your knowledge and skill and a belief that your services have an inherent value will give you a winning edge. Believe in yourself. As you learn and get experience, your confidence will increase. You'll be able to achieve more in less time.

Your confidence and enthusiasm will be transmitted to your client. A client who is shy about doing something really different from what they are accustomed to will gain boldness and daring and be willing to make the "leap" if you are confident and reassuring. But know when to back off if they are overly reluctant. Probe further to find out what is making them hesitate. You can often overcome objections by simply taking more time to listen and then explain your ideas more fully.

For all you know, the client may be thrilled with a suggestion personally, but apprehensive about a spouse's anticipated response or that of the agent or overly worried about potential buyers. It would be good to know this.

Your pride and confidence can be the difference between a professional who lands a few projects and one who lands many or is invited back to service the agent's clients again. These sentiments, pride and enthusiasm, are not, and must not be manufactured. They are a result of practicing creative problem-solving with your clients and sincerely believing in your talents and the benefits you have to offer.

Your Professional Image

As a professional home enhancement specialist, you are not only selling your expertise, you are selling your good taste and your own personal image. Before you can say a word, as soon as you enter the home of the seller or the real estate agent's office, your prospect begins to evaluate you and whether your personal image is consistent with the image they were expecting.

It is important for you to project a personally powerful and successful image of your own, preferably on the same level as your client. Dress the way you would expect someone else to dress if you were the client. Your client will look to you to set a standard of taste, and will want to feel that your style is similar to and compatible with theirs at the very least. Your voice, your wardrobe, your accessories, your marketing materials, and your vehicle together convey a personal message about you. So will the tools you bring with you and the manner in which you transport them.

While it should be common sense, I still have to mention to make sure your hair is well groomed and stylish. Make sure your makeup is applied appropriately. Keep your fingernails clean. No chipped polish, please. Use deodorant at all times and freshly brushed teeth. Use breath mints. Make sure your clothes are appropriate for the project and not wrinkled.

My moving and design tools are all professionally stored in a black "sales" case on wheels. I'll discuss the tools later in another section. But I just mention the case here, because you want to arrive compactly and professionally. A case gives you a neatly organized place to keep your tools while at their home or office. You want to be able to find things quickly and easily and you don't want to leave anything behind. It also provides a logical place to keep tools when you are not using them instead of spreading them around the home. Your image is also fashioned by your attitude which was discussed earlier. Bring plenty of confidence and eagerness, a sense of humor, a humble spirit, and eagerness to  serve, all mixed with a happy spirit and you will find you are conveying the image of a successful, competent home enhancement specialist.

Your Professional Ethics

You will never go wrong in this business (or any business) if you always give your clients MORE than you promise, charge a fair price, offer a guarantee and stand by it 100%. My best advice is to treat clients and vendors the way you would want to be treated, and focus on how you can best serve them.

Home sellers view their consultants as their personal advisors. Therefore, you need to be aware of professional standards of ethics used by other design and real estate professionals. These standards will probably be the same or similar to all business fields. If you handle your affairs in an honest, ethical manner, you should find your business will develop an excellent reputation within your community and this will enhance your business growth and personal satisfaction.

Sometimes I get asked, "What about selling other products to your clients?" I know of plenty of re-designers/home stagers who offer a Buying Service as well. I personally consider that, for me, would be a conflict of interest, but that's my private view for myself. Later on I will give you a list of other types of services and products you can offer.

Some people may encourage you to call up your competition and pretend to be a prospective client to "spy" on how they answer the phone, give a quote and so forth. I consider this unprofessional and unethical. Never pretend to be other than what you are, even for a short time. If word gets out that you did such a thing, you may damage your reputation in many ways and generate resentment from others in your community. This is never good.

Entrepreneurial Skills

Not everyone is cut out to be an entrepreneur. You have to be highly motivated, persistent, professional and persevering. You have to be able to overcome your fears and reservations, learn what you need to learn.

You also need to acquire or have the ability to research, assess facts, make decisions, minimize your risks, and be involved in all aspects of your business, getting your hands involved in the "touching and doing" labor.

Entrepreneurs are self starters. They are stubborn, creative and focused. They derive great pleasure from their achievements. They are people willing to be the CEO as well as the janitor. They are flexible, creative, problem solvers. Would it surprise you to know that 65% of businesses owned by women have no employees whatsoever? And that percentage is growing every day. To keep costs at a minimum, many wear many "hats" and do a wide variety of tasks.

You can cultivate and develop these skills, but it's best if you have them naturally. If you have trouble getting up in the morning, if you're a chronic procrastinator, I'm not saying you won't be successful, but you clearly have to overcome these tendencies. As an entrepreneur, you're not going to get paid if you don't work.

Initially you'll have to do all of the marketing as well as the running of your business. The most successful businesses, however, in time will be those business owners who eventually spend the majority of their time "marketing" their businesses instead of "running" their businesses.

If you have performed every aspect of your business yourself, however, you'll be able to properly supervise others as your business grows and you begin to delegate responsibilities to employees to handle. So whether you have plans to build a large business or keep it a small home-based consulting service, look at your basic entrepreneurial skills. Take training to acquire ones you don't have.

Finding Your Niche

Identifying Real Estate Agents

This is pretty simple, actually. Pull out your local yellow pages and look under the category "Real Estate". In alphabetical order, you should find a host of real estate agents and brokers. Brokers usually have an office to which several agents are attached. A broker is also a real estate agent, but a broker does more than an agent does. Reaching a broker can many times provide you with easy access to all of the agents in the broker's office.

Go on the computer and type the words "real-estate-agents" into your search bar. Then add a space and type in your city or town. If you live in a two word city or town, add a hyphen between the words. That will be a hard target search for just the real estate agents in your immediate vicinity. If you live in a city or town of any size, you should get back a whole crop of agent prospects.

Visit the websites that pop up. Look up the names, addresses, phone numbers and email addresses of every agent you can find. Make a list. This will be the list you begin with. I'm assuming that you'd like to work with people as close to home as possible.

Most Well Known Real Estate Agencies

Here is a list of the most popular real estate companies who have agents nationwide.

- www.remax.com (REMAX)
- www.century21.com (CENTURY21)
- www.realtor.com (REALTOR)
- www.era.com (ERA)
- www.coldwellbanker.com (COLDWELL BANKER)

Agents Who Suit You

In the process of asking some specific questions, realize that you are in a position to be interviewing the agent in every sense of the word. Recognize that this is not a matter of the agent choosing you. It is a two way street. You are also in a process of choosing whether you wish to work with this particular agent or not. You are to be interviewing them from that perspective as well as finding out as much about the property as you can.

You're not going to want to work for every agent you meet. Happily you don't have to. Don't put yourself in a situation where you are stuck with an agent that you dislike or distrust for any reason. Life is too short. The money isn't **that** good. Sometimes you have to be willing to pass. If your first impressions are negative about the agent, you should dismiss them. There is a reason for those feelings that you subconsciously pick up on but might not be able to explain.

Choose only agents with whom you feel comfortable working. Choose people you like. Choose people you trust. Choose people who appear professional and easy to communicate with. So much of what you do relies on great communication. You don't want unnecessary problems brought about by an inability to communicate.

Choose an agent you perceive to be sharp and on top of his/her "game". You don't want someone who fails to return phone calls, who procrastinates, who ignores details, who is overloaded. Look at the office. Look at the desk. Is it messy and unorganized? You can pick up a lot of clues just by being in the agent's office as to whether he/she is a good match for you.

Home Owners Who Suit You

Typically potential homeowners fall into three basic groups: 1) High end clients (upper income level households); 2) Medium end clients (middle to upper income level households); and 3) Low end clients (lower middle income to low income households).

Generally speaking, your target market for home enhancement services will be Group 1 and 2: high end to medium end clients. High end clients have the ability to hire any service to be done for them. They typically prefer to have a professional service them as they know their time is better spent doing other thing. Low end clients are a tougher sale because they just won't have the money to hire someone. They can't afford your services, won't be looking for anyone who offers what you do, and need to spend their available income on necessities like food, clothing and utilities and mortgages.

So your best target market is homeowners who are middle income and above. You just have to remember that if you find the house empty and need to rent furniture and accessories, you need to choose furnishings that are consistent with the quality of the home. You won't be shopping at Walmart for a multi-million dollar estate. See what I mean?

Having said that, you will need to pre-qualify all prospects. Not everyone who can afford your services is a good candidate for becoming your client. What?

That's right! You don't want just anyone and you want to pre-qualify your home owner sellers in the same manner you do the agent. Of course, one of the first areas of pre-qualification will be to make sure they understand your service and the nature and amount of your fees to provide your services.

But you also need to make sure that your potential client is someone that you like and feel you can communicate with. You don't want to be miss-matched with a homeowner any more than being miss-matched with an agent.

So you really need to choose your client carefully. They will be making a choice about you too. But it's not a one-sided street. Don't develop tunnel vision about landing a job that will pay you money that you choose unwisely. It will be a miserable experience if you do.

If you find yourself at the home and you're visiting with the seller and you just find you will be sorry if you service the seller, then my best advice is to provide a detailed itemization of what is needed, collect your consultation fee, and say you are too swamped to do the enhancement itself. Encourage them to do it for themselves. Life is too short to get entangled with a problem client. We are always "too swamped" for that.

To boil it all down, your niche market is a homeowner who wants to sell their property and wants it to show the best way possible to stimulate lots of offers. Perhaps the home has been on the market for a while and the owner is frustrated with the lack of offers. Perhaps it is the real estate agent who is pushing for a professional to give the home a nicer ambience.

Or perhaps the homeowner has a nasty disposition, is ultra picky and hard to get along with. You don't need this in your life - walk away.

Finally, do a careful analysis of your business strategy to make sure it matches both your personal goals and the probable needs of your potential clients. I can guarantee you that you will have times when you need to pass. Whenever I refused to listen to my gut instincts, I was always, always sorry. You have been given instincts by God. Use them and choose wisely.

Scouting Your Neighborhood

Drive around the residential neighborhoods in your immediate vicinity and look for homes that are up for sale. If the home is listed for sale by an agent, write down the phone number and name of agent and give the person a call to set up an appointment to meet. Don't try to sell your service -

just get an appointment. If the home is for sale by the owner, contact the owner for an appointment.

Visit Open House Listings

Look in the newspaper for open house showings or watch for signs in the neighborhood and on light poles in your area. Go and visit the open house showings for homes for sale. If the home isn't squeaky clean and impressive leave your card or a brochure or one of our staging postcards when you leave. Try to get an appointment with the agent or the seller to discuss the need for staging services if you feel the home needs your help.

Real Estate Prop Companies

Visit the companies in your area that sell marketing tools and supplies to the real estate market. Often these companies have bulletin boards where you can post your business card, one of our postcards, or even leave brochures of your services. Ask the owner of the store if they would be willing to add your postcard or brochure into every bag of items they sell in exchange for a referral fee when you get a project as a result.

Contacting Builders

As home staging becomes more known, some builders are getting involved in helping their customers sell their homes so they can purchase the new home built by them. By contacting them, you could become the official stager whose services are recommended. Perhaps the builder will even cover some or all of the costs of a consultation to help people sell their present homes swiftly and close the deal.

Create Networking Relationships

Here is a list of all kinds of real estate related companies that you could contact and work out some kind of joint venture deal or referral payment plan. Or perhaps you might consider purchasing ad space in their publications or on their websites.

- www.moving.org (American Moving and Storage Association)
- www.moving.com (Pick up information about moving which you can pass on to your client)
- www.monstermoving.com (Another site to pick up tips on moving out, tools and information)
- www.bbb.org (The Better Business Bureau)
- www.ehomes.com, www.erealty.com, www.forsalebyowner.com, www.fsbo.com, www.owners.com, www.listforless.com, www.listlow.com, www.owners.com, www.ziprealty.com (By Owner Sales Information)
- www.americanhomeshield.com, www.countrywide.com, www.ctic.com, www.fnf.com, www.firstam.com, www.quotesmith.com, www.stewart.com, www.landam.com, www.ticortitle.com (American Home Shield, Title and Escrow and Warranty Information)
- www.aia.org (American Institute of Architects)
- www.ashi.org (American society of Home Inspectors)
- www.askbuild.com (Building Site Information)
- www.nahb.com (National Association of Home Builders, Remodeling Council)
- www.nrca.net (National Roofing Contractors Association)
- www.smarthomebuy.com (Environmental Hazards Property Reporting Site)

Distance You Are Willing to Travel

Another consideration you need to make is the distance you are willing to travel to serve a client. When I was actively servicing corporate art clients, the projects were generally much larger and the potential profit could be huge, considering the time and effort required to complete the project. So it was well worth my time to travel an hour or more away to do a project. But when it comes to my rearrangement services, I'm far more reluctant to travel very far.

Rearrangement design is typically isolated to just one room in someone's home - sometimes more, but the average seem to be just one room. It is not that often that a client has the money to have you rearrange an entire home all at once. You're typically going to be spending half a day, counting your travel time. So you need to make some advance decisions with regard to how far from your home or office you are willing to travel and what your time is worth.

Home staging is different, however, because it is more likely to include the entire home, not just one room. This will require multiple trips and day-long labor. Due to the higher fees and larger projects, it makes sense to travel further to service a client than if it was a simple one-room redesign for half a day.

While you won't have any hard, fast rules that are inflexible, it's good to make some decisions in advance so you don't get into a project that is too far away to be practical.

Your Ideal Homeowners

Consultation Only Homeowners

How Much Should You Charge?

Your prospect will always ask for an estimate. Give a complimentary estimate and you'll probably get hired if you structure the estimate fairly and cite plenty of benefits to the homeowner. Keep in mind that this is only an estimate and estimates can be a bit off. However, unless something unforeseen takes place between the estimate and the actual job itself, an estimate should be fairly accurate. You will no doubt feel a little uneasy at first, but you'll get better at estimating when you have a few projects under your belt.

Don't be surprised if the home seller gets more than one estimate. Just like any service, pricing in the home staging industry can vary over a wide range, sometimes escalating simply because of locale. You may want to charge an hourly rate or at least base your price on an hourly rate. Factors to consider are the average amount of time you expect the home to be on the market in your area, and the asking price of your prospect's home.

The homeowner should be willing to pay for staging services in accordance with the asking price of the home. If you bring in rented furniture and accessories, the price will be considerably higher, especially if you're looking for furnishings that compliment the home itself in terms of quality. Remember, if you charge too much you will make it unrealistic for the homeowner to benefit. Don't forget that the average seller plans to move OUT of the home in the near future, the sooner the better. Don't lose sight of that. They will be reluctant to invest a huge amount into a home they are selling, no matter what the asking price.

Know in advance what your costs will be. Anticipate a reasonable increase in price based on your services. The rule of thumb is that the higher the asking price, the higher your fee - but it still has to be reasonable.

What About Agent Participation?

Some agents will be willing to share in the cost, because it is to their advantage to make a quicker, more profitable sale. They will be analyzing their profit margins. They will want to weigh the cost of staging with their costs of advertising the property.

Experienced agents will have a good feel for those homes that are in need of a staging service. A home that has nothing in it, where the seller has already moved out, is a prime candidate for a staging service. An agent should value the homeowner's best interest. Many of them have an amount set aside in their marketing budget for staging services already. If you're good and your services are reasonable, they will want to enlist your help. Everyone wins. The goal is a speedy sale at the best possible price. Staging is certainly a viable way to achieve just that. If you find after throwing out certain price ranges that you are not getting hired and someone else is, adjust your pricing slightly.

Full Service Home Sellers

Ideally you want every home that you give an initial consultation service for to turn into a full service staging project for you. That is where you'll make your serious money. But they won't all do that and some you'll just be paid to give them a list of recommended tasks for the seller to complete on his/her own.

Faster Sale/Higher Price Tip

Take a close look at the home's condition before you make recommendations and, certainly, before you quote a price range for full service staging. Tell the seller that they usually only have one shot at impressing potential buyers so the decisions need to be made carefully. Remind them that your services will be a lot less expensive than the loss they are likely to encounter on having to reduce their asking price the first time. Tell them you will only do what you honestly believe is absolutely necessary to get them a speedy sale for top dollar. Depending on the home, you could very easily provide all the service they need for no additional cost. If the home is furnished and you have a lot of furnishings to utilize or eliminate, your job becomes much easier. While it is time consuming to pack things up and remove from the premises, it's less expensive for the seller than having to rent new furnishings because the house is bare.

Benefits to Home Sellers

The purpose for decorating one's home is to provide a comfortable, functional and attractive environment for the people who live there. However, your job is to do all of that as sparingly and neutrally as possibly to look attractive to new buyers.

Comfort - In a day when most people work and are gone from their homes for the better part of the day, coming home should be a pleasant experience. They are tired. They may be irritable. They need to relax. So the more comfortable that experience is, the happier they will be. You need to convey comfort and relaxation to a buyer without all of the usual props and trappings found in a home where people are planning to live for a long time. You'll quickly discover that a home enhancer merely "suggests" an activity is possible. The stager doesn't necessarily go all out to provide what is needed, but just leaves enough to "suggest" an activity or feeling.

Function - The staged home needs to convey that the rooms are fully functional for the types of activities that are normally conducted in the room. Typically one watches TV in the family room. The seating in that room should attempt to convey that possible activity. In the bedroom, the standard expected behavior is sleeping, so it makes sense to include a bed with plenty of room to navigate around it. Model home designers often place smaller beds in a room than would be normal. The bed suggests relaxation and sleep, but the smaller bed size makes the potential buyer feel that the room is quite large and easily navigated. It's not uncommon at all to find twin and full size beds in model homes rather than king and queen sized beds.

Attraction - Making the rooms look attractive is a given. The home enhancer must look for furnishings on the premises (or rent them) that are compatible with the colors of the background of each room. If you're going to change the wall color or floor color, this needs to be determined before furnishings are selected for the room. Attractiveness can be boiled down to two critical elements: color and placement. Get that right and the room will look terrific. Just think about a fine hotel room. It is designed to make you feel comfortable, relaxed and happy, but they only include the barest of furnishings and accessories. The rest is left to your imagination.

Why Homeowners Need Help

After over a decade of rearranging other people's homes and visiting homes where my services have not been sought, I have come to the conclusion that most people don't know that their furniture and accessory arrangements are poor. If they don't know there was a need for a redesign service all the while they were in the home, they can't possibly be expected to know how to make the home attractive for other people.

If you don't know basic design concepts, you might not know that what you've done is ineffective. The most common problems I see are a failure to address a room's natural focal point, failure to create seating arrangements that encourage conversation, failure to balance a room, failure to create a sense of unity, form and rhythm, huge disparities in sizes, failure to account for proportion and scale, failure to acquire a sufficient amount of accessories, failure to properly assess lighting and traffic issues.

So what I find over and over again are homes that look and feel chaotic, disjointed and totally unappealing. I personally wouldn't want to send 5 minutes there, much less live there. And if I were contemplating buying the home - forget it.

So while most people do a pretty good job of selecting reasonably nice furniture and accessories (to whatever point they have acquired these things), their sense of where to place them leaves much to be desired. So too their ability to make the home presentable to buyers will leave much to be desired. That's why there is such a need for home enhancement services.

So this is one of the areas that is an enhancer's biggest challenge - convincing sellers that they have a need that you can dramatically resolve. Those stagers that can really speak to the benefits they can bring to the home will find themselves hired and making a really nice income.

Working with the Decision Maker

It's important to work with the person who mostly makes the financial decisions for the home. They have the most input to give you and usually are the most vocal and concerned about the final outcome in the staging business. There is more at stake in staging a home for sale than there is in redesigning a home for living. It is imperative to work with both the husband and the wife whenever possible. You'll want the input of both people as they will each have their own opinions, frustrations and goals.

You do not need both the husband and wife's signatures on any agreement forms you present for signature, but it's always a good idea to have both people sign. Hopefully you'll never be faced with a client that refuses to pay for services, but should you be in that situation and need to present paperwork in a small claims suit, for instance, it would be advantageous to name both parties in the suit, not just one or the other one.

You should also verify the names on the trust deed. Deal with the owner of the property and no one else.

What Home Sellers Need Most

The competition in this specialized service is growing every day. You are wise to be starting your business now while you have a chance to dominate the market in your area. People prefer to deal with people that offer more than one service, however, so you might give thought to other services or products that you could also offer. Later I will be giving you a list of other types of services you can offer if you so choose.

Home sellers need people who are confident and really know what they're doing. They need someone who has a good head for details, is organized and methodical, knows redesign techniques, understands the importance of repairing and cleaning - someone who can literally take over the whole project and manage it and orchestrate every detail in a timely, orderly manner. Will that someone be you?

If there are specific areas of design that you just prefer to avoid, do so. But consider building business relationships with other professionals who would be happy to give you a referral fee to service your clients in those areas. You'll want to pre-develop working relationships with people such as: gardeners, handymen, plumbers, electricians, painters, rental companies and so forth.

What will separate you from your competitors is your professionalism and service. Traditional design concepts, organizational skills, cleaning and repairing services and so forth have been around for decades. But the uniqueness of you, your ideas and creativity, your genuine warmth and commitment to service will be observable. Always be professional. Good things will return to you.

First Steps First

Long before I ever made a single presentation to an agent or seller, I did my homework and practiced. Sometimes you will find someone will hire you simply because of the confidence you showed. Confidence is everything. In starting your business, set your first appointments with agents and potential clients outside your immediate area. This is the best way to begin practicing and perfecting your approach. Don't ruin the chance to work with local real estate agents close to home by practicing your presentation skills on them and failing. Unless the agent is a good friend who is also willing to serve as a mentor to you, practice on someone else and don't make any presentations locally until you are reasonably confident in your professional demeanor. Do some role playing with your spouse and a good friend. You'll be amazed at how much role playing will help.

Meeting with the Agent

As I stated earlier, if an agent is involved, you want to get all the information you can from the agent before you ever start a project. You want that agent to act as your ally. Don't do anything to antagonize the agent nor to undermine his/her relationship with the seller. You must have an attitude of 3-way partnership with the agent and seller for the common good of everyone involved.

With that in mind, try to set up appointments that are early in the morning and let the agent know in advance how much time you will likely need. There's nothing worse that to sit on appointment with someone whose mind is elsewhere because time is short and they have other places to go or things to do. You want that agent's undivided attention. Make sure you get it. Having said that, don't be late. Every minute you are late is one less minute you will have to make your case. The best agents are extremely busy. Don't waste their time. Don't waste yours. Believe me, you will be the big loser if you fail to arrive on time or slightly ahead of time.

Presentations to Agents

You are in a very visual business. This requires good visuals if you hope to adequately and professionally entice an agent to hire you or to recommend you to their clients. You can approach the subject with them in a "left brain", intellectual mode, but is that the most effective way to communicate? No. While there are plenty of facts and figures you could toss around with the agent, the bottom line is that everyone deserves to "see" what a home enhancement service can actually do. When they see the service in action, through before and after slides, they will be touched on an emotional level. Remember earlier I mentioned that people "buy" from an emotional frame of reference, not so much from an intellectual one?

I have found that the simplest, most effective way to communicate with an agent, especially one who has never heard of the concept of home staging, is to make use of a good, professional, concise Powerpoint presentation. You can, of course, create your own if you have Powerpoint software on your computer.

46 Questions to Ask Agents

Your actual meeting with an agent, or even over the phone, will be an excellent time to ask questions and get feedback. In most cases, you should rely quite a bit on the insight the agent will be able to provide you, especially if they have been in the field for many years. You're likely to find it a give and take exchange. You will have certain types of information and data you need to give, as well as gather. The agent will have data and recommendations to make to you, as well as questions to ask you.

Be prepared to take lots of notes. Not only will you be less apt to forget something important, you'll be viewed as someone who really cares what the other person is saying. So let's briefly discuss some questions you might want to ask the agent. These are not in any ironclad order. You will find as you begin talking to an agent that the order will be affected by what the agent is saying to you. You will probably think of questions of your own to add to the mix, especially if something the agent says triggers an unusual request, suggestion or comment.

- How long have you been an agent (broker)?
- Have you ever heard of home enhancement before (home staging, staged homes, ready to sell services, etc.)?
- If not, may I show you a brief presentation which will show you what it is and how it can benefit you?
- Have you ever used a home stager/enhancer before on other properties?
- What can you tell me about the property you are selling right now?
- Are there any open house dates currently in place? When?
- Has any company already inspected the property?
- Are you the listing agent?
- What can you tell me about the owners?
- How long have they lived in the home?

- How old is the home? What style is it?
- Are they selling because they want to or because they need to?
- Is the home currently on the market?
- How long has it been on the market?
- What can you tell me about any offers it has received?
- What feedback have you received so far about the property from buyers, other agents?
- Do you have pictures of the home?
- Do you have measurements of the home?
- Do you have a floor plan? Is it drawn to scale?
- What kind of neighborhood is it in?
- What is the asking price?
- Are there any other terms that I should know about?
- Will you be absorbing the cost of staging yourself or will I need to make a presentation to the seller?
- What do you feel the major problems are in the home's current condition?
- Are you interested solely in an Enhancement Plan or are you seeking a stager/enhancer to handle all of the necessary tasks?
- When can we preview the property?
- Will the seller be present during the preview?
- What price range do you have in mind for the services you feel are needed?
- Do you feel the sellers are "do-it-yourself" types or will they want full service?
- Have you already discussed a home staging service with the sellers?
- What has been their reaction so far?
- Is the home fully furnished, sparsely furnished or bare?
- Do you anticipate the need for rental furniture?
- How would you describe the general condition of the exterior?
- How would you describe the general condition of the interior?
- Will the sellers be moving into a new home locally or are they moving some distance away?
- What can you tell me about the personalities of the sellers?
- Are there any special deadlines I should be aware of?
- What is the size of the family?
- Do they have any pets? What kind and how many?
- Is there a pool/Jacuzzi/sauna?
- Where is the property?
- How long have you known the sellers?
- Are there any special personality issues I should know about in advance?

You will discover very quickly that this Q & A can move all over the place. You may be with an agent who has a huge amount of information to tell you and willing to do so, or you may discover the agent either has very little information or is tight-lipped. Some agents will be open and friendly; others will be reserved and hesitant to share information. Obviously we'd all prefer the ones that are open, upfront, detailed and thoughtful. Don't be surprised if you're asking questions that they've never considered before.

Terms to Settle First

By the time you have thoroughly discussed the needs of the property and the wants and wishes of the real estate agent concerning it, you will probably already have some clue as to whether the agent will be paying for the service or expecting the home seller to pay you. Whether you have a clue or not, now is the time to find out and get an agreement signed and dated if the agent is going to pay for the service. If you are only being hired to make recommendations in a consultation format, you can easily quote a price for that at this time. However, if there is the possibility of being hired to actually do the work for the seller, you won't be able to make any quote until after you've seen the property.

As I've already stated elsewhere, some agents have already allocated an amount of money from their advertising budget to cover some or all of the cost of a home enhancement service. Usually they will have set aside a percentage of the asking price for that. Other agents may want the seller to bear all costs and some agents pay for it up to a certain limit and expect the seller to pay any overages. You will want to find out what type of agent you are dealing with at this point, if you don't already know.

When I have never worked with someone before, I always request payment in advance as a precaution. Then if I get more work from them, I will ease into a business relationship where I perform the work and then submit an invoice for payment. If you work first and get paid later, it would be a good idea to have them fill out a credit application. Don't worry, they won't be offended. They will actually have more respect for you. It is customary business practice to have another business that seeks "credit terms" to fill out an application for a **Net 30 Account**. A Net-30 account is where you provide the service or product, then submit an invoice, and the business that hired you or purchased the product agrees to pay you within 30 days of the date of the invoice.

There are other reasons for wanting a business to fill out such a form. It gives you a comfortable way to collect information such as their social security number (if a sole proprietor) or their Federal Tax ID (if the business is a corporation). You will also be able to collect the address and phone numbers of the business, but also the personal addresses and phone numbers of the people opening an account with you. In the past, individuals who are directors of or employees of a corporation were not legally liable for the debts of the corporation. Because of the abuses of this loophole, many businesses now hold the individual personally responsible if the corporation fails to pay or fulfill the contract. By having the representative of the corporation fill in their personal information and sign a personal guarantee at the same time on the same form, you are protecting yourself with information you will need in the event you don't get paid. To properly seek redress in a small claims suit, you need to have the social security numbers or the Federal Tax ID number, along with other pertinent individual information.

You can find generic forms of this nature at your local office supply store that you can either use as is, or use as a sample to create your own. If you get paid in advance, however, you don't need to take this step.

Meeting with the Homeowner

The First Preview

Try to set up your meeting with the seller so that all introductions are done outside the home at the curb. Then, before you do anything else, ask to preview the property just as a potential buyer would preview a property. Ask the seller to remain outside while you "walk the home", escorted by the agent. Pretend you are a buyer. Take nothing with you. Write down nothing. Just react to the home. Take your time. Look. See. Experience the home. This is your one and only opportunity to get a first impression. It will be one of the single most important things you will do as a home enhancer.

Take note of the direction you naturally move through the home. Don't let the agent lead you. The agent has been at the home before. Tell the agent you want to react to the home naturally, the way most buyers will react. Make your own way through the home quietly, silently. Simply react. Note what struck you the most favorably. Note what struck you the most negatively. When you are done, return to the seller out front and ask to sit down somewhere comfortable to all so you can talk, ask questions and formulate a plan.

This would be an excellent time to praise whatever it was that most affected you in a positive manner about the home. Remember, that even though the seller is going to be leaving, they still want someone to appreciate the home and perhaps how it was decorated. You will get much farther with a seller if you can genuinely compliment them on some aspect of the home: how you love the view, or how you love how spacious it looks, or how you love the pattern on their sofa, or how much personality they have put into the family room. Something. Anything. No matter what the condition of the home, you should be able to find something to compliment the seller regarding. Do not under any circumstances go outside and say anything derogatory. You will instantly kill any opportunity you might have to manage the entire transformation of this home into a property that can sell quickly for top dollar.

The Initial Interview

Whether or not you are being paid by the agent or the seller, you're going to need to meet with the seller of the home and gather all of the data you will need to make recommendations or to proceed with an actual staging of the home. So when you are ready to do that, you need to call the seller to make an appointment. If the agent wants to set up the appointment for you or to go with you, that's fine and probably best anyway. Try to get the agent to make the call while you are there so that a convenient time can be discussed more easily.

If the agent is with you at the time you first meet the seller, you'll have to play it by ear to decide when you should actually "take over" the meeting. In the beginning it's good to allow the agent to introduce you and be in control. But at some point you're going to have your own set of questions to be answered and want to work in the manner that is best for you. I cannot tell you when that point will arrive, because it is different every time out. Having already spent some time with the agent, you should have gained clues as to their personality style. Some will be Type A personalities who like to be in charge, work fast, make quick decisions and are highly energetic. Others will be more laid back, quiet, analytic types who might just love for you to jump in and take charge from the get-go. There are no rules here. You have to play it by ear.

After you have begun the process of taking over the appointment, a good place to start is by asking your seller the questions you want or need answers to and doing a walk-thru of the property. Why questions? Questions give you critical information, help verify assumptions and clarify understandings. They involve the seller, reveal the sellers goals and so much more. They help you understand the seller's priorities, any special agendas and their personality style. They help you re-qualify the correct decision-maker, and just as importantly, they let you demonstrate your interest in helping the seller achieve their goals.

You can start by explaining to the seller that you have a number of questions you *always ask* that you would like to pose. Then explain that, after you get the answers to those generic questions, you'll want to tour the property at which time you'll likely have even more questions. Then ask if there is a place where you can all sit down and talk.

The room the seller chooses is often the dining room, an office or the living room. Whatever room is chosen, try to position yourself opposite the seller. If you are directed to a specific chair, take that one. Place your check list of questions on a clip board. It's even a good idea to have a pencil on a string attached to the clipboard. A clipboard signals to the seller that you are an experienced stager. You are just going through procedures that you use with every seller. You want the seller to feel comfortable, especially since you may be asking some questions that might be perceived as very personal or you might be forced to make comments about the home that they aren't necessarily going to like.

It's a good idea to preface your questions and ensuing comments with a statement that you're going to be looking at the home with "buyer's eyes" and that you see it as your job to be especially critical, even more critical than a buyer might be, and that you only have their best interest in mind. Perhaps mention an analogy, like visiting a dentist. No one likes to visit the dentist and is apprehensive of what the dentist is going to say or do. But in most cases, usually the dentist is going to have to do a filling, or pull a tooth or make some adjustment to your teeth. It's not personal, just something that has to be done in order to have a great smile and health.

Ask them to view you as a "house dentist" and to know that your only goal is to help them sell their house quickly and for top dollar. That may require you pull out some furniture and accessories. It may require you do a "filling" by painting a wall a different color or some other cosmetic change. Get the seller to acknowledge that they understand the analogy and remind them that you would not possibly suggest certain changes if they were going to continue to live in the home. Some repairs and changes might be crucial for no other reason than they are selling it. There is a very specific difference between the two and you want to really drive that point home so that the seller doesn't become hurt or offended when you start to make recommendations that require change. Then proceed with your questions.

60 Questions to Ask the Seller

Here are some specific questions you might consider asking at this point to help you understand your seller and the goals they have. These are not the only questions you might ask but will, hopefully, serve as a starting point. Feel free to put them into any order that makes sense to you. Continue to ask questions and get feedback until you feel you comfortably have enough information to proceed. Depending on whether you've already discussed the home with an agent or whether you're talking to a "do it yourself" owner, you may already know the answers to some of the questions and can drop them out of the list.

- How long have you lived in the home?
- Are you the first owners?
- Why did you decide to sell and move?
- Are you selling because you want to or because you need to?
- Is there any crucial time table when the house needs to be sold?
- What has been the most enjoyable aspect of owning this home?
- What has been the least enjoyable aspect of owning this home?
- If you were to pick your favorite part of the home, what would that be?
- If you were to pick the most annoying aspect of the home, what would that be?
- Is your house currently on the market?
- When was your house listed?
- Who is your listing agent?
- What is your current listing price?
- Is anyone living in your home currently? If so, how many residents are there?
- If your home is unoccupied, are there any furniture, accessories or other personal items in the home?

- Do you feel your home is already "market ready"?
- If not, what do you feel the house needs before it will be "market ready"?
- Can you put any personal items, furniture and accessories into storage while your home is on the market?
- Is there anything currently in your home that you must have immediately?
- Is there anything in your home currently that you can't wait to eliminate?
- Since you purchased the home, what have you added?
- Since you purchased the home, have you removed or replaced anything?
- When you first arrived at the home, what do you remember being the most favorable part of the home that made you want it?
- When you first arrived at the home, what do you remember being the least beneficial part of the home that made you hesitant, if anything?
- Do you know of any serious defects the home presently might have?
- Do you plan to do any major repairs on the home yourself or hire outside labor to do for you?
- Has the home been inspected officially yet?
- What has been the response of any agents that have previewed the home?
- What has been the response of any potential buyers that have previewed the home?
- Have you received any offers to date? What has been the disposition of those offers?
- What is your biggest frustration at this point?
- Are you looking just for consultation services or are you looking from someone to take charge and do all the necessary work for you?
- Have you ever heard of home enhancement before (home staging, staged homes, ready to sell services, etc.)?
- If not, may I show you a brief presentation which will show you what it is and how it can benefit you?
- Have you ever used a home stager/enhancer before on other properties?
- I will need to take pictures and measurements of your home. Will that be ok?
- Do you have a floor plan? Is it drawn to scale?
- How have you enjoyed the neighborhood here?
- Are there any problems with neighbors that I should know about?
- Do you have any pets that get nervous when strangers are in the vicinity?
- What do you feel the major problems are in the home's current condition?
- Have you already removed any furnishings or accessories that are highly valuable or irreplaceable?
- I may be suggesting the removal of up to 1/2-2/3rds of the furnishings presently here. Are you open to us moving them to a different location?
- How would you describe the general condition of the exterior?
- How would you describe the general condition of the interior?
- Will you be moving into a new home locally or are you moving some distance away?
- Is there a pool/Jacuzzi/sauna?
- Do you plan to live here while the house is on the market?
- Will you be living here until escrow closes?
- If you are planning to move out before it goes on the market, will you be taking everything out of the home when you go?
- Do you anticipate the need for renting furniture and accessories?
- Do you have a budget for the services of a home enhancement specialist or stager?

- What is your budget?
- $500 or less? $500-$1500? $1500-3000? $3000 or above?
- Is there anything you can think of that would be helpful to me to know in advance?
- Do you have any questions for me before we proceed further?
- May we take another tour of your home now together?
- After I tour the home with you, I will need to tour it again on my own to take detailed notes, measurements and pictures. Is that ok with you?

Depending on the responses of the seller, you might not need to cover any more probing ground than what these questions trigger. But you'll probably find that the answers to these questions will trigger other questions not covered here.

Questions can also be useful in confirming your understanding of what the seller wants, expects and needs from you. Those questions usually begin with, "Let me see if I understand you - is what you're saying . . . . .?" Or you rephrase or repeat something the client said and add the tag, "Does that sound right?" or "Did I understand you correctly?"

These types of questions help you clarify points and assure both of you that you are "on the same page". During the interview process, your questions will probably be a mixture of different types of questions, but the majority of your questions should be open-ended questions, the kind that encourage your client to talk.

THE GIVE AND TAKE PROCESS

Regard the whole process as a "give and take" exchange. The person who asks the questions is the person in charge, not the one answering the questions. You want this time to be light and enjoyable for the client and to create a feeling of having a conversation. Do not handle it in such a way that the seller feels they are being interrogated. So periodically, intersperse questions with information, comments and occasionally an example of what you've done for some other homeowner that may relate to the topic. Keep those examples to a minimum, however. If this is done very sparsely - a comment here, a similar experience there - the seller will get the impression you've had lots of experience, know what you're doing and have great confidence in you.

In the beginning you may have little to no experience. If you can, see if you can do a project or two for a real estate agent who is a friend or acquaintance. Do it for free if you have to. Consider it part of your training experience. I always start my business experience with a willingness to do something free or for a discounted fee just to gain the experience. There's no shame in that. You just want to keep it to a minimum. You shouldn't need to do more than 2-3 projects for free or at a discounted fee. You'll be amazed at how quickly you "catch on". And always remember, that you probably already have more knowledge than the average homeowner just because you've taken this training.

The Initial Tour of the Home

When you start the first tour of the home with the seller, you're going to quickly find out that it moves quickly and if the seller talks fast you can easily find yourself unable to write everything down that is being communicated. Don't be overly concerned because you're going to come back on your own (either now or on another day) and take copious notes of every room. Your job right now is to listen, listen, listen. Your job is to ask questions as you see things that concern you. This is when you need to have your "buyer's eyes" wide open and take note again of anything and everything that bothers you now or bothered you on the preview tour when you first arrived. If it bothers you, it's going to bother other people as well. Write down only the things that give you poor first impressions that distract you from focusing on the house. Much of these impressions you will remember later, but some are really going to jump out at you and others you might tend to forget. Those are the ones you really need to write down.

As human beings, we tend to remember forever the things that deeply affect us emotionally and we forget the things that didn't reach our deepest emotional levels. So that is why I want you to make notes about things you didn't like seeing that were more of a minor irritation, because these will be the ones that are harder to remember later.

Take a large note pad with you on the tour. Use at least one page per room. Note the name of the room at the top of the page. Jot down your negative reactions only, especially the minor ones.

Taking the Seller's Tour

Keep the seller talking as much about the home as possible. Ask them to try to be brutally honest about any defects they know about as you would appreciate their help in pointing out things that buyer's might not appreciate or relate to. Make them part of the critical team. Praise them on their ability to separate their emotions connected with the home and their efforts to view it as a "house" and no longer as their "home". Make no value judgments. Make no comments unless you are asked specifically about something. Save everything for the end report you will be making. Listen to what your seller is saying, but also listen for what they are **not** saying. Hopefully your seller will be totally honest about any problems in the home, but don't count on it.

If you are doing all of the talking, the seller isn't going to be very impressed. The seller wants to be heard and made to feel important and a part of the process. They may be apologetic for some portions of the house and its condition. Tell them you totally understand. Reassure them that minor defects can be easily fixed and that just a little tender loving care might be all that is needed. Be reassuring and positive. Be kind and understanding. Sometimes the homes will be in a state that is not normal for the family. You may not be privy to extenuating circumstances such as divorces, deaths in the family, some other critical issues such as loss of employment or other factors that can put a home into disarray. Be free of any judgment on their lifestyle.

Selling a home is a very stressful time for anyone. For some people it's like having a death in the family. I think about my own home of over 30 years and how I might feel if ever I was to move out. All of my family's history is in this home. It's undergone many changes through the years. It has aged with me and holds memories that are both near and dear and memories that are painful. There is a lot of history embedded into its walls that will remain long after I am gone. It isn't always squeaky clean. It isn't always orderly and organized. It certainly isn't in any kind of condition on the average day to be shown to a potential buyer. So you will not be privy to the deepest feelings, longings, stresses of the family that lives there currently and is going to be moving out. Whatever its condition, try to always show nothing but total respect to the seller.

You're not likely to find a home that is in pristine condition. If it were, they wouldn't need you, would they? So the run of the mill will be homes that need help - some needing desperate help. It would be easy to fall victim to some kind of urge to be critical of the people themselves and not just of the condition of the home. Be on guard for that, especially if you enjoy a home that is far superior in quality to begin with.

Using Your Check List

In your training you are being provided with a pretty extensive checklist of items that are typically needed in the preparation of most homes for market. These items are broken down by room, starting with the front exterior of the home and moving throughout the interior of the home to the back and side exteriors of the home. You can use either our check list or one of your own to help you when you do your own private tour of the home. One the key values of using a check list, is not only to serve as a reminder of all of the tasks that you might encounter in each room or area, but to help you as a home enhancer to estimate the amount of time, labor and costs that you might encounter for each and every task you perform on the behalf of the seller (or to help you advise the seller on what they should expect by way of time, labor and costs).

If you are creating your own check list to use from home to home, and you want to be able to easily hand the seller a list of tasks that you have checked off as necessary or recommended tasks, you could have your entire list pre-printed on NCR paper. Any local printing company can do this for you. It can be rather expensive to have your list printed on NCR paper, but the value is that you won't have to use carbons or worry about making copies. I wouldn't take this step, however, until or unless you are well entrenched with plenty of projects and know that you will regularly use these lists to help you conduct business. Until such time, just make copies of your working papers as needed or carry some carbon paper to use.

Evaluating Time Frames and Costs

Here is the place where you really need to devote serious time and attention. Evaluating the time and costs of a task is crucial for several reasons. First, you want to make sure that what you specify is as close to real time as possible. If you under-estimate the time needed, you will under-estimate the final quote. If you over estimate the time factor (or the costs), you run the risk of losing the project because the seller might think your services are too expensive. So there is a fine balance in trying to arrive at a price that is fair to you but in line with your competitors who may be bidding on the same project without your knowledge.

While you may be in an area of the country where home staging is relatively new or unheard of, that doesn't mean the seller (or agent, for that matter) isn't having another company/stager come in before you or after you to give a report and quote. You should always assume you have competition, even if you don't.

Developing Estimates or Bids

Don't be overly concerned. It is a trial and error proposition we all have had to cope with, even your competition. If you do a thorough job, and you properly alert your seller to all of the tasks that are necessary, and you charge a fair price, you'll get your fair share of the work. You have to know that you'll win some and you'll lose some. That happens to everyone.

As you gain more experience and expertise, you'll get better at it and you'll also get faster too. You may even one day emerge into a home enhancer that prefers to price a job by a percentage of the selling price. This has it's advantages and disadvantages. One of the advantages is that you can relax some on the front end, knowing that you don't have to nail down every single task in advance of giving a quote. You will be paid a flat fee for services based on the advertised price of the home at the time you start the work. The downside is that you may need to do more work on the property than the percentage justifies. But usually any overage or underage you experience will balance itself out over time as you do more and more projects.

In any event, you can structure your business any way you wish. 1% of a $500,000 home is $5000.00. You could easily afford to spend 5-10 days working on a home in this price bracket and make out pretty nicely, assuming you have no additional costs like renting furnishings, etc. Obviously the higher the price of the home, the more you would make for the same time and labor. So you might even want to work out more than one scenario for pricing your services. Work from a check list for the tasks you will perform and price them accordingly for homes that have a low sales price; consider a percentage of the sales price for higher priced homes. No matter how you structure your pricing, just do your best to make sure you adequately cover yourself for your time, expertise, labor and costs while at the same time trying to be fair to the seller and recognizing that sellers never want to pay very much for this type of service, no matter how much they need it.

The more you stress how time consuming this will be for the seller to manage for themselves, the more you stress all of the details that will have to be tracked, the more you stress how you've benefited other sellers, the greater your chances become of landing a lucrative project. As you grow in the business and become better at your job, you can always adjust your pricing up or down the scale. As you become better at your job, you will learn about short cuts you can take, how to group tasks better to cut down on time and so forth. All of these things add up in the end and help you make more money for the time and energy you expend.

Making Your Recommendations to the Seller

There are many different ways you can do this, all equally good choices. Obviously, if you're just providing a consultation and you already know in advance that the seller plans to do all the work themselves, you can go through your check list rather quickly and arrive at a list for the seller. If your check list is on NCR paper or you have carbon paper, it is totally possible to hand them a copy of the list of items to be done and recommendations and invoice to pay right on the spot. Some enhancers are more comfortable doing it this way than others. Never hand a home seller your list of recommendations without first agreeing on a price for this consultation. Get paid first, then give up the list. There is nothing worse than handing over all of your expertise on paper and then having to fight to get paid for it.

I don't do work for free unless it's my idea. So in every situation where I am expected to give counsel only, I demand at least 50% up front and the balance the moment I get done. I expect (and get) payment right on the spot. It's tough for a home owner to look you in the eye and refuse to pay you. If you require it while you're there at the home, you're much more likely to get it.

Now on the other hand, you may feel uncomfortable with doing that and feel that it is more professional to go back home or to your office and draw up an official, typed report on your computer, together with an invoice or whatever. You, of course, can do that, but you will decrease your assurance of being paid after the fact. My suggestion is to always get paid on the spot. You can always promise to send the seller a formal checklist and letter of recommendations after you get back to your office, but make every attempt to be paid for your services at the time you are there in their home. I have found that most people will do whatever you tell them to do and will conform to the expectations you place on them.

The more time that goes by between making your recommendations and getting paid, the greater become the chances of never getting paid at all. Recommendations are ideas, concepts and thoughts - as such they are more easily dismissed as being worthless, or should I say less worthy of being paid for than an actual service or action. So this is another reason why you should always strive to first be paid in advance, or at least to be paid before you leave the home the first time if you are only going to be providing a list of recommended tasks to make the home ready for market.

If the agent is paying for the consultation, get paid in advance as well. Be sure and give or send the agent a copy of your official recommendations as well as the seller.

What Does it Cost?

Fortunately, enhancing a home doesn't have to be expensive to be effective, though that has to be balanced with the income level of the seller. A basic staging consultation, in which a home enhancement specialist evaluates the home and submits a report of what needs to be done, usually costs between $150 and $300, depending on the market and the size of the home. Experienced stagers suggest that the seller should pay for staging. "The agent doesn't pay for the home inspector to inspect the house or the roofer to put on a roof," they say. "So why expect the agent to pay for enhancement? It's the owner's home." Nevertheless, as I've already stated, many agents absorb this cost as a marketing expense, probably because they either lack the ability to promote it correctly or just find it easier to get it accomplished if they absorb the cost themselves. They also probably are more inclined to pay for it themselves because it is hard to convince a home seller that it is truly needed. When there is a leak in the roof, they don't have to be told that a new roof is needed or that it needs repair.

"I give complimentary staging to my clients," says one agent. "It's an added service that I can offer to give clients truly remarkable service." This agent will also cover a few hours of a stager's time to do some simple furniture placement and de-cluttering. If the stager suggests bringing in props or doing substantial work in the home, however, he gets the seller's approval, then passes the costs on to the seller. To me, this is a pretty fair way to operate.

The second phase of staging, when the actual cleaning, packing away, and enhancement are done, can get expensive. Costs for hiring a professional stager to actually carry out staging recommendations can range from $500 to $15,000 depending on the extent of the work to be done and the income level of the seller. So if you're looking for some kind of formula, it doesn't exist, and you need to factor in all of the advice I've already given above on this subject. You're talking about a custom service and you need to sell it as such no matter what income level the seller is at. It's doubtful that any home seller can compare one stager with another, because likely each person will list a different amount of services they will render. You may be talking about 20 items, 50 items or more. That works in your favor because it is so difficult to really compare apples with oranges.

Homeowners who are willing can usually do some of the staging themselves, making the option more affordable for mid-range sellers. Another way to make home styling less costly is to suggest that homeowners purchase items to stage the old home that can be reused in the new one. That way, they get the desired temporary effect without wasting money, assuming the new purchases are rather neutral to appeal to the broadest number of buyers. Some home sellers have actually been so enamored with the furniture that a stager brought in they decided to buy it once the house was sold, adding even more profits to the stager's bottom line.

Professional stagers should always attempt to stay within a seller's budget, however. Charge at least $350-450 for staging an average three-bedroom, two-bath house (arranging furniture only). Keep your fee fairly low because of your creative uses of the seller's own furnishings. Charge more for services above and beyond that. This is about as close to a formula as you're going to get, and it's not a hard-fast rule either. Remember, I've also talked about taking a percentage of the selling price of the home as a flat fee for services.

It's also critical that the home enhancer avoid interfering with the work the agent is trying to do. An enhancer needs to walk the line between what helps the agent and what the client wants. That's why I spent so much time earlier talking about the different types of questions you should be asking the agent so that you really grasp where the agent is coming from and avoid antagonizing the agent whenever possible. The stager's advice is very important, but the agent knows the market and often can be helpful in determining how much staging needs to be done. Some will be clueless and give you carte blanche – others will want to have their imput.w

A stager should also know how to get the job done effectively — where to find the best buys on decorating items and good values on cleaning and other services that sellers may want to use. And, as in the case with any vendor, it is important that the home enhancer complete the work in a timely fashion and keep the agent apprised of deadlines and possible delays.

While some stagers feel that a real estate background is more critical for a successful stager than one in design, experience is what will ultimately count. Understand the real estate market and the stress of what it's like to be a seller. A designer may understand design, but stagers who understand sellers and the needs of the market can act a lot quicker and cater to those needs.

As the industry evolves and cut-rate brokers put more pressure on full-service real estate practitioners, success may ultimately hinge on an agent's ability to provide extra value. The ability to offer home staging does just that.

The way we live is not the way we should sell our home. By repainting the walls a neutral color and replacing the floral bedspread and repositioning the bed, one of my students turned this bedroom around so that it really looked inviting and showed off the home to its best advantage.

When a kitchen is completely bare it has no personality. This is not good, even though it is not cluttered.

With some careful placement of accessories, the kitchen looks charming and a place where one would love to fix a meal.

52

Chapter Two

Providing a Full Service Enhancement

Full Service Agreements

While I know that you're probably eager for me to provide you with a bona fide contract you can use with agents or home sellers, I cannot do that for liability reasons. I will not provide actual contracts but I will provide a rough sample at the end of this manual. If you want a contract to use that protects you, you'll need to contact an attorney in your state or country to arrange for one to be drafted for you. There are too many differences from locale to locale, from state to state and from country to country. I will, however, provide you with a loosely written example of a simple agreement for you to draw ideas from right here. I in no way warrant it as any kind of iron clad agreement that will protect you in the event of a dispute. That is something you'll need to construct on your own. With that disclaimer stated, here are some brief ideas.

The Waiver Form and Payment Agreement

THE WAIVER FORM - Now this is the tricky part. You're probably going to be tempted to skip this part but I advise you not to do so. For many years now, our society has become a "sue happy" society. People will sue other people at the drop of a hat. And there is an erroneous but common conception that you cannot be sued for things not involving any kind of negligence on your part. It's true that you must be found negligent for a plaintiff to win, and damages awarded can be miniscule, but the costs to defend yourself against a frivolous suit will still be incurred.

This is why I insist that all my clients sign a Liability Waiver. Mine isn't long and not full of legal jargon, but you'll have to decide what's right for you. Seek legal advice. While I am certainly not an attorney, nor do I claim that the following waiver statement will totally protect you in the event you have a problem of this nature (and I do recommend that you speak with an attorney for all legal issues pertaining to your business), here is the one I currently use.

This is just a brief statement on a sheet of paper that I ask my clients to sign at inception.

"While _____ (your company name) and it's owners and employees always take every precaution when handling a client's furnishings and accessories, and while we have never broken or damaged anything in the past, it is our policy to have every client sign a Waiver of Liability. Please read the paragraph below, fill out the address and date and sign the waiver. Thank you for your understanding and cooperation.

"I hereby acknowledge that I understand there are some risks involved in the moving of my furniture and accessories as part of the enhancement services I have contracted _____ (your name or name of your company) and associates to

---

do on my behalf. I hereby waive any and all monetary claims for damage or injury to myself or members of my family, my furniture and my accessories, whether owned, rented or borrowed by me or members of my family, relatives or friends and assume all legal and financial responsibility myself for such. I shall not now nor in the future make claim against _____ or any of her family, partners, associates, helpers or employees for any injury to persons within my home or damage or destruction of possessions or property belonging to myself or others in and on my property beyond the value of the services performed and agreed to in advance. I further warrant that I have the authority to authorize the movement of all of the furniture and accessories within this home."

_____

Signature

_____

Address of Property Chosen for Enhancement Services

_____

Date

Most people will be agreeable to signing the Waiver but you may encounter someone every once in a while that needs reassurance. Up until this point they probably haven't given a thought to whether anything might get damaged or broken in the process, and suddenly now they become apprehensive. Try to verbally reassure them about how careful you always try to be, that you've never had a problem in the past (hopefully you haven't), but then let them know that this is company policy and that all your previous clients have been agreeable and have signed the Waiver. They will probably sign it at this point.

If you are unlucky enough to get someone who refuses to sign the Waiver, then you have a choice. You can say to them that they will have to do all of the moving of the furniture and accessories themselves and you will simply direct where it should go; or you can say you can not take the job and leave; or because it is your business and you must decide what risks you are willing to take, you could dismiss the Waiver and do the job anyway. I advise against the latter choice, but it is really up to you.

PAYMENT AGREEMENT FORM - Once the Waiver is signed, you should also bring out a Payment Agreement Form that you have prepared in advance which states the nature of the financial agreement between the two of you. If you are charging a flat fee, the amount should be stated on the form. If an hourly fee, the anticipated time involved and the hourly rate should be clearly defined. Some home stagers charge a base minimum figure and then add an hourly rate if the project takes longer than a specified time. Whatever agreement you have already made with the client, the form should give you a place to indicate what the charges will be, which room(s) or exterior(s) you are addressing, the address of the location, the date, and any other particulars you feel will clearly describe what you have been hired to perform.

Construct a form that covers every area you can think of, because whoever draws up the agreement in writing (in this case you and your company), that is the party that is held responsible for any ambiguities that might arise later. I have operated before with no official agreement other than verbal, but times are clearly changing, and if you've ever watched any court TV shows like the People's Court, Judge Judy or any of the rest, you quickly see how much better it is to have all your business agreements in writing. They don't have to be complex and shouldn't intimidate the client. But they should adequately cover the basics of what you have agreed to do and how much the client will pay you for that service. Of course, if you're involved in acquiring rental furniture, it becomes more complicated and an official contract patterned off of contracts that furniture rental companies use would be very advantageous. I personally prefer to have the rental of the furniture be handled by the seller and not by me. I just don't like being in the middle of such arrangements. I will go back in and arrange the furniture and will even accompany the seller to the rental company's showroom and pick out the furniture, but I prefer for the seller to contract with the rental company themselves, even though I will miss out on any profits I could have made should the seller decide to buy any of the rented goods.

Get It In Writing

You should always conduct business with some kind of written agreement. While oral contracts are binding, you must prove to a judge that there was, indeed, an oral contract (a meeting of the minds) and that can be difficult to do sometimes. When it's in writing there are not the problems because the terms of the contract or agreement are down in black and white, dated and signed by both sides of the agreement. The very least amount of information you should have on an agreement are: the date, the client's name and address and phone, your name, address and phone, the project start date and projected end date, the specific details of the project, the anticipated hours, the hourly rate or a flat fee amount, any warranties promised, any disclaimers, any outside costs and how they will be handled, the deposit amount, how you want to be paid and when.

One Last Word About Costs and Pricing

Put yourself in the shoes of the seller. No one wants to spend money on home improvements, particularly if they aren't going to be around to enjoy them or benefit from them. While they will likely benefit from a higher sales price, there's really no guarantee of that, at least not in their minds. But turning in the lowest price is no guarantee that you will get hired.

Shrewd and savvy business people will get 3-5 estimates and will not pick the lowest price. Why? Because they might feel the materials or service will be less than desired. They might feel the company with the lowest price will cut corners on quality, be slower than others, or be less reliable. They want their projects to be done right and done quickly, and they have a right to expect that. So you don't want your estimate to be the highest one and you don't want it to be the lowest one. You want to fall right in the middle of the pack in most cases. But even more than that, you want it to be a fair price and you want to get back what you need to not only survive in business, but to prosper.

Value starts with you and what you determine your value is. Don't cheat yourself just to get the project. You won't be happy and it will show up somewhere in your work or attitude.

And while they will know that it is impossible to compare "apples-to-apples" in the home staging industry, they will still try to do it. So you'll have to test your pricing over and over again. There is no hard, fast formula. You can't even honestly compare a MacDonald hamburger with a Burger King hamburger. What goes into each is different; the weights and the condiments may be different. If you can't compare something as simple as a hamburger, how can you realistically compare home staging services? So don't get overly concerned about this. Do what's right for your clients. Work hard. Give them more than you promise. Believe me - you'll get referrals that will be worth gold that you won't even have to bid on to get. Just make people happy. When you give them what they want, you'll get what you want in return.

Line Up Outside Vendors to Help You

I'll write about this again later, but I cannot stress enough the importance of building solid relationships with outside vendors whom you can rely on to do some work for you at the drop of a hat. They need to be quality workpeople who offer great service at an affordable price. Work out a referral fee to bring them on board. Have them bill the seller directly so you're not involved in case anything goes wrong. But get your labor force in place and get them to give you a percentage of the profit for referring them. This is a way to make extra income without having to do the work yourself.

Beginning a Full Staging Service

Taking the "Before" Pictures

Once you have completed the interview process and your Liability Waiver is signed, your agreement is signed, you've done your seller assisted walk-thru and you've done your private walk-through, you are ready to begin taking pictures. Get out your camera and do that. Explain to the client that you always like to take "before" pictures so that you will have a reference later for your records. If you plan to use the pictures as "before and after" examples on your web site or in your literature (which I do all the time), you might also mention that you use the photos to give examples of your work to other prospective clients and add, "if that's ok with you". I've never had a client say it wasn't ok. In case it should be a problem in the future, you can always refer back to this brief conversation confirming that you did get the client's permission to use the photographs later. Technically they are yours and part of your work process, so you really have the ability to use them however you want without permission, but it's a nice courtesy to mention it.

Now let's cover how to take the "before" pictures. You want to take an adequate supply of pictures because you don't know how they will come out. Most pictures have a tendency to come out too dark, at least for me, but then I'm no camera whiz. You want to do this part as quickly as possible. However, I rarely use my standard film camera any more because I have two top notch digital cameras which I use almost exclusively now. One has a powerful zoom for close-ups, and the other one has the digital industry's best wide angle lens for taking distance shots of two walls simultaneously.

My zoom camera is a Lumix with a 12x optical zoom. It's made by Panasonic. Having said that, it's no doubt out of date by now compared to new cameras developed in the interim. My wide angle digital camera is made by Olympus and is the Camedia C-7070. They are both fairly pricey so don't go jump into these types of cameras until you're well on your way to an excellent business to justify the costs. I haven't tried this one, but look into the Kodak EasyShare V705 7.1MP Digital Camera with 5x Ultra-Wide-Angle Dual-Lens Optical Zoom for under $300.

I try to take a picture of every wall in the room from the opposite side of the room. I also try to stand in every corner of the room and get a shot or two of the opposite corner. When you do this, your camera is going to pick up parts of two walls. You want to pay particular attention to getting a shot of the parts of the room you just know look "awful". You want there to be as much difference in your *before* shots from your *after* shots as possible. It is the dramatic difference between the before and after that will have the greatest impression on future clients.

You're going to need more detailed pictures for home staging than you will ever need for the redesign business. To back yourself up later, you're going to want to take plenty of distance shots, plenty of close ups, even take pictures of problem areas like stains, chipped paint, etc. - just load up your camera with as many pictures as you can take. You can't easily come back and grab more pictures, so I always take far more than I know I will need, just as a backup. Don't rely on your memory for every detail of every room and exterior section.

If you see smaller sections of the room that need improvement (the top of a desk or table, a shelf unit or such), take close up shots of those areas. Remember what areas you took pictures of as best you can because you're going to want to try to show those areas again in the *after* shots and how you improved the appearance of that desk, table or shelf unit, furniture arrangement, painted wall, repaired table leg, etc.

Unlike redesign, you may also want to take pictures of the inside of closets, drawers, cupboards, the garage, the laundry room - places that you don't normally work with or bother with in the redesign industry. Taking good, detailed pictures is also a precautionary step as well. Should you have a later problem with getting fully paid for services, you'll have plenty of proof (both before and after) to show all of the work you performed. And you never know what you'll want to incorporate into your portfolio. In a nutshell, take a vast amount of pictures.

If you feel you have time, you might want to try to take both digital and traditional photographs. But be sensitive to your client. If the client is busily doing something else, like cleaning or fussing with kids, etc. then you have more time, but if the client is standing around and waiting on you, then get this part over as soon as possible.

When done, put your camera(s) back with your tools. Always keep all of your personal equipment and tools in one place out of the way. Don't be a source for further mess. You're going to be facing plenty of messiness as it is in most cases. Don't add to it.

Taking Measurements

Measurements in a home staging project can be critical to a successful outcome, particularly if you're going to need to bring in more furniture and accessories. If you're assisting in the rental of furniture, you absolutely don't want to rent too much furniture or furniture that is too large or too small. Measurements will back you up when you have to make decisions away from the home.

It's really helpful if you have some 1/4" graph paper to use. In the design business, 1/4" is always equal to one foot. So if the room measures 20 feet in one direction you can easily draw a line 20 boxes long on your graph paper. Indicate where there are breaks in the wall, such as doorways, windows or other architectural elements (thermostats, light switches, etc.).

Continue on around the room until you have drawn all four walls and so you have a good feeling for the basic architecture of the room and the amount of space you have to work with. You'll later match up your drawings and measurements to the photos you've taken.

This way you will easily be able to identify the natural traffic patterns that the room dictates. You could draw arrows on your layout at this point showing the traffic patterns. You'll need to make sure there is access to the windows and doors at all times.

TRAFFIC PATTERNS

Here are some general rules for traffic patterns. You always want to make sure you have enough clearance so that the room is both functional and safe:

- For major traffic paths, leave four to six feet open.

- For minor traffic paths, leave one foot-four inches to four feet open.
- To have foot room between seating area and the edge of the coffee table, leave at least one foot.
- For foot and leg room in front of a chair or sofa, leave 1-1/2 feet to 2-1/2 feet open.
- Leave three feet open in front of a piano chair or bench.
- For occupied chairs, allow two feet per person left open.
- Leave 2 feet to three feet as the open space to get into chairs.
- Leave 1-1/2 feet to two feet of open traffic path around the table and occupied chairs.
- For making a bed, leave 1-1/2 to 2-1/2 feet open around a bed.
- Between twin beds, leave a traffic path of between 1-1/2 feet to 2-1/3 feet open.
- In front of dressers, leave at least three feet of walk space to allow you to open the drawers.

After you have the room's measurements and you have noted the traffic flow for the room, I advise you to take the measurements of the major pieces of furniture in the room that will be staying. You don't have to measure any furniture that will be leaving the premises, only if it will be used somewhere in the home.

The only measurements you will really need to take are the length and width. Occasionally you might need to measure the height of something. Jot down on your paperwork the name of the furniture and it's measurements and what room it is currently in or what room it will be moved to. As you begin to work and try to decide if a certain piece will fit a certain place, your measurements will all be readily available and you should double check them first before moving something, particularly if it is heavy or expensive. If it's a specially cherished piece, it's a good idea to temporarily remove it from the home altogether for safety.

Removal List

As soon as is feasible, make a list in each room of all of the pieces of furniture and major accessories that will need to be removed. Make one list for furniture leaving the premises. Make another list for furniture to be moved to a different room. Have a third list for furniture that will be staying. A little later I'll provide a list of common items that are often removed.

Retain List

Before you start to reposition furniture in a room, make sure all furniture that will not be left in the room is removed. This is the best way to function quickly and efficiently. You'll probably need a few muscular men to carry large pieces out or at least a large dolly. If you don't have a set of furniture sliders for moving heavy furniture on carpet and hard floors and a furniture lifter, the job of moving furniture becomes more tedious

Shopping the Home

You're also going to want to "shop the home" for furniture and major accessories that you could use that may be in other rooms or in storage in the garage. Clients will not be looking at the home with the same mindset you have, so you just may find some pieces they have tired of that would work perfectly for the staging of the home. When you're doing your initial walk-thru, you might spot pieces, but it's a good idea to revisit every room and the garage for the specific purpose of "shopping" the home, because its easy to forget when your mind is tracking in so many different directions on the previous tours of the property.

Adding to the Mix

While the whole goal of a good home enhancer/stager is to try to prepare the home for market without the seller having to spend any additional money (other than for your services), this is quite often an impossible task. It's really going to boil down to the size of the home, the number of pieces the seller has there for you to work with, the quality and color and so many more factors, as you can imagine. You're going to try to pull from their own garden some plants and flowers for arrangements, but they just very well may not have enough furniture to really do a proper staging. Many homes go on the market completely barren of anything.

So don't be surprised that you'll have to have a conversation on bringing in some additional furniture and accessories, even if you're taking some out at the same time. You'll have to be very careful when suggesting that some furnishings the seller owns won't work yet you want to bring in something rented instead. You really have to use all of the diplomacy you can muster here. But then again, some home owners will readily admit to you that their furnishings are all wrong or too beat up or whatever it is that makes them less than ideal. So you just have to play it by ear on this issue.

Evaluating Home's Architecture and Views

Just like you would do as a re-designer, you're going to begin every room with looking carefully at the room's architecture to see if there is any natural element in the room that obviously is the dominant feature in the room. You'll need to analyze that focal point to see if it is what you want to continue to feature and whether there is any aspect to it that needs to be repaired or cleaned up. This is crucial.

If the room has a large bay window but the scene out the window is a neighbor's wall with their utility boxes, you're not going to want to feature that view at all. So draping the window might be in order. If the room has a fireplace but it is in some kind of disrepair and the seller balks at repairing it for some reason, you're going to need to draw attention away from the fireplace rather than featuring it prominently.

So you'll want to inspect the room's natural focal points carefully to see if they need service, highlighting or "hiding". Let's say that large bay window overlooks a grand floral pasture or beautiful woods but the window is covered with heavy drapes. You'll want to consider removing the drapes and hanging some beautiful sheer curtains where the scenery will open up and pull the buyer into the room to admire the view.

Evaluating Background Design

After you've identified the focal point and decided upon featuring it or de-emphasizing it, then you'll want to turn your attention to the walls and the floor - the background of a room. Many people, in their decorating to live in the space, have chosen some pretty bright, busy wallpapers or dungeon dark paints and so forth that really make the home look small and dingy and foreboding. The carpeting may be in terrible shape and need replacing. The walls may need to be stripped of the wallpaper and re-papered or painted. The paint may be scuffed and marred or chipped. What we are willing to live with ourselves is not at all what we should suggest someone else accept - not if we want to sell quickly for top dollar.

Many people have chosen colors, intensities and values that are all wrong for the space. The walls and window treatments press in and attract too much attention to themselves. They don't blend in and stay in the background where they belong. Perhaps the seller has painted the walls dark and then installed bright white crown molding that just jumps out and grabs all the attention to itself, making the room look pieced up.

Your job as a home stager should be to try to minimize some of the decorating faux pas and correct them by taking the background from glaring to subdued, from gaudy to neutral, from high contrast to a blended look. By doing this you will help the seller go a long, long way to making the entire home look more spacious and less cluttered. You will take it from poor design choices back into a safer, neutral zone that will appeal to the broadest possible range of potential buyers.

Evaluating Natural Light Sources

Next you're going to want to focus on the natural light sources of each room. Natural light is very important in making a room appear bright and cheery and welcoming. If a room has a lot of natural light, you won't have to make sure that artificial light is brought in, except for maybe one lamp for evening viewing. Let the light in as much as possible, unless it's the middle of August and the room is baking hot. Then you're going to want to do what you can to cool the room off during the worst times of the day.

Adding Artificial Light Sources

When designing rooms for a family to live in, one normally wants to make sure there are at least 3 light sources that are positioned so that they form a giant triangle in the room. It's called triangular lighting. But for a staged home, you may want to drop the lighting sources (lamps) down to just two. You want to light the room adequately, but you have to balance that with keeping the room from looking cluttered. Always remember you want each and every room to look as big and spacious as possible. So in some cases you may be faced with a trade off. More light vs. fewer items. Just use your best judgment here.

Bringing the Outdoors Inside

I'm a big, big fan of plants, both live and artificial. Plants are the easiest accessories to bring into a room and do absolute wonders for a home that needs staging. But the plants have to be in good condition. You can't have any half dead plants or plants with dead leaves. That's nasty. Toss those babies out. But as a home stager you can keep a supply of plants on hand for just this purpose. You'll want to make sure that they are in excellent condition and marked on the bottom as being your property. Plants will soften the hard edges of a room and the furniture and if you bring in a large spreading tree, put it in a corner and that's all you need. They are a home enhancer/stager's best friend. Having said that, don't overdo it. A little bit goes a long way.

Another reason I like plants so much is that they virtually go with any color and any style. You can use them with cool colors and warm colors. You can use them with modern furnishings and traditional furnishings and everything in between. Love 'em. You will too.

Exit Re-evaluations

Finally, before you ever leave the home on your first visit, the last thing you should study is how each room appears to you and the home as a totality upon **exiting**. Remember that the last impression can be almost as important as the first impression. What your eye is drawn to as you leave the room, or as you finally leave the home itself will create the lasting impression. Think of it like judging "Dancing with the Stars" or "American Idol". The last lift, the final position the dancers take is the last impression the judges will get. That final "high C" or that last musical "run" to end the song will be the last thing that Simon Cowell will hear. It's pretty important to leave a great lasting impression.

So make sure when you're taking your "before" pictures that you grab pictures of the doorway you will exit from in every room you enter. If that's the last view you will get, that is the last view the buyers will get too. You'll want to make sure that view is as positively strong as their first view upon entering the room.

The Less is More Effect

The popular design mantra "Less is More" was never more true than in home staging. This is probably going to seem pretty extreme, but when you start to de-clutter the home for the market you are going to take it from "full" to just this side of "stark". Seriously. You want to remove all sense of clutter and you want to make each room look as big and spacious as possible, but by the same token you don't want the home to look completely lifeless. Homes that are stark bare do not sell quickly. It's too difficult for buyers to imagine themselves living in the home. So you have to "suggest" activities by the furnishings you place (or leave) there. A completely bare room (or home) subconsciously transmits the message that the owners **have to sell**, that they are on the verge of becoming desperate to sell. This is not a good message for buyers to feel. You always want your client's home to look "lived in".

Check out the number of doors in each room. If the doors are a different color from the wall, paint them the same color or remove them and store in the garage. You really want all doors to disappear from view. Doors, especially if a different color, have a way of cluttering the room visually because they chop it up. When I visited my Mom a couple of years ago, her living room/dining room combination had 7 doors in a dark chocolate brown. The walls were off-white. The rooms were narrow and long and she has lots of furnishings. When I left I instructed her to have a painter change out the color of her doors to the same color as the walls. She was ecstatic with how much better the rooms looked and felt. Now her doors were not competing with her furnishings for attention and both rooms looked far less cluttered and relaxing.

Open doorways won't block the view either. I have a door between my kitchen and office which I removed years ago. The space is far more open and inviting and also I'm free from the annoyance of opening and closing the door all the time.

Check List of Removal Items

In order to properly de-clutter a space you'll invariably be involved in boxing up accessories and other non-decorative items that are in each room. You'll need to use boxes that you provide as part of your service or boxes that the seller has. Either way, as you box things up you'll want to mark each box with a label that states which room the box came from. It's also a very good idea to fill out a contents form and tape the contents form to the outside of the box. There's nothing more frustrating than to be looking for an item and being unable to find it after it's packed away. A contents list can be a valuable additional service to offer that your competition probably isn't offering.

Some of the items you will box up will go into the seller's storage. Other items may be designated for donation to Goodwill or another charity. By encouraging your seller to donate items you will be helping other people who need inexpensive sources for household goods, even clothing, shoes and other items. If you offer a **garage sale management service**, you may find yourself boxing up items that will be sold through that venue, either before the house goes on market or even at a different location, such as official swap meet venues or at a relative's home.

Think constantly "less is more" and let that be your guide. Home owners become attached to items that they should have let go of years ago, so you can also provide a needed service of helping them look at many of their possessions with more objective eyes. If the seller puts enough items into a well-managed garage sale, they might even pay for the entire cost of hiring your staging services. One never knows.

But a word of caution. A homeowner's possessions often have nostalgic emotions tied to them. They might have really significant emotional feelings that get aroused by the sight of certain possessions. Be thoughtful and concerned about the memories that other people cherish that are associated with their furnishings - and the home itself.

As you begin the process for the seller, remind them that it's going to look worse for a while before it all starts to look better. Weeding out and sorting possessions is a time consuming cluttered process. Remind the seller that all this upfront work will actually make their final move so much easier and has to be done anyway. It will also have another benefit when they get to their new home because it will make the unpacking process go so much more smoothly as well.

TYPICAL THINGS TO REMOVE

- Excess sofas and chairs. You only need one sofa and one chair per room.
- Small throw rugs.
- Excess end tables. You only need two.
- All bookshelves except one.
- All ottomans.
- Boxes, bins, cabinets (more commonly found with home based business owners).
- All lamps except one table and one floor, unless room is extra dark.
- All small appliances except perhaps toaster or microwave.
- All stacks of newspapers, bills, notes, magazines, etc.
- All magnets, notes, bulletin boards.
- All large beds. Put in smaller beds with only one nightstand.
- One table and chair is enough in master bedroom unless room is very large.
- Television and stand in bedroom.
- Bureaus and dressers, unless room is quite large.
- All things on bathroom counters that are utilitarian.
- All but one bath mat.

Check List of Items Often Retained

You can temporarily fill out a check list of items you want to keep in the room or get from another place in the home and tape this list to the door of each room. Just remember to remove these lists later when your services are complete. Items commonly kept are: sofa, loveseat, sofa chairs, end tables, coffee table, console table, very large area rugs, dining table, dining chairs, smaller beds, night stands, table lamps, large trees, some plants, centerpiece, headboards, chest of drawers, large artwork, microwave, toaster. See Bonus Section for an actual form.

Cleaning and Repairing the Home

Tools of the Trade

Here is a list of the main tools of the trade you might consider having with you:

- My portfolio (I usually don't need it, but always good to have it if I do)
- A 25' metal measuring tape
- A paint chip sampler (for color discussions)
- A note pad or 1/4" graph paper, pencil or pen
- My digital camera
- A wide angle lens traditional camera and tripod (optional)
- An artificial tree
- Assorted artificial plants of various sizes in baskets
- A Thomas Brothers map
- A liability waiver form
- An invoice
- A Services Agreement Contract
- A client card
- A testimonial and referral request sheet
- A professional sales case/caddy on wheels
- A dust rag
- Deodorant
- Allergy pills (if you are allergic to dust mites)
- A padded dolly for moving furniture inside and outside the home
- Clean white cotton gloves
- Supply of rubber gloves (long)
- Clean white soft cotton rags
- Polishing cloths
- Duster
- Padded trays for carrying small objects at one time
- A supply of cardboard or foam core sheets to protect works of art
- Extra pads
- Raffia (assorted colors for tying)
- Scissors
- Plenty of Assorted Felt Tip Markers (for labeling boxes)
- Krud Kutter Stain Remover
- PureAyre Odor Eliminator (Gallon)
- PureAyre Cleaning Kit
- Painter's Tape
- Masking Tape
- All Purpose Glue
- Hammer
- Phillip's Screw Driver
- Regular Screw Driver

- Needle Nose Pliers
- Assorted nails, hooks, wire
- Wallpaper removal tools
- Small Level
- Large Level
- Furniture Sliders for Carpet
- Furniture Sliders for Hard Floors
- Wood Polishing Cream
- Leather Polishing Cream
- Assorted Paint Brushes
- Staple Gun
- Yard Sign to Advertise Your Services (metal stake kind)
- Cell Phone
- Contact List of Vendors
- Check List of Possible Services to be Considered
- Extra Business Cards
- Furniture Arrangement Kit
- Storage Boxes
- Sealing Tape
- Trash Bags
- Garment Bags
- Blankets
- Van/Truck (or rental trucks)
- Giant plastic bags (for covering beds, appliances, etc.)
- Gardening Tools

PROPS YOU MIGHT INVENTORY

- Sofa or Loveseat
- Dining Table with chairs
- Bar Stools
- End Tables
- Coffee Table
- Assorted Table Lamps
- Slip Covers (neutral color)
- Artificial Trees (6 and 7 foot)
- Artificial Floor Plants (3-5 foot)
- Artificial Table Plants (1-2 foot)
- Artificial Table Floral Arrangements (assorted colors)
- Artificial Fruit and Pastries
- Assorted Plug-in Room Scents
- Area Rugs (neutral) 3x5, 4x6, 5x7, 9x12
- Neutral Table Linens
- Colored Light Bulbs
- Supply of Good Used Hardbound Books
- Assorted Vases
- Tray Table for Master Bed
- Reading Glasses
- White Throw Pillows
- White Pillow Shams

- Assorted Colored Candles and Candle Sets
- Assorted Landscape Art (framed under glass or canvass)
- Free Standing 3-Panel Room Divider

Carry the essential items in a professional sales case on wheels or in some other enclosed case. Do not walk in to anyone's home carrying your tools in your open hands or in a box. This will instantly devalue your credibility. Even though you will be dressed casually because you are going to be doing physical labor while there, you want your appearance to be professional and organized.

Cleaning Check List

I'll get into more specifics later, but here are some quick guide tips on what to expect in the cleaning area of a staging business. First, you'll pretty much have to remove (or at least move) just about everything. Next you'll be consolidating, not only what will be packed and sent elsewhere, but what will be remaining. The cupboards should remain well stocked, but you don't want them to look crammed and you'll be facing all labels to the front. Things, including clothing, that face outward from the side should all face the same direction. You'll leave enough clothing in the closets and drawers to look like someone lives there, but eliminate any look of being jammed in.

Paint what you can't clean. Paint the insides of the closets. Scrub everything else thoroughly. Use a plain white shelf liner. These are some of the "extra" goodies that will really impress a buyer. You'll be wiping down all glassware, pottery and bottles and facing them toward the front. Group them in like kinds: all cans together, all bottles together, etc. Use plastic containers for things that may move around in a drawer or small items. Storage boxes are a must. Fold all the linens in a tri-fold style. This prevents the edges from showing and looks more professional.

Look at the quality of the hangers that the seller has. Replace old bent ones and use the same type of hanger throughout each closet. Hang the clothes facing the same direction. You can even group them by color. Shoe racks and boot racks would be another nice touch.

The windows should be cleaned with a good glass cleaner to prevent streaking. Wipe dry with paper towels. You can even use newspapers, but the ink does come off on your hands. Check out the sills and make sure they are free of debris or dead bugs. Remove any knick-knacks on the window sills or plants that may block sunlight from streaming into the house. You always want plenty of sunlight to stream through all the windows. Don't forget the skylights. You might not think they are that dirty, but you may be really surprised how much additional light they let in when they are clean.

And don't forget the glass on the framed art, the mirrors and the frames themselves. Be sure to check first to see if the glass is real glass or plexi-glass. You do not want to use a cleaner on plexi-glass. Just use a damp cloth or sponge to clean plexi-glass. Lastly, be sure to clean the light bulbs in the lamps and in the ceiling and wall fixtures. If they are dirty, they won't be able to cast light to their full potential. To get the brightest possible light, put in new bulbs.

Curtains and drapes should be professionally dry-cleaned or laundered. If they are in poor condition, suggest sheers for the softness, ease of installation and inexpensive costs. The floors should be mopped and waxed and polished to a high sheen. Carpets should be cleaned and deodorized. All woodwork needs to be wiped down and polished. Painted surfaces will need to be inspected and touched up or repainted.

Carpet Care and Stain Removal Guide

Day to Day Care
1. Vacuum frequently
2. Clean spills promptly
3. Have periodic professional carpet cleaning. (Brite-World)

Appearance
1. Sprouting - Shoe nails, pet claws, or defective cleaning equipment can pull tufts above the level of the rest of the carpet. Trim sprouts with a sharp pair of scissors.
2. Shedding - Short broken fibers can become trapped in the yarn during the yarn making process. After their carpet is installed, these short, unattached fibers show up on the surface of the carpet as fuzz. Some shedding is normal for the high quality spun yarn used in a fine carpet. A few weeks of vacuuming will eliminate the condition.
3. Shading - Heavy traffic sometimes cause tufts to lie in opposite directions. The tufts that remain upright appear darker than those lying on their side. A thorough vacuuming or combing the pile with a pile rake will lift compressed tufts and reduce shading.
4. Mildew - Gulistan carpet is designed to reduce mildew. However, when humidity is high or the carpet is continually moist, your carpet could develop mildew. If mildew should appear, first eliminate the moisture problem, then have a cleaning professional treat the carpet with fungicide.
5. Pilling - Pills are small, fuzzy balls that stick to the carpet surface. They are caused by strong, unbroken fibers clinging to weak fibers broken by defective or improper cleaning equipment. Gulistan carpets should not pill after the first few weeks. If pilling continues, the fibers should be carefully trimmed and all cleaning equipment inspected for worn or broken rollers, beater bars and brushes. Pets may also cause pills in the carpet.
6. Furniture Dents - The weight of heavy furniture will crush the pile underneath and cause an indentation, Holding a steam iron over (never against) the indented area will help restore the pile. If possible, you should rearrange your furniture periodically to reduce permanent damage indentations.

Preventative Care
1. Dirt isn't just dirty. It can actually harm your carpet. If allowed to accumulate, small particles will wear individual fibers, weakening the carpet.
2. Place walk-off mats at all outside entrances, use runners in high-traffic areas, and rearrange furniture periodically to reduce wear and dirt. The most important preventative measure you can take is proper vacuuming. Vacuum your carpet at least once or twice weekly, depending on the amount of traffic.
3. A vacuum cleaner with a motor driven brush attachment will work better than one that uses suction only. Follow your machine's directions for carpet height adjustment. Do not vacuum sticky or greasy stains.

Spills and Stains
1. Your carpet gets rough treatment everyday. Sooner or later, accidents will happen. Fortunately, your Gulistan carpet features the latest stain-resistant fibers. So cleaning is easier than ever before.
2. As soon as you discover a spill, follow theses steps. A. Remove as much of the spill as possible. Scrape up the solid material with a putty knife or other flat, blunt tool, moving from the outside of the spill to the center. Blot wet spots.
B. Refer to the Stain Removal Procedures for cleaning instructions. C. Let the carpet dry completely, then brush the pile to restore texture. D. Repeat procedure if necessary. E. Consult a

professional carpet cleaner if the stain persists. Tell the cleaner the type of stain, type of carpet fiber, color of carpet, style of carpet (cut pile, cut and loop pile, loop pile), carpet age, general condition, and cleaning method already used.

Stain Cleaning Methods (see explanation of each method below the list)

Acid Toilet Bowl Cleaner E
Acne Medication E
Alkaline Drain Cleaner E
Asphalt D
Beer A
Beet Juice B
Bleach E
Blood A
Candle Wax I
Carbon Black (soot) E
Carbonated Cola (dark) A
Carbonated Fruit Flavored Soda A
Ketchup A
Chocolate D
Coffee H
Cooking Oil/Soil D
Cough Syrup (FD & C colors) A
Cranberry Juice H
Crayon D
Dimethylsulfoxide E
Dirty Motor Oil D
Drink Mix A
Egg A
Feces C
Furniture Polish E
Furniture Stain D
Gelatin A
Grape Juice B then H
Grease D
Hair Dye E
Ice Cream D

Ink (water soluble) A
Ink (ball point) D
Insecticide E
Iodine A then E
Jam/Jelly (fruit or berry) A
Latex Paint A
Lipstick D
Liqueur A
Liquid Fruit Punch A
Marking Pen (permanent ink) A
Medicine (FD&C colors) A
Mouthwash A
Mustard with Turmeric A
Nail Polish G
Oil Paint D
Orange Juice A
Plant Fertilizer E
Prune Juice B
Red Clay Soil F
Red Wine H
Rouge D
Rust A
Sauce, Spaghetti & Bar-B-Que D
Shoe Dye E
Shoe Polish D
Tea H
Topsoil F
Urine C
Vomit C
Watercolors A

Cleaning Method A
1. Blot excess stain or liquid with paper towels.
2. Wet stain with a minimal amount of water, soak 1 minute, blot with paper towels, and repeat until no stain is evident on towels.
3. Apply small amount of liquid detergent. Massage into stained area with finger tips, blot excess, and repeat until no stain is evident on towels. Rinse with a minimal
amount of clear water, and blot.
4. Cover stained area with a layer of paper towels, weight down with a heavy object such as a brick or book. and allow to dry.
5. Repeat Step 4, each time adding a minimal amount of water; until blotter no longer picks up any stain.
6. Brush up pile of carpet and allow to dry thoroughly. (Turmeric will fade under strong light)

Cleaning Method B
1. Blot excess stain or liquid with paper towels.

2. Wet stain with a minimal amount of water, soak 1 minute, blot with paper towels, and repeat until no stain is evident on towels.

3. Apply first 3% hydrogen peroxide then ammonia to stained area. Blot, rinse with clear water; and blot up excess with paper towels.

4. Apply small amount of liquid detergent to stained area. Massage in with fingertips, blot excess, and repeat until no stain is evident on towels. Rinse with a minimal amount of clear water, and blot.

5. Cover stained area with a layer of paper towels, weight down with a heavy object such as a brick or book, and allow to dry.

6. Repeat step 5, each time adding a minimal amount of clear water, until blotter no longer shows any stain.

7. Brush up pile of carpet and allow to dry thoroughly.

Cleaning Method C

1. Blot excess stain or liquid with paper towels.

2. Vacuum up particulate. Soften stain with a small amount of dry-cleaning solvent, blot with paper towels, and repeat until no stain shows on blotter.

3. Apply small amount of liquid detergent. Massage into stained area with fingertips, blot excess, and repeat until no stain is evident on towels. Rinse with a minimal amount of clear water and blot.

4. Cover stained area with a layer of paper towels, weight down with a heavy object such as a brick or book, and allow to dry.

5. Repeat step 4, each time adding a minimal amount of clear water, until blotter no longer shows any stain.

6. Brush up pile and allow to dry thoroughly.

Cleaning Method D

1. Blot excess stain or liquid with paper towels.

2. Wet stain with a small amount of alcohol or dry cleaning solvent, blot dry immediately, and repeat until no stain shows on blotter.

3. Apply small amount of liquid detergent. Massage into stained area with fingertips, blot excess, and repeat until no stain in evident on towels. Rinse with a minimal amount of clear water and blot.

4. Cover stained area with a layer of paper towels, weight down with a heavy object such as a brick or book, and allow to dry.

5. Repeat Step 4, each time adding a minimal amount of clear water, until blotter no longer shows any stain.

6. Brush up pile of carpet and allow to dry thoroughly.

Cleaning Method E

1. Blot to remove excess stain or liquid with paper towels.

2. Rinse stain with a minimal amount of clear water, and blot dry with paper towels.

3. Have damaged areas replaced (plugged) by a professional carpet installer.

Cleaning Method F

1. Allow residue to dry.

2. Vacuum up particulate.

3. Wet stain with a minimal amount of water, soak 1 minute, blot with paper towels, and repeat until no stain is evident on towels.

4. Apply small amount of liquid detergent. Massage into stained area with fingertips, blot excess, and repeat until no stain is evident on towels. Rinse with a minimal amount of clear water, and blot.

5. Cover stained area with a layer of paper towels, weight down with a heavy object such as a brick or book, and allow to dry.

6. Repeat Step 5, each time adding a minimal amount of clear water, until blotter no longer shows any stain.

7. Brush up pile of carpet and allow to dry thoroughly.

Cleaning Method G

1. Blot excess to remove stain or liquid.

2. Apply a small amount of nail polish remover, blot immediately and repeat until no stain shows on blotter.

3. Apply small amount of liquid detergent, massage into stained area with fingertips, blot excess, and repeat until no stain is evident on towels. Rinse with a minimal amount of clear water, and blot.

4. Cover stained area with a layer of paper towels, weight down with a heavy object such as a brick or book, and allow to dry.

5. Repeat Step 4, each time adding a minimal amount of clear water, until blotter no longer shows any stain.

6. Brush up pile of carpet and allow to dry thoroughly.

Cleaning Method H

1. Blot to remove excess stain or liquid.

2. Wet stained area with a minimal amount of club soda or tonic water, blot with paper towels, and repeat wetting and blotting until no stain is evident on towels.

3. Rinse with minimal clear water.

4. Apply small amount of liquid detergent. Massage into stained area with fingertips, blot excess, and repeat until no stain is evident on towels. Rinse with a minimal amount of clear water, and blot.

5. Apply 3% hydrogen peroxide. Let stand 4 hours, blot, and repeat procedure. Allow to stand 24 hours, blot, then allow to air dry for 48 hours. If stain is still evident, repeat procedure until stain is no longer visible. Rinse with clear water and blot dry.

6. Brush up pile of carpet and allow to dry thoroughly.

Cleaning Method I

1. Allow wax to harden.

2. Freeze with ice and chip off excess.

3. Wet stain with small amount of dry cleaning solvent. Blot immediately with paper towels. Repeat until no stain is evident on blotter.

4. Apply small amount of liquid detergent. Massage into stained area with fingertips, blot excess, and repeat until no stain is evident on towels. Rinse with a minimal amount of clear water, and blot.

5. Cover stained area with a layer of paper towels, weight down with a heavy object such as a brick or book, and allow to dry.

6. Repeat Step 5, each time adding a minimal amount of clear water, until blotter no longer picks up any stain.

7. Brush up pile of carpet and allow to dry thoroughly.

Making the Rounds

Obviously if you don't want to do the cleaning yourself, there are plenty of professional services that can be hired to come in an do a thorough cleaning. I hate to clean my own place. I'm certainly not going to go clean someone else's. So I highly recommend hiring a cleaning service. But it's your business and maybe you don't mind cleaning.

Bring together two large baskets with handles or some light weight tote bags. Put your tools in one. Leave the other one empty. As you move from room to room, you'll have an easy place to put items that are out of place in the empty tote. Later you can place them in other rooms or in the area where the packing will be done. Whatever you can do to cut down on unnecessary steps and effort will help you zip through this less than appealing part of a home enhancement service.

Use your cleaning check list to mark off tasks as they are completed. With so many different tasks needing to be done, it's easy to forget.

A small carry round cleaning supply kit will usually find these types of items included:

- screwdriver
- single edged-razor (for removing paint drops, glue, caked dirt, etc.)
- a hand vacuum
- plastic garbage bags
- paper towels
- a small bucket with warm sudsy water
- glass cleaner
- can of cleanser
- rust remover
- scratch filler or cover
- your check list, notepad and pencil

A small paint kit might find these items included:

- throw away paint brushes, assorted sizes
- stir sticks
- plastic wrap by the roll
- masking tape
- razor or x-acto knife
- small can of white paint
- drop cloths
- step stool

Polishing

Look at all of the wood in the home, whether it be a door or paneling or the floor. As wood gets used it starts to dull. A good polishing will restore it's natural beauty and give the home a glowing warmth that only wood can give. You can get wood soap and a scratch cover which will cover up small scratches and chips. It will deepen the color of the wood and you'll be amazed at the transformation. There are also professional services that will come in and do this kind of work if you don't want to do it and the seller will pay for it.

Care of Wood Furniture

Ultraviolet rays will be harmful to your client's fine wood furniture, so keep them away from strong florescent lighting or bright sunlight. This is another reason why it's good for your client to periodically rearrange their furniture. You don't want a particular side to get sunlight all the time and deteriorate.

Be careful of extremes in humidity as this can cause the core wood to contract and then the veneer might buckle. If there is excessive humidity, the wood will absorb the moisture and then it might swell causing it to warp. Tell your client to keep the humidity as moderate as possible where you have placed fine furniture.

Tips on How to Clean and Preserve Fine Wood Furniture

There are a lot of misconceptions or myths that continue to circulate on how to care for wood furniture. And just try and find instructions when you buy that lovely armoire, coffee table, sideboard or other piece. I don't know about you, but I tend to neglect mine, or I inevitably do something wrong, and then I've ruined it for all time.

First of all, we all need to understand that wood is alive. What? Yes, it is a living organism. It has pores just like we do. It reacts to climate and temperature changes by expanding or contracting. Therefore, it is subject to reacting to humidity, pollution, sunlight and water.

Just as we use soap and water to cleanse our faces as a good and basic maintenance for every day, using a wood soap on your furniture acts like a deep-pore cleanser. It takes away the pollution from beneath and gets rid of the impurities that have collected.

And just like our skin, that needs a moisturizer after we clean it, wood needs a moisturizer as well. It comes as a commercial cream and makes the surface more flexible. It is then less apt to crack or split because of changes in the weather.

Don't apply the wood cream directly to the wood. Put it on a damp cloth, then work it into the wood by rubbing the wood in the direction of the grain. How often? Well, fine furniture needs to be cleansed and polished four times per year with the changing seasons.

Polish is the final application. You could compare it to makeup. To create a healthy glow that is vibrant, rub the wood with a soft, dry cloth along the grain. Look for a non-silicone cream and polishes that have a sun screen built in. Always read the labels before buying any furniture polish and follow the directions for best results.

Repairing and Painting

This is an area that I totally job out to a handyman as I'm not much good with making repairs. I know my limitations. So you should look at your own background and confidence level in any of these tasks. If you don't have the proper background and experience, don't risk botching the job and ruining your relationship with the seller by trying to do things you're not equipped to do.

Check out your local area to see if there are any Handymen Repair Organizations. Start with a search on the internet, making sure you include your city or county in the search requirements. You might have a husband or relative that is pretty handy. Repairs must be done right the first time as they can really be costly and time consuming to fix if they are botched. So before you hire anyone, check out their references in advance and know what they are qualified to do and what they are not.

I've found good professional help by asking around at my church. Even as I write this, I am waiting for my electrician to arrive to install new outdoor lights and put together a ceiling fan and install it. When it comes to things like electrical work, be sure to hire a professional. You definitely don't want any problems to come back on you if things are not done properly and according to code.

Steer clear of doing anything that requires you to place yourself in a dangerous position, like getting on roofs or extremely high ladders. It just isn't worth the risk in my opinion. Let the professionals do that kind of thing. You stay on the ground where you're safe. I refuse to do anything that requires me to stand on anything higher than a step stool or chair. Period!

Painting

I actually love to paint. Maybe because I'm also an artist and have had a few of my paintings published. But I guess I also love seeing one color disappear and a new one emerge. It's a change of pace for me from all of the computer and mental tasks I do. And it's quite amazing how a new coat of paint will change your entire feeling about a room.

You'll want to make sure you are dressed appropriately with comfortable clothes. Don't wear anything with long sleeves or puffy sleeves. Nothing too baggy. Always wear shoes. Make sure the room is well ventilated. My partner once was painting a space at night and did not make sure the area was well ventilated. He fainted while standing on the ladder and fell. The only thing he remembers is that he had the presence of mind to say to himself, "Keep the brush off the carpet!" He kept the brush from hitting the carpeting, but he broke his collarbone slightly in the process. So make sure you have plenty of air circulating in the room before you start.

To eliminate that paint odor, put one teaspoon of vanilla in a gallon of paint and stir it up before you start. You'll find there will be no significant odor and it won't change the color of the paint. Use a large plastic drop cloth and masking tape to protect the floors and keep paint from getting where you don't want it. Prime the surface with primer first (old paint can also work as a primer). It will help when you put the finishing coat on. Be sure to have some spackle to plug up little holes in drywall, then lightly sand the surface before painting.

Guide to Choosing Paint

The great thing about paint is that it is one of the least expensive methods (and one of the easiest) to change the whole look of a room. Almost anyone can paint a room in a decent manner and if you don't like what you selected, it's not that difficult nor expensive to change it.

But before you go and invest in paint, you need to know what kind of paint to buy for the surface you are going to treat. So here is a basic guide. Be sure to check the labels by the manufacturer before buying paint for a client, however.

APPLICATIONS	UNDERCOAT	OIL-BASED GLOSS	OIL-BASED EGGSHELL SEMI-GLOSS)	WATER-BASED EMULSION LATEX//VINYL	SOLID EMULSION (LATEX)	ENAMEL	TEXTURED PAINT
SURFACES TO USE ON	Use on primed surfaces. Do not use on plastic, copper, brass or stainless steel.	Woodwork, metalwork. Can be applied to plastic and copper without using undercoat.	Walls, ceilings and woodwork. Ideal for bathrooms and kitchens.	Walls and ceilings. Vinyl silk/satin can be used as a base coat for paint effects.	Walls and ceilings. Do not apply directly on to new unpainted plasterwork.	Metalwork, woodwork. Best for small areas.	Walls and ceilings. Particularly useful for covering uneven surfaces.
EQUIPMENT	Wide paintbrush, roller or spray gun for large areas, small paintbrush for details.	Wide paintbrush, roller or spray gun for large areas, small paintbrush for details.	Paintbrushes, roller and tray, or spray gun	Paintbrushes, roller and tray, or spray gun	Roller for large areas and paintbrush for details. Usually sold in its own tray.	Paintbrushes for small areas, roller or spray gun for larger areas.	Shaggy (coarse nap) roller and tray.
DILUTING	White spirit or	white spirit or	White spirit or	Use water to	Should not be	White spirit or	Should not

	turpentine can be used to thin the paint	turpentine can be used to thin the paint	turpentine can be used to thin the paint	thin the paint if necessary	thinned	turpentine can be used to thin the paint	be thinned
POSSIBLE PROBLEMS	Can be used as a top coat, but must be covered with matt varnish to avoid marking	Go back over painted surfaces to brush out drips and runs	Patchiness can occur if surface is not thoroughly prepared and completely dry	Oil-based paint and water-based paint are incompatible when wet	Too absorbent to take most paint effects. Not recommended for kitchens and bathrooms.	Shows up imperfections of surface, so thorough preparation is necessary.	Extremely difficult to remove
DRYING TIME	2-6 hours. A second coat can usually be applied after 6-16 hours.	4-6 hours. A second coat can usually be applied after 16-24 hours	4-6 hours. A second coat can usually be applied after 16-24 hours	2-4 hours. A second coat can usually be applied after 2-4 hours	1-4 hours. A second coat can usually be applied after 1-4 hours	2-4 hours. A second coat can usually be applied after 1-4 hours	1-4 hours
CLEANING	Use white spirit or turpentine to clean brushes immediately after use.	Use white spirit or turpentine to clean brushes immediately after use.	Use white spirit or turpentine to clean brushes and equipment.	Brushes and other equipment should be cleaned with water and soap.	Roller and tray should be cleaned with water and soap.	Use white spirit or turpentine to remove paint from brushes.	Use white spirit or turpentine to remove paint from roller and tray.
NUMBER OF COATS	1 or 2	2	1 or 2	1 or 2	2	1 or 2	1 coat, followed by a coat of emulsion (latex) or gloss
SPECIAL PROPERTIES	It has a high pigment content and covers well. Chalky texture as top coat.	Undercoat is not always necessary. Durable and easy to clean.	Smooth finish with dull sheen. Easy to clean and withstands condensation.	No primer required. Dries quickly to a smooth finish.	Particularly good for ceilings and stairways because it is non-drip.	No primer required. Some brands also contain rust inhibitors. Hard, shiny finish.	Much thicker than regular paint. Can be used to create various surface patterns.
COLORS	Limited to a few basic colors	Wide range of colors, some coordinating with water based ranges	Range of colors	Wide range of colors	Limited range of colors	Range of colors	Colored paint is applied to textured surface

Depersonalizing

So far we've discussed removing the clutter from the home, cleaning the home and repairing what needs to be fixed. There are two last major strategies left to properly prepare the property to go on the market and sell quickly for top dollar. The first one I like to call **de-personalization**, because the idea here is to remove from the home anything that fits into a small niche where it would only appeal to a very small percentage of buyers. Any time a home is highly focused on a very specific style or color, you run the risk of the home being categorized in a smaller segment. This is not good. You want the home to appeal to the absolute broadest segment of society. You, ideally, want anyone to walk into the home and instantly **know** that their own furnishings could fit and look good.

To accomplish that goal, the home must be depersonalized. To many sellers this will totally ruin the decor they worked so hard to achieve and that will be upsetting. They will tend to look on it as a criticism of their taste. So you have to be gentle with them. You have to explain why it will work to their advantage to remove the elements that target the home into a narrow classification. When explained properly, that it is in no way a reflection on them and their style and taste, most sellers will be able to handle any drastic changes you might recommend or implement without feeling overly dismayed.

So if the walls in the family room are covered with zebra patterned wallpaper, it has to go. If the bedroom walls are bright pink and green, those colors have to go. If the living room is full of stylized oriental furniture, it needs to be pared down to just a minimum and turned into a more eclectic feeling with a mixture of furnishings from other non-Asian countries. I personally love Asian furnishings, but it's too small of a niche market. I love all kinds of styles and colors. But I'm in the design business. Most people aren't. So you need to make sure that the home is neutral enough to appeal to the broadest segment. In other words, it should actually have **no style** - at least no definitive style - to be the most effective it can be.

Advising Client on Styling

Let me help you break it down into easy segments. You should note the style or combinations that the client has in the home, make suggestions on how the style can be relaxed or reduced. Here are some reminders in that area:

- Elegant
- Conservative
- Flamboyant
- Ordinary
- Dull
- Youthful
- Playful
- Luxurious
- Amusing
- Grandiose
- Strong
- Bold
- Graceful
- Offbeat
- Plain
- Formal
- Informal

- Ostentatious
- Amusing
- Dramatic
- Sedate
- Common
- Whimsical
- Opulent
- Powerful
- Understated Elegant
- Understated Casual
- Modern
- Serene
- Dignified
- Simple
- Graceful
- Quaint

Were I to pick from the list above and choose the best place to be in, I'd choose the following: understated elegant, understated casual, graceful, conservative, simple, dignified, traditional, plain. You get the point, right? By the way, slipcovers are a great item to utilize to de-emphasize a poor color or style. Consider stocking some white slipcovers of various sizes for sofas, loveseats, dining chairs, lounge chairs, and so forth. Have an inexpensive white comforter or bedspread on hand to depersonalize a bedroom. They don't have to be white, necessarily, but any color that is in the neutral white/beige/tan category would be very useful no matter what home you're working in.

Finding Vendors

Depending on how involved you wish to get in the Home Enhancement market, you would do well to set yourself up with some vendor companies who are professional, have great reputations, and who have the ability to step in and provides goods and services that your client sellers will need.

So with that in mind, set up accounts in advance with the following types of vendors:

1) A furniture/accessory rental company;
2) A painter;
3) A roofer;
4) A housecleaner;
5) A carpet cleaning service;
6) A landscaper or gardening service;
7) A tree trimmer;
8) A handyman;
9) A wall paper hanger
10) A storage facility
11) A moving company
12) An interior plant service

and any other type of supplier of products or services that you feel would enhance your services. But before you hire any of these companies, you should decide whether you wish to be the one that "contracts" for their goods and services or whether you wish the home seller to deal with them directly. If you hire the services, you will be legally responsible for the quality of the products and services they provide. If the homeowner is unhappy, they will want you to make good. This is another reason why you need to carry liability insurance.

If you merely provide the homeowner with the names and contact information, and make sure (in writing) the home seller deals directly with each company independently, then if the home seller is unhappy with anyone they will deal directly with the specific vendor company and you are out of the loop, so to speak.

Either way, you need to check out the people and companies that you enlist to help you with providing all the services the home seller needs. An unsatisfactory job committed by any one of these types of vendors will have negative repercussions on you and your business.

Home Enhancement Strategies

I believe in taking the risk of repeating myself because I think some subjects I'm teaching bear repeating. So if you find I'm going back over some concepts and strategies, bear with me. If you've never written a training manual, updating it frequently as needed, you'll never know how difficult it is to segment it and approach different aspects in a logical sequence at all times. Choosing what information belongs where can sometimes be difficult, so I find myself occasionally being a bit redundant, but this subject is too broad to write in one sitting and ever changing and evolving. So when I revisit certain subjects just to make sure you fully comprehend their importance, I recognize I risk making you impatient, even irritated, but I trust you'll continue to be gracious with me. Sometimes concepts stated in a different manner penetrate at last.

Your goal as a home staging professional is to lure buyers from the roadside, sitting in their car, onto to the sidewalk, up the driveway or path, up to the front door and into the home. It is the **curb appeal** that lures buyers into the home. However, it will be the **hearth appeal** that gets them to sign on the dotted line. Without both of these strategies in place, your client's home will probably stagnate on the market while other homes in the area are selling. And just as bad, if one or the other of these strategies is not done properly, the seller could lose thousands and thousands of dollars if and when they finally get an offer.

Creating Curb Enhancement

While it is easier said than done, you've got to help your seller look at the home through the eyes of potential buyers. Anything and everything that enhances the outside of the home, particularly the front of the home, falls into the category of **curb appeal**. What did you first notice when you drove up to the home? Did you approach the home from more than one direction? If not, go out to your car and drive up to the home from as many different directions as possible. Only then will you see what a buyer will potentially see. My home can be approached from 3 different angles: left, right and straight on. Different aspects of my front yard are more noticeable from one direction than another. If I didn't look at every angle, I would not understand the importance of driving up from all three directions and inspecting the home each time from a different perspective.

The seller might have children who are popular in the neighborhood. Perhaps there are two bicycles lying on the lawn. The seller might find it necessary to do car repairs in the driveway to save money, but hasn't thought about the stains on the concrete left as a result. A buyer will look at these issues as junk on the yard and a home that hasn't been cared for very well.

Here are a few quick tips to pass on to the seller. I say pass on because you're not going to be there every day to look after the home once you have completed your tasks, or you may have just been hired to consult with them and not actually do the work.

- Keep the lawn mowed and watered and green
- Keep the shrubs pruned and cleared
- Store all tools, gadgets, toys, sports equipment, and other utilitarian items
- Garage all cars or park them anywhere but in the driveway or in front of the house
- Plant some flowers along the walk
- Place some plants near the front door
- Keep all windows sparkling clean
- Keep doorbell in working order; install new doorknocker
- Keep house numbers clearly visible at all times
- Sweep sidewalks and steps daily and keep clear of clutter
- Replace or repair walkways, stepping stones, bricks so they are in first class condition
- Fix or replace all outdoor lighting; keep all lights on at night
- Clean the new welcome mat daily

Creating Hearth Enhancement

The longer a potential buyer hangs out in the home, the better for the seller. If they are in and out quickly, you can be pretty sure they weren't impressed or it just didn't meet their needs. Since buyers and agents pre-qualify a home using some major criteria before even setting out to visit it, a quick preview is most likely caused by negative impressions the seller should have addressed but didn't. So it is the **hearth appeal** that will cause them to hang around, discuss how they would enjoy living in the home culminating in an offer of some kind.

So let's make sure we understand the criteria that buyer's most want from a home. If you don't understand what they want, you can't possibly try to give it to them.

1. They want a home that is spacious (or at least one that is clutter-free);
2. They want a clean home (they don't want to see bugs, pets, food, mildew, odors or junk lying around);
3. They want a home that is sturdy (free from squeaks, loose objects, broken objects or rusted and dirty objects).

Any home can be made to look spacious, even if it isn't. Believe me, the buyer already knows the square footage before arriving. But looking spacious is a feeling they get once they arrive. The seller could have a home with a very large square footage, but if it is highly cluttered and messy, it will look much, much smaller and cramped. Counters that are bare can make a small kitchen look much larger.

Here again are some quick tips to pass on to the seller if you're not hired to do it for them or for when you are no longer around.

- Get rid of anything that hasn't been worn or used in the last 2-3 years. Have a garage sale or donate it.
- Remove excess furniture. Store it or sell it or donate it.
- Clean out and organize all closets and cupboards and drawers.
- Oven, dishwasher, microwave should be spotless.
- Keep ceiling fans, light fixtures clean; replace all bulbs with new ones.
- Tighten, repair or replace: hinges, switch plates, doorknobs, moldings, hardware.
- Repair anything that leaks, squeaks, rattles or bangs.
- Repair or replace anything worn, stained, smelly, frayed, broken, aged, discolored.
- Remove smudges, nicks, cracks, marks, chips.
- Remove daily any trash, litter boxes, undone laundry.

Questions to Ask Yourself

Here are some very basic questions you should ask yourself while pretending to be a potential buyer. Set about answering these types of questions in a positive manner for the greatest number of people and your seller will have multiple offers to choose from.

- What is there about this house that would appeal to me? To other buyers?
- Can I easily entertain in a house like this? Would I want to?
- Will my growing family fit in here? Or is this too much house for me?
- Will this home be suitable for my particular lifestyle? For my business? For my hobbies?
- How much work might I have to do to make it work for me?
- How proud could I be of giving out this address to friends, relatives and others?
- Can I live with any of the negatives I've seen?

What's Wrong With These Pictures?

Remember all those "before" pictures you took? If you don't have a digital camera, you need to get to a one-hour photo development shop and have your prints made. You're going to use these at this point to begin pulling your ideas together of how to totally enhance this home and turn it into a great profit center for the client. If you used a digital camera, you'll need to print out the photos you took. To save printing ink, you might want to take all of the photos from one room at a time and insert them into a Word document on the same page. You can easily rescale them so that you get as many photos on a page as are necessary. You can easily label the page "Entry" or "Master Bedroom" or "Living Room". If you are using prints from a non-digital camera, it may help to use double sided tape and put the pictures for each room on a page or two together. Some people prefer to leave them each as individual prints for more flexibility. Just choose the method that works for you. The natural place to begin will be at the curb. Lay out the photo prints in the order you would naturally move through the home if you were a buyer. Remember back to your first preview of the home, pretending to be a buyer. Where was your eye most naturally led first? Retrace your steps in your mind and lay the photos out according to the path you took.

Once you have the photos laid out, whether individually or on pages, look at each photo and ask yourself this question, "What's wrong with this picture?" If there is anything in the picture that forms a negative impression in your mind, that is a detail that will need to be corrected. This is a great way to identify the things that a buyer will most likely notice. Your goal as a home stager is to remove all of the negatives you can find, whether you do it yourself, you hire help or merely assign the task to the homeowner.

You can make notes right on the sheets of paper where the photo appears or make a separate list of the tasks to be done for each room. If you have taken your photos correctly, you should have one shot from the main entry to each room, shots of all of the walls and floor and ceiling in the room, and a shot from inside the room of the doorway where you will exit. Remember, we're not only looking for creating a great "first impression", we also want to create a long-lasting great "last impression" for each room in the house, and the house itself.

Evoking the Right Feelings

I'm going to give you some specific ways to evoke the perfect feelings in a room a bit later. But for now I just want to make mention of the fact that it's not enough to make the home look spacious and de-cluttered, clean and in good repair, it will greatly aid the sale of the home if you also are creating the right feelings. What do I mean by that? Well, let's say the home is a very modern style, with high ceilings, a high-tech kitchen, lots of straight edges and lines. Hopefully the owner hasn't tried to turn it into a Country home, but you never know what you're going to find. As you could imagine, to leave the home in a Country style might not be the best "feeling" for buyers. You're going to want to convey to a buyer that it doesn't matter what background they have, what furnishings they have, if they love the home and it works for their family's needs, then they can make it their own. This is why it's so important to bring the home into a neutral color scheme and depersonalize any particular style. When you've achieved that, you'll have created the right feelings for the greatest number of people who preview the home.

Remember to look for ways to suggest with the furnishings and accessories that a room can be use for more than one purpose. Buyers have different needs, so the more functions a room can be used for, the better. Think of each room as an opportunity to communicate with buyers some alternate use they hadn't thought about.

The Basics of Enhancement Design

The final step in preparing a property for market is the most creative and fun step. We have already discussed the need for **Consolidating** (de-cluttering), **Sanitizing** (cleaning), **Restoration** (repairing), **Depersonalizing** (neutralizing). Our last step to creating the right impressions and feelings is **Enhancement Design**. This is the sizzle. This is the unspoken method that makes a buyer fall in love and feel themselves owning and living in the home. This is where and how you'll get in touch with their deepest feelings - the ones that make them want to return, move in and enjoy living in the home.

Up until now we've discussed the tasks that you will provide that will meet the initial criteria a buyer discusses with their agent as "must haves" without ever seeing any property at all. But is that enough? No. Ultimately people buy a home because they fall in love with it. Falling in love is an emotional response borne out of a psychological need. To get them to fall in love with the property they need:

- to feel totally comfortable in the home
- to see it as a personal haven from the hectic life outside

- to enjoy the beauty of the structure or view
- to see it as a place to be proud to own
- to see it as a place to show to family and friends
- to see it as a place to live safely and see their family happy

If a buyer can connect emotionally with the home you stage, the competition in the immediate area doesn't stand a chance. To get what they love, buyers will often sacrifice a feature that was on their list. They might even dig deeper into their pocket and pay a higher price. But falling in love with the home is the key factor. That is why home enhancement is so valuable.

By using vignettes in a room you can easily focus the buyer's attention in a specific direction. Remember, you're not leaving a room brim full of furniture and accessories. You're going to be trimming it severely. So you'll want to decide from the outset what type of room you want it to be featured as and whether the room can double for a second activity or not. For instance, when you work in the master bedroom, see if you can make it more than just a bedroom - such as a bedroom suite. Look for a way to create a small seating area in addition to the sleeping area.

Have you ever noticed that in design magazines the rooms look charming, warm and inviting? There is usually a suggestion of family unity - yet not many pictures show people in the room? Practically none! Yet the homes depicted look like you could relax, enjoy TV, enjoy a book, bake cookies, sleep restfully, entertain with gusto and enthusiasm. These are the types of feelings you want to elicit.

Each room should speak to you in its own way. Maybe it speaks relaxation. Maybe it speaks comfort. Maybe it speaks organization and study. Maybe it speaks of solitude and refuge. Go with that aspect that the room is naturally speaking to you about - then also consider if you might tweak one or two of the rooms to suggest something other than the obvious.

Look for small ways, free (or very inexpensive) ways you can reach a buyer's senses - sight, smell, sound, touch. The more successfully you can tap into their emotions, the sooner the sale will take place and the higher the price your client will get.

Redesigning the Furniture and Accessory Placement

As the West Coast Pioneer of Redesign in 1986, I really want to emphasize what a positive impact you can easily make on a home by just rearranging the furniture and accessories in a professional manner. Astonishing as it may seem, I rarely walk into a home (unless it is one that was designed by an interior designer) and marvel at the way the home furnishings were placed. This is the biggest problem homeowners have and why redesign is such an affordable and popular service to offer. But it is a very important aspect of home staging you must look at carefully if you want the buyer's to feel comfortable once they are inside the home.

It doesn't matter what style of furniture the client owns, nor what style of furniture you might rent on their behalf. It doesn't even matter what color scheme you are dealing with, nor how old or how expensive the furnishings are. If they are not placed properly in the room, it all falls flat. When deciding the placement of furniture, focus first on the largest piece for the room. Get it where you want it and the rest tends to fall into place. Try not to force a buyer to walk around a piece of furniture in order to get into the room. You don't want to obstruct their path. But by the same token, the room needs to feel warm, inviting and functional. So you have to pick the most important criteria and work that first.

Watch out for very tall pieces. Make sure they don't obstruct the flow and openness of a room. You don't want the furniture to create any barriers. Your buyers will be a wide variety of heights. If you happen to be tall, remember that the average height of people is 5'6", so you need to know that half the population is shorter than that. Keep this in mind as you arrange the furniture.

You're going to find out that the placement of furniture for a staged home might very well be quite different than for a redesigned home for a family that will be living in the space for some time. In redesign you're more looking to pull furniture away from the walls and out into the middle of the room facing the focal point. But that might not be at all right for a staged room. I cannot give you a formula. One doesn't exist. There are so many variables: size of room, shape of room, placement of focal point, placement of windows and  doors, existence of a great view or not, size and type of furniture, usage of the room, secondary usage options (if any) - so many variables.

This is about as close to a formula as I will get and these are only just really very, very basic tips:

- Keep the size of the furniture in scale to the size of the room. Pushing large furniture into a small space will make the room feel cramped and crowded.
- Don't put undersized furniture against a really large wall. You don't want furniture to look crowded into a space, but you also don't want it to look lost in the space.
- Large furniture should face other large furniture in order to balance the room.
- When you can, place the largest furniture in the middle area of the room rather than around the perimeter.
- Angling the furniture can make a room feel larger, especially in a small room.
- Try to focus on only one focal point in a room.
- Group like kinds together when arranging accessories.
- Remove anything in the room that doesn't blend with the colors of the room.
- Remove much of the art. It should not look like an art or photo gallery.
- Remove all area rugs, especially small ones. Leave only larger rugs but only if they are defining a furniture arrangement.
- Avoid huge contrasts in height. Don't place something very short right next to something really tall. The height difference will be too extreme and make the buyer feel uneasy.
- Make sure each room has plenty of natural and/or artificial lighting.
- Go white or as neutral as possible.
- Group accessories in 3's. Less is incomplete; more is too much. Vary the heights.
- Flowers and plants work miracles. Don't over-do a good thing.

Unless you have a degree in interior design, this is really mandatory training for you to get under your belt. It's one thing to decorate your home. It's one thing to decorate for free for your friends. It's a whole **other** thing to decorate for a fee and you don't want to be stumped for a logical answer when you are asked questions. So fortify yourself with the proper design training.

Anticipating Costs for Enhancement Design

The goal, of course, is to do everything that is needed without spending a penny, but this is often pretty tough to accomplish. Still you want to try. That's where having some furniture and accessories of your own to "loan" or "rent" to the seller can help out. If you see that the seller just doesn't have enough of the right type of accessories, try to get them to give you a spending budget for adding the necessary ingredients to pull it all together. Remind them that they can take these items with them in the end.

This is where knowing what your own favorite stores carry and the costs of items will be particularly helpful to you. I would suggest you stay away from designer showrooms which tend to only handle high end furnishings (unless you're staging a really expensive home worth several million dollars). You want to keep the items reasonable (even inexpensive) as a rule. Tell your buyer that it is not that unusual to spend $1000 yet get an additional $17,000-20,000 more on the purchase price as a result. Don't guarantee them anything. But just let them know that it's a good investment for them to make.

Handling the Client's Possessions Guide

Before you move anything, you need to survey the room and look for any and all potential hazards that might be present. Hazards? Yes, things like small toys, slippery rugs, breakable accessories in precarious places, cords and other things you could trip over and such. Remove all such things immediately.

Even though you have a signed Waiver safely tucked in your case, you always want to take the greatest of care whenever handling someone else's property and treasures. Something might look old and beat up to you, but it could be a family heirloom, for all you know. Something might look very durable and in reality it is not. A sofa could have a broken leg that you cannot see. If the client has not already removed the most breakable objects from the room, have them do so at this point. It's better if they remove these things than if you do. Believe me, you won't have them arguing the point with you since they have signed the Waiver.

This is one reason why I charge a flat rate. I have done it long enough to know what kind of time frame I am most likely to incur and I make sure I've allowed enough time and charged accordingly for that time. When a client knows they are paying a flat rate, no matter how long it takes, they will not be pushing you to move quickly. You will not be pushing yourself either. When neither one of you is unduly concerned about the time factor, you will proceed more cautiously and this will lessen the likelihood of an accident. You definitely don't want any accidents to take place - not by you nor by your client. It can be guaranteed to ruin the day for both of you. So take your time. Be as careful as you can be. And enjoy the creative part of the project into which you are now about to enter.

Moving Tips Guide

MOVING WOODWORK AND FURNITURE

- Try not to move woodwork or furniture by sliding or pushing along the floor, as legs or bases can be easily broken. Our steel furniture lifter gives you perfect leverage (when placed near the corner or leg of furniture to lift the truly heavy pieces) to push a slider under the leg or corner. Sliders then are easily placed on all four corners, making the actual move of heavy furniture and appliances very easy. You'll want to acquire both the lifter and the sliders for sure. They come in sets of 4 sliders each and we have them for

moving furniture over carpet and we also have them for moving furniture or appliances over hard surface floors. I recommend more than one set of sliders.

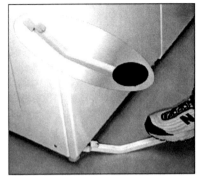

- Whether you have sliders or not, if you choose not to move some of the furniture all by yourself, take an assistant or get the homeowner to help you.
- Lift chairs under the seat rail, not by the backs or arms.
- Carry tables and other types of furniture by the solid part of their framework and not by the ornamentation.
- Make sure your hands are clean before touching any upholstery on the arms, seats or back of chairs or sofas.
- Don't stack furniture when moving it.
- Remove contents from drawers unless you can safely remove the drawers and the contents together.

- Remove marble or glass tops altogether before moving the bases. Carry them in a vertical position to avoid breaking them.
- Be careful of surrounding furnishings and the walls so that you don't knick them in the process of moving something else.
- Don't be in a hurry. Mistakes happen when you are hurried.
- Report any and all damage immediately to the homeowner. Never try to hide it.
- Another indispensable tool I love is the all steel furniture lifter. You slide it under or near the leg or end of the furniture you want to lift, press down with your foot enough to lift that end so you can slide one of the sliders under the leg. Then you do the same to the other legs. It's a really handy tool to help you get your sliders in position. I never go anywhere without it. See Chapter Six.

MOVING PAINTINGS AND OTHER ARTWORK

- Move only one painting at a time, no matter how small.
- Carry paintings and other under-glass works of art with one hand underneath and the other hand at the side where the frame is solid. Don't carry a painting by the top of the frame or by the stretcher bar or by the wire.
- Extremely large works of art should be carried by two people.
- Don't stack paintings one on top of another.
- If you absolutely must stack or lean works of art against each other, separate them with foam core, cardboard, a soft towel or blanket. Place the largest one first, followed by smaller ones. Do not stack or lean more than 5 works of art in any single stack.
- When resting paintings or other framed art on a floor, place on pads or something soft. It is really easy for frames to get scratched.
- Never try to clean a painted surface. Do not attempt to remove or improve slight scratches, dirt or any other mark with a cloth, your hand or anything else.
- Have a set of clean white cotton gloves with you. Clean hands are not enough to protect light-colored, matte-finish or gilded frames. The perspiration spots can easily ruin a frame's appearance.
- Check out the condition of everything you move BEFORE you move it. Report any damage, no matter how slight, to the homeowner.
- Should any part of a framed image loosen or come apart, save all the parts. It is much easier to have a framer correct the problem if all parts are provided.

MOVING SMALL OBJECTS

- Don't move anything if you don't have to. Use extreme caution and take your time.
- Move only one object at a time and carry it with one hand underneath.
- Watch your traffic path very carefully to make sure you do not trip over anything.
- Don't lift small, fragile accessories or objects by their handles, rims or any other part that is projected out. Those parts may have been broken previously and are just glued in place. Carry each piece underneath, gently but firmly.
- Consider having one or more padded trays made for transporting smaller objects. Separate delicate objects on the tray with sufficient cotton or padding to keep objects from contacting each other while on the tray.
- Always make sure your hands are clean.
- Use gloves or tissue to handle objects that are glazed, have polished metal surfaces or have other highly finished surfaces. These surfaces show finger prints quite easily and are generally difficult to remove.
- Use gloves or tissue when moving objects with matte finishes or painted decorative pieces as well, for the same reasons as above.
- If an object is very smooth or shiny, they are typically harder to handle and therefore gloves or tissue aren't advisable when moving them. Just use extra care for these pieces.
- Use extreme caution when carrying any object on a tray. Make sure the objects are not too high above the edges of the tray where they might be in danger of falling off.
- When placing any object on a wood table or chest or shelving unit, make sure the object is set on a soft surface to avoid scratching the wood.
- Ivories and small wood carvings are affected by sudden or extreme changes in atmosphere or temperature. Do not place such pieces near open windows or doors, particularly during the winter or in climates that experience extreme cold or wet climates.
- Metal objects, such as armor, arms and such, are vulnerable to handling. Always use gloves. Finger marks can cause rust. Don't place them in areas of dampness or high humidity.
- Never handle a client's jewelry.

MOVING LARGE ACCESSORIES OR OBJECTS

- Do not attempt to move large sculpture. Just don't do it.
- Even if you are able to lift it, sculptures should always be moved on padded dollies and carefully tied to the dolly for moving.
- If you just must move it, examine it well for any points of weakness in advance. If in doubt, don't. Tell the homeowner to hire a professional mover. Redesign the room around the sculpture, right where it is.

MOVING RUGS, TAPESTRIES OR LARGE TEXTILES

- Never let the fabric bear the weight.
- Use the supporting bar, roller or stretcher for lifting.
- Avoid stretching it, tugging it or pulling on it. Textiles can easily tear the older they are, but even if it's new, use extreme caution.
- If you need to roll one up, remove all screw eyes, wires or other projections first, with the homeowner's permission, and then roll them evenly to avoid wrinkling or creasing them. If the textile has a lining, roll it separately, face out.
- When picking them up, use two people. Don't grasp the bar at the middle. One person should support each end.
- Do not place one rolled textile on top of another. You don't want any of the threads to break. These can be impossible to repair.

- If removing anything from the wall that requires a ladder, make sure one person is stationed at the foot of the ladder to steady it.

MOVING SMALLER TEXTILES

- Remember, when moving a textile, handle it by the stretcher or frame. You can cause damage by slight pressure on the fabric.
- Do not fold textiles, laces or costumes unless you get permission from the homeowner first. If you must fold anything, place tissue paper in the folds to prevent creasing.
- Make sure your hands are pristinely clean.
- Many fabrics can never be cleaned and are consequently very fragile.

MOVING DRAWINGS, WATERCOLORS, PRINTS, RARE BOOKS

- Have the homeowner move anything of this nature that is not framed under glass.
- Have the homeowner move anything that is an historical artifact, a specimen or anything they own of a historical nature and value. Art objects of a historical value, archaeological value and such will be rare and you most likely won't encounter them, but if you do, simply have the homeowner be responsible for the moving and relocating of these types of objects.

The entry of a home is an important part of the home because it establishes the entire look and feeling for the rest of the home. To neglect this area is a big mistake.

Pick the most advantageous place in the room to feature. It may be a large wall, a bay window to a great view or the wall one sees first when entering a room.

Chapter Three

Implementing Enhancement Plan

At long last we've reached the point of actually creating an Enhancement Design Plan and implementing the plan. In this section I've broken down the main components of most homes into areas or spaces, such as: the front exterior, the driveway, the entry, the living room, bedrooms, bathrooms and so forth. In each segment or space, I've outlined suggested steps for consolidating the furnishings, for sterilizing the space, for restoring the space and furnishing the space, for depersonalizing the space and for enhancing the space. You could even use this section like a detailed check list which will help you identify the tasks needed, the amount of anticipated time each task will entail, and helping you arrive at a quote for the client that is fair and that makes sense.

Front Exterior/Driveway

CONSOLIDATING AND DE-CLUTTERING

- Make sure the street in front of the home is free of debris: leaves, twigs, trash. Look up and down the street for any other litter and have it cleaned up.
- Check the front yard for weeds, debris, fallen twigs, dead leaves and so forth.
- If there is a lawn, it should be freshly mowed, watered and free of weeds. Put new sod in any bare spots and edge it.
- Crop and trim all plants, shrubs, trees, flower beds. It should look neat and orderly.
- Remove any toys, bicycles, extra vehicles from the driveway.
- Remove any hobby machinery such as auto repair tools and gadgets, wood working machinery and tools. Have them stored in a storage place or temporarily moved elsewhere.
- Remove all lawn accessories and ornaments.
- Neatly store the gardening tools and equipment in the garage.
- Remove any dead plants or those about to die. Replace them with new plants.
- Remove anything that is just being stored that will not be vital to the sale of the home.

SANITIZING

- Remove all stains from the driveway (or hire someone to do it)
- Remove all debris from the gutters.
- Hose off all eaves.
- Wash any vinyl or aluminum siding. Professional services are available with the proper cleaning products.
- Sweep or wash off the walkways with a hose.
- Kill and remove all weeds along the sides or between cracks.
- If in winter where snow abounds, use salt or sand on ice patches. Make sure the edges are neat and tidy along all walkways after shoveling.

RESTORING

- Inspect the roof as best you can. If it looks to be in poor condition or the seller admits to leaks, recommend the roof be replaced. If it just needs repair, have any broken or missing shingles replaced. Repair all flashings. It's best to hire a professional roofing company to inspect and do all repairs.
- Check the gutters and down spouts. Replace or repair if needed.
- Check the driveway for cracks, separations from the house, broken pieces. Use a driveway patch and sealer to give the concrete a like-new feeling.
- Look for cracked or broken steps. These should definitely be replaced. It is dangerous for the buyers and detracts from the appeal of the home.
- Have a professional check the foundation of the home. Repairs to the foundation are critical and necessary and should be done immediately.
- Check the fence and any gates. Make sure gates open easily, that the latches work and that they don't make noise. Use WD-40 on hinges. Paint the fence if it looks old and dull.
- Check all windows from the outside. Look for cracked or broken glass, wood rot, broken or uneven caulk, torn screens, chipped paint. Repair or replace as needed.
- Check all exterior doors. Make sure the doorknobs are tight, easy to lock and unlock.
- Open and close the doors and listen for squeaks. Use WD-40 as needed.
- Check sliding doors for sticking or jamming. Have seller purchase new rollers if needed. They are inexpensive, easy to install and make a world of difference.
- Press the doorbells. Make sure they work and can be heard easily inside.
- Check the finish on the front door. It should shine.
- If there is an old fashioned front porch, check the condition of the paint and the condition of the pillars. Repaint if necessary.
- Check the garage door. Make sure the opener works. Use WD-40 if necessary to minimize noise.
- Look at the exterior paint. If it looks pretty bad, urge the seller to have the home painted immediately. If that is absolutely not an option, then suggest that the trim be repainted. Look at the other homes in the neighborhood. Suggest exterior colors that blend into the neighborhood. Keep it conservative and rather subdued to appeal to the most buyers.
- Check the immediate area for fire hydrants, post boxes, lamp posts and other items that are the city's responsibility. If they need paint, ask for permission to paint them.
- Look at other structures in the immediate vicinity. If you spot graffiti, arrange to have it removed immediately.

ENHANCEMENT DESIGN

- Add new plantings to the garden that bring harmonizing color.
- Potted plants along the walkway look smashing.
- Clusters of annuals along the walkways, beneath a tree or lamp post always look great.
- Plant more than you need, close together, to give it an instant full look.
- For cold climates, try evergreens in a pot.
- Group like kinds together for more impact.

- Repetition of the same plant will create a feeling of unity. Variety is great, just don't overdo it.
- Check for bare spots and fill in with inexpensive plants with lots of blooms: begonias and impatiens can be quite useful.
- Add gravel or wood chips around trees and shrubs for a professional manicured look.
- Don't forget to dress upwards, say with hanging baskets brimming with flowers and greenery. You can even use artificial flowers and plants.
- Get more impact from three of a kind than a single added feature.
- If there are empty window boxes, add plants to soften and fill the area. In cold climates, use greenery from the garden and pinecones to fill the window boxes for a lush and inviting appearance.
- Check the condition of the mailbox. Repair or replace it if necessary. Add some winding greenery up the pole on free standing boxes.
- Make sure the house numbers are in excellent condition and readable from the street.
- Add potted plants right by the front door if space permits (see previous photo).
- Make sure the welcome mat looks welcoming. It should be in excellent condition and clean. Dump it if it has sayings like "Wipe Your Paw Prints Here" or is personalized with the name of the owners. A simple "Welcome" is all that is needed.
- Polish the wood and fixtures on the front door or add a new coat of paint. It should be a welcoming focal point.
- Add a new door knocker that gleams, cast-iron address plate, shutters to the windows if they look too plain and ordinary.
- You can never go wrong with an all-season welcoming wreath.
- A spot of color can set off the front, like a tub of white geraniums, a pot of colorful petunias, a basket of red roses, a black or red door. Select colors that most people like, but avoid such colors as shocking pink or chartreuse.
- A new light fixture by the front door is almost mandatory. They aren't very expensive.
- If it's necessary to park a vehicle in the driveway, make sure it is cleaned and polished.
- Solar lights will make the home look inviting at dusk and into the evening. This is important especially during colder months. If the home is in inclement weather much of the time, then electrical lights along the walkway are a better choice.
- If there is a front porch, highlight it because newer homes don't have porches of any substance. Set out an old rocker or two, especially white wicker, if possible. Add colorful pillows. Hang potted plants in baskets between the pillars. Place a needlework project on a chair. Drape a quilt or blanket over the swing. A bucket of toys or a doll carriage will suggest the porch is a great place for kids to play. A book on the table with a tray, lemonade in a glass with a pitcher nearby will convey it as the perfect place to read and refresh one's self in the summertime.
- If it's Christmas time, go easy on the decorations. Lights, especially white lights, are always nice, however.

Landscaping Decisions
Sometimes it's not what you add that is important, it's what you take away.

Here's an example – Years ago I had several large trees in the front yard. One was so full, the branches were being weighed down and it was pretty ugly. On top of that, it was dislodging the asphalt driveway. So it was suggested that the trees be completely removed, including the roots.

I had the trees cut down, but did not want to spend the money to have the stumps and roots removed. I did replace the driveway with concrete. I turned the stumps into platforms. I built up the dirt around the stumps, planted flowers around the perimeter and placed a large potted plant on each stump. I cannot tell you the number of people who stopped, as they were driving by, to say how much they loved the new look.

Front Exterior/Driveway Summary:
It is difficult for buyers to visualize making changes to a home. If they don't like what they see, they move on to the next home on the list. And if they can look past things they want to change, they expect to buy the house for a reduced price to make up for that. This is not good for your seller. This is why it is so important to make the exterior and the interior as generic as possible.

Never lose sight of the fact that buyers don't want to replace anything and they don't want to fix anything. So the more you can get your home-seller to make the necessary revisions, alterations and changes, the better off they will be.

Popular colors change from year to year. If the house is old and dingy, a fresh coat of exterior paint will really make a difference. If not sure what colors to use, drive the neighborhood and pick out homes that have an appealing color. I once went up to a homeowner and asked what colors she used on her home. She was more than happy to give me the information and felt complimented at the same time.

New front doors can be very expensive. If the budget will allow, it's not a bad investment. However, if the budget will not permit a replacement door, put on new hardware that is decorative as well as securely built. If that is not possible, remember you can always re-paint the door and polish the hardware.

Entry

CONSOLIDATING

- Check the floor to make sure there are no cluttering elements like shoes, boots, umbrellas and such. Remove or store such items out of sight.
- Remove most the coats and jackets from the closet. You want it to look as roomy as possible.
- Hang everything facing the same direction.
- Hang all apparel on wood hangers, if possible. At least make all the hangers the same. No wire hangers, please.
- Remove all skis, tennis racquets, bowling balls, fishing poles, wrapping paper.
- Remove all mail, or at least place it in a decorative box or basket.
- Remove or create special place for keys.
- Remove bulletin boards (if any).
- Remove anything that infringes on the walkway. The entry should be open and inviting.

Before Staging (left – entry is too empty)

After Staging (right – an armoire is brought in from another room to balance the area and make a strong statement when a buyer enters the home)

SANITIZING

- If the entry has windows, they should be cleaned until they sparkle.
- Clean the walls and check the ceiling. What you can't clean, paint.
- Launder or dry clean drapes or curtains. Replace them if needed.
- Scrub and polish the floor or have it done.
- Wipe down all woodwork and polish it.
- Polish all doorknobs and any light fixtures. Make sure there are no dead bugs in the light fixtures.

RESTORING

- Repair or replace any cracked or broken windows.
- Oil the hinges and tighten the doorknobs.
- Check the floor. Repair if needed. You can rent a sander and refinish the floors yourself or hire someone to do it.
- Replace switch plates or outlet covers if cracked or broken with new ones.
- Repair any furniture that is scuffed, cracked, broken.
- Replace all light bulbs with new ones. Don't take chances on bulbs burning out, especially in the entry.

DEPERSONALIZING

- If the walls have dated wallpaper, remove it and paint the walls white or a neutral color.

ENHANCEMENT DESIGN

- Make sure entry has a dramatic focal point.
- Showcase unique piece of furniture or artwork.
- Group small table lamp with vase for elegance.
- Add large beveled mirror to brighten entry. Make sure frame is in excellent condition.
- A beautiful tapestry can be colorful and add size without clutter.

- Add drama with fresh flowers from the yard or the florist.
- Potted plants will last the duration of the showings.
- Add plants or a tree but don't crowd the space with too many.
- A bag with cedar chips or a pomander ball filled with potpourri hanging in the closet is a nice touch. It will send out a fresh scent when the buyer opens the closet (and they will open the door).
- Add warmth, color and texture with an area rug. Depending on the size of the entry, you may need a runner instead. The rug should fill a good share of the floor space so that it doesn't appear choppy.
- Add dramatic new lighting fixtures.
- Add new switch plates that are decorative if the budget will allow it.
- During Christmas season, add a red poinsettia to table in the entry.
- During bleak months when flowers aren't blooming, add an arrangement of dried flowers. Silk flowers are equally nice in a breathtaking spectacular arrangement.
- Add an antique umbrella stand for rainy day visitors.
- Add a bentwood coat rack for scarves and hats during cold months. Leave the heavy coats in the closet, however.
- If there is no entry hall, try to create the look of one by the arrangement of furniture. Don't block the view of the living room, but try to somehow separate the two areas.
- A console table with sconces and a mirror can also help create the illusion of a separate hall area from the living room area.
- Low partitions can also be useful in dividing the space to give the feeling of a definite entry area.

Make sure that the home's entry is perfectly arranged. This is a very important part of the home because it is the first thing one sees when entering and it sets the stage for the rest of the home. Your first priority is to look for a way to make the focal point dramatic; fill in from there.

Living Room/Family Room

Before Staging

After Staging

The room is too full in the before picture. By removing just one chair, and rearranging the coffee table, the room opens up and invites buyers to enter. Sometimes all that's needed is a simple adjustment.

CONSOLIDATING AND OR DE-CLUTTERING

- Remove all magazines, newspapers, mail and so forth from any tables.
- Remove all coasters, glasses and cups sitting on tables.
- Remove unhealthy plants and excess plants.
- Remove hanging plants as they tend to intrude on light streaming from windows.
- Remove all paperback books.
- Remove dust jackets from hard bound books.
- Remove from 1/2-2/3rds of the furniture in the room (unless it is sparsely decorated already).
- Remove all family photographs and extremely small art.
- Consider removing all heavy drapes that prevent light from streaming in the windows. If they stay, at least tie them back.
- Remove any furniture that is broken, frayed, discolored, stained.
- Remove and store all videos, DVDs, CDs, gaming equipment, small TVs or radios, photo albums, TV Guides and remotes.

SANITIZING

- Clean all windows till they sparkle, even the ones at the top of vaulted ceilings.
- Paint the walls white or a soft neutral color.
- Unless the doors are custom, paint doors, wainscot, wood trims, grate covers and so forth the same color as the walls. This will unify the room and eliminate the feeling of brokenness.
- If you spot black soot on the walls or ceiling above air vents, that is a sign of the possibility of the presence of dangerous carbon monoxide. Have the vents cleaned throughout the home by a professional before painting.
- Dry clean or launder drapes and curtains.
- Dust, and if necessary, clean all blinds. Repair or replace all window treatments that are not in pristine condition.
- Polish all wood furniture and woodwork, including any wood floors with a fine wood oil.
- Rent carpet cleaning equipment or hire a professional to clean and deodorize the carpeting and rugs.
- Clean and polish all light fixtures, including ceiling lights as well as lamps.
- Remove all ashes from fireplaces and clean the grates.
- Polish all of the fireplace tools and make sure they are tightened, if they have screw-on handles.
- Clean and polish all musical instruments, including the keys to a piano.

RESTORING

- Repair or replace any cracked or broken windows.
- Patch and repair walls. Paint is great for covering smudges. Well, it's just plain great and inexpensive and covers a multitude of problems, so if you have smudges, just paint the wall.
- Repair squeaky floors. A little baby powder in the cracks can help.
- Replace old, worn or highly stained carpeting. New carpeting should be very neutral - not too dark and not too light. A middle value color is best.
- Replace all switch plates and outlet covers.
- Paint all rooms that flow into each other the same color for the best unity. Choose white, off-white or a light neutral color.

DEPERSONALIZING

- Don't depersonalize to the point where a buyer thinks it looks like an untouchable museum room. On the other hand, remove that "lived in" look. Look for a balance between the two extremes.
- Remove busy, overly strong wallpaper.
- Remove area rugs unless neutral and very large and being used to section off seating areas. Persian rugs and country braided rugs are too stylized. Remove them.
- Remove all family photographs or art that would be considered raw or bizarre. This is not the time to display nudes or even that strange drawing or watercolor by Aunt Sally.
- Retain any generic or neutral art but reduce the number to a grouping of no more than 3-5 pieces. Work to create a geometric shape with the outside edges.

ENHANCEMENT DESIGN

- Place an instrument (like a guitar) against the wall in a corner to suggest a place to practice or a place to entertain guests.
- Open sheet music and place on the piano.
- Place a partially done jigsaw puzzle on a table or a chess set half played.
- If there are high exposed beams, place some artificial plants, herbs or dried flowers up high to attract attention to the beams. Baskets are nice too.
- Other high ornamentation can come from a chandelier, a spectacular hanging mobile, or possibly tree branches.
- Send the attention to the high beams with a couple of spotlights focused upwards.
- Drape a beautiful tapestry over the oversized TV to hide it if it attracts too much attention or looks out of place.
- Hide all cords and outlets in the room.
- Place all remotes in a decorative box or basket. Don't leave lying around loose.
- All toys should be kept in a container out of sight.
- Close all entertainment center doors and drawers. If equipment shows through glass doors, consider covering the inside of the door with black paper to hide the electronics from view. That kind of stuff is always distracting.
- Place a stack of 4-5 hardbound books on the coffee table that look interesting and whose covers blend with the colors in the room.
- Leave an opened book on an end table.
- Leave a bowl of M&Ms or fruit on a table to suggest family activities.
- Place wood logs on the fireplace grate and on the hearth. Birch logs are more dramatic if you can find them.
- A large work of art or large mirror should always be placed above the hearth to dramatically set off the natural focal point of the room.
- If no logs, place white or off-white candles on the grate in the fireplace, especially if the back of the opening isn't that attractive.
- Update the fireplace screen or tool set if needed. You could even make one.
- Drape an afghan over an easy chair or sofa.
- Add decorative pillows to sofas and chairs.
- Add fresh flowers or plant to coffee table.
- Add art pieces to a bookcase for multiple use. Don't overdo it.
- Enhance cozy feeling with floor or table lamp.
- Arrange furniture according to solid interior design concepts.
- Smooth out the cushions on the upholstered seating. Plump up the pillows.
- Rearrange the bookshelves. Don't try to fill all the space. We're just looking for a suggestion of books, plants, figurines.
- Place some books standing up and some lying flat with their spines facing out.

- Add variety to the bookshelves but use repetitive items and colors to create unity.
- Remove family photographs from frames. Insert decorative scenic greeting cards in the frames for the look of "small art" for the shelves.
- A large decorative plate on a plate stand is always good to add here or there.
- Instruct owners to keep the TV off at all times when buyers are going thru the property.

PRIMARY SEATING ARRANGEMENTS

Now for more detail. The living room or family room usually requires the most attention to the placement of furniture and accessories to do the home justice. Assuming that you have either already been trained or are in the process of getting trained in the area of arrangement design, it is common sense to begin your room rearrangement with the main seating arrangement The sofa will be the anchor for the room in most cases and will literally dictate where all the rest of the furniture will be placed.

If there is an entertainment center or a large screen TV, let's hope that it is already in the ideal place or can be moved to the ideal place without much problem. I have often found that the TV is situated in the wrong place in the room and the owner is reluctant to move it because it is hooked up to the outside antennae or cable cord and a complicated adjustment would need to be made to accommodate it elsewhere in the room. Whenever this situation arises, it doesn't mean the situation is hopeless, but it does make the arrangement choices more limited and more complicated.

Under no circumstances should you become involved in moving cables or doing any electronic work. If the client is willing for the TV to be moved, under the condition that they will have another licensed professional make any necessary changes to the homes wiring that may be necessary, then go ahead and work with the client to move the TV to a more useful place. Otherwise, try to work with it just where it is, even if it is not the ideal place. Definitely explain all of this to the client, however, no matter which way it ends up.

Of all of the homes I have rearranged, it is the TV/Entertainment Center that has caused the most difficulty in getting the room properly rearranged. But you can only accomplish what your client will allow you to accomplish.

SECONDARY SEATING ARRANGEMENTS

Once the main seating arrangement is in place, look for ways to start to accommodate any other furniture you have chosen to remain in the space.

In most cases you're going to want your main seating arrangement to be no more than about 8-9 feet from the focal point (measuring from the back of the seating to the front of the focal point). So unless the room is unusually small, there should be plenty of room left for other interesting furnishings under normal circumstances. But if the room is extra large, consider a secondary seating arrangement, like a chair with a small table and lamp. Consider a desk unit with a chair - perhaps a grouping of plants. But don't add extra furniture unless what is there looks way too small for the room.

If at all possible, work to include as many areas for the general activities of the room and you will stimulate the imagination of most potential buyers. I have found that most clients never think beyond the main seating arrangement, so here is one of the areas of the arrangement in which you will really be able to surprise them and delight them at the same time. As I already stated, you want to ever so slightly suggest multiple uses for a room whenever possible, so long as you don't make a space feel cramped or cluttered.

PLACING OTHER FURNITURE

Chances are by this time you've created all that you need for this type of room. Look over the room. Be sure there are plenty of spaces in the room where the eye can rest so that the room appears as spacious as possible.

The goal is to look for ways to balance the room. This can best be done by a good distribution of the furniture throughout the room. You want to avoid having one side of the room heavily laden with furniture while the opposite side has little to none. But you want the room to literally invite people to enter it from each entrance to the room and you don't want any of the furniture to block entry into or block the view of the room.

You also want to avoid creating a roller-coaster look in the room, where there are huge height differences between one piece of furniture compared to another piece placed next to it. The heights of the furniture should move up or down in gradual increments and there should be no cliff-like drops from one item to another. It's much more pleasing to the eye.

You're also going to need to check the color balance in the room. The various colors in the room, from the lights to the darks, need to be well distributed throughout the room to achieve the best balance.

So it may start to get tricky at this point. Your job as an enhancement specialist is to make sure you have incorporated all of these elements together into a cohesive unit: balance, rhythm, color distribution, height distribution, focal points, traffic patterns, lighting, electronic needs, the room's activities. When you have done this, you will have succeeded - assuming you have preserved the feeling of order, spaciousness and function.

PLACING ACCESSORIES

Do not start placing any accessories until all of the furniture is in place. Even veteran arrangers make additional adjustments with the furniture as they go along. There are many times that I just don't know if I'm going to be happy with a particular arrangement until I try it. There are also times when I've convinced myself that putting something in a particular place just isn't going to work. Then I move it there later and discover that it looks perfect in that place.

But when you are ready for this stage, start with the lighting. Make sure that the lighting is well distributed and put in places where it will be functional and not create any hazardous conditions. In other words, you don't want to put a lamp where the cord might trip someone, yet you want to provide adequate lighting for people using the room.

Remember that there may be accessories your client has in other rooms that you can use. There may be accessories out in their garage, stored in boxes. So if you don't find what you need, be sure and communicate all of your ideas and wishes to your client.

Dining Rooms

CONSOLIDATING

- Remove any extraneous furniture from the room, other than the dining room table, a maximum of 4 chairs and perhaps a china hutch.
- Remove most of the accessories.
- Remove any area rugs.

- Remove all family photographs or small art from the walls.
- Remove all papers, magazines, newspapers, mail, other types of clutter.
- Remove pretentious greenery from curtain rods. Simplify window treatments.
- Remove any distracting art that is overly stylized.

SANITIZING

- Clean and polish the dining room table. If a glass table top, use a glass cleaner. If a wood top, use a wood furniture polish.
- Make sure the carpeting is clean and free of any stains, spills, crumbs of food.
- Vacuum thoroughly; wax floor to high polish shine if hard flooring.
- Shampoo cushions. Replace if loose and soiled.
- Clean light fixture, especially if dust collector like a chandelier.
- Wipe down walls.
- Remove busy wallpaper; paint walls white or soft neutral color.
- Clean draperies or curtains. Tie back heavy drapes. Use white sheers whenever possible.
- Clean and polish china hutch, highboy, baker's rack or any other wood furniture in the space.
- Spray clean any silk flowers or plants.
- Clean all dishes, Chinaware, vases, or any other pottery that will be seen.
- Remove any equipment in the room.
- Polish the silver if it is to remain or is to be displayed.
- Any windows should be cleaned to a sparkling glint.

RESTORING

- Repair or replace any broken or cracked windows.
- Remove heavy draperies and let the sun in, especially if they are worn, torn, frayed, discolored, stained.
- Fix any broken, chipped, damaged furniture.

DEPERSONALIZING

- Remove all family photographs, either on the wall or sitting on furniture.
- If cushions are removable, consider replacing with neutral, plain cushions.
- If wood is marred or chipped, cover with slipcovers in white or a neutral color that blends.
- If table top is marred, scratched, chipped or damaged, cover with a plain, white or light neutral tablecloth. Iron before placing on the table.
- If replacing cushions and adding table cloth, try to purchase a set for the most unity. Using fewer chairs will decrease the client's expenditure for slipcovers.

ENHANCEMENT DESIGN

- Add a bouquet of fresh flowers on table.

- Make table decoration attractive from all angles, either in a circular or square shape, or an oval shape.
- Display a single, large interesting serving piece.
- Add candles or art piece on table or server to extend length or size fitting in scale to the size of the table.
- Add new table runner in a blending color. The runner will make the table appear longer thus making the table appear in better proportion to the space.
- Group accessories on buffet in small grouping of no more than 3 items forming a triangle by their heights.
- Do not set every place on the table. It appears contrived that way. Just put out a couple of place settings to suggest entertaining.
- Create simple place setting for the seller to put out during different times of the day. For morning showings, set out a luncheon or tea setting. For afternoon or early evening showings, have the seller put out a dinner place setting. The dinner setting will be more formal than the luncheon or tea setting.

- A luncheon/tea setting will be more colorful, casual. Use stoneware plates, placemats, and cut flowers from the yard, if possible, for the centerpiece.
- An evening dinner setting will be set on a nice tablecloth, conservative dinner plates, polished silverware or stainless ware, perhaps one goblet per setting. Don't go overboard here. Less is more. You're just creating a mood and it needs to fit into the style of the home.
- Make traffic lanes easy to navigate for several people passing through the room at the same time.
- Remove one or two leaves from the table if you need the room to appear larger.
- Place a drop-leaf table against the wall for a surprising look.
- If the china cabinet is really large and very tall, consider removing it from the space. You don't want it to dominate and make the room feel smaller.
- If the cabinet has glass doors, remove enough china and glass to keep it from appearing crowded and cluttered. Group like kinds together. Place taller items at the back to fill the vertical space between shelves.
- Hang a large mirror on a wall opposite the window, especially if the outdoor scene is attractive.
- Allow as much light to filter into the room as possible.
- If the dining room is especially large, create a room within a room, by adding a small secretary desk and chair to suggest other activities the room could also accommodate. A small lamp and a box of stationery will completely the suggestion of a place to pay bills or send out Christmas cards.
- Or move the old spinet piano from the basement into the dining room, or the old sewing machine. These will lightly suggest a room that can be filled with family activities or an arts and crafts center.
- Or move the large bookshelf to the end wall and suggest the inclusion of a family library. Include an easy chair and floor lamp. It's amazing how many subtle suggestions for alternative uses you can make in an overly large room. While the seller's family may have 10 kids, the potential buyers could have small families and need ideas to make the room serve more than one purpose.

The Kitchen

You should know that the kitchen, to many people, is the most important room in the entire home. Get this room right and you will definitely impact the buyers and probably generate a lot of offers for your client.

CONSOLIDATING

- Clear off all the counters.
- Store all small appliances, pots and pans, bowls, utensils (spatulas, wooden spoons, knives) out of sight.
- Clean out all of the utilitarian things, such as rags, ant spray, oven cleaner, sponges, and cleansers. Just a few very basic cleaning supplies should remain. You want the buyer to know the seller is continually on top of the situation when it comes to cleaning. Face all items toward the front.
- Clean out all of the drawers. Clean or paint the inside of the drawers white. If not painting the inside a fresh coat, line the bottom of the drawers with white drawer lining. Buy it by the roll and cut to fit.
- Clean out all of the cupboards too. Remove and box up most of the plates, bowls, paper products, serving platters and all of the other stuff that seems to collect in a kitchen.
- Group like kinds together and leave plenty of open space.
- Place silverware in new organizers in the drawer. Eliminate all but the most essential tools for cooking and eating.
- Place all items in the "junk drawer" into an organizer. You can buy one at container stores. Organize items such as paperclips, pencils, scissors, tape measure, screwdriver, hooks, nails and stuff. Leave these items there because you want people to know there is plenty of room in this kitchen to accommodate a junk drawer.
- Remove all refrigerator magnets, notes, bulletin boards, memo pads, children's art or report cards, etc. Remove all papers containing private information such as names, addresses, phone numbers, etc.
- Add an organizer shelf to the inside of one of the doors for the detergent and cleanser. A piece of linoleum or carpet on the floor in this area is a nice touch.
- Store cleaning products in a small bucket or other container. This helps to let necessary products remain without making the area look cluttered and messy.

SANITIZING

- Thoroughly clean out the refrigerator. Throw out all old food, food whose expiration dates have passed. Store in the freezer only half of the food it will handle.
- Clean all shelves with glass cleaner. Wipe off all the food containers, bottles, jars, cans and face them toward the front, putting like kinds together.
- Add an opened box of baking soda to remove odors and make the interior fresh smelling.
- Clean out the area under the sink. Paint the interior white.
- Use a soft cleanser on laminate shelves inside.
- Use a glass cleaner on the outside of laminate cupboards and drawers.
- Use wood soap on wood cabinets, followed by a scratch cover.
- Wipe down small appliances before storing away. If they do not look squeaky clean, remove them from the premises.
- Be sure to clean the top of the refrigerator and any high shelves.
- Make that oven sparkle.
- A single edge razor will help remove stubborn grease. Follow up with a good glass cleaner meant for removing grease and oil.
- Replace the oven light bulb.

- Clean or replace the burner liners.
- Put new light bulbs or florescent lights in. You really want this room to look bright, cheery and sparkling clean.
- Clean the vents and exhaust hoods.
- Plug in an air freshener.
- Clean and polish the sinks.
- Use a toothbrush to break up mineral buildup around the faucet.
- Remove all stains with cleanser.
- Clean the tile grout. If it won't clean up, re-caulk it.
- Cut up a lemon and run it through the garbage disposal to add a fresh fragrance that just says "Clean!"
- Make all windows sparkle and shine.
- Clean all curtains, drapes or blinds. Replace if necessary.
- Clean all light fixtures making sure there are no dead bugs inside.
- Wash and wax the floor to a brilliant shine.
- Wipe down all woodwork and polish, using a scratch cover. You'd be amazed at the transformation this can make.
- Clean out the inside of the dishwasher. Make sure no dishes remain in the dishwasher.
- Clean pantry thoroughly.
- Clean broom closet and organize it.

RESTORING

- Repair broken latches or broken parts of the appliances.
- Check the walls for cooking residue, grease, marks, holes, scratches and so forth.
- Check all of the hinges and knobs. Tighten loose knobs, use WD-40 to loosen tight or squeaky hinges.
- Repair or replace chipped countertops or tile.
- Check the appliance lights and timers. Make sure everything works or fix as needed.
- Repair or replace leaky faucets.
- Repair or replace the garbage disposal.
- Repair or replace leaky pipes under the sink.
- Check for broken or cracked glass on the windows. Repair or replace as needed.
- Open and close shades, blinds, shutters, drapes to make sure they function properly. Repair or replace as needed.
- Replace old worn, darkened flooring or tile.
- Patch and repair any flaws in walls or ceiling.
- Replace all switch plates or outlet covers with new ones. Choose white or the color that blends the best with the walls.
- Throw out all old rags, sponges, linens.
- Replace trash receptacle with a new one lined in plastic.
- Check for odors of any kind and eliminate them, especially in the vicinity of the trash container.

DEPERSONALIZING

- Remove busy or dated bold wallpaper. Paint the walls white.
- Paint the cupboards white to instantly transform them and make the kitchen look as large and clean as possible.
- Replace worn or dated flooring with a neutral linoleum.
- Remove family photographs, notes and reminders.
- Clear away all papers, personal items, books, photos, private documents such as invoices and the like.

ENHANCEMENT DESIGN

- Counter tops should be virtually empty.
- Open colorful cookbook on a stand.
- Group set of cooking oils next to cookbook.
- Create neat, clean look with new burner covers.
- Add covers to toaster and other small appliances or remove them entirely.
- Add one new throw rug by the sink. Store it away between showings to keep it fresh and clean.
- Set decorative serving bowl with fruit on table or a wire basket with eggs.
- Place a few carrots on a wooden cutting board or a white ceramic mixing bowl with a wire whisk on the counter.
- Add a blooming plant to counter.
- Add colorful bouquet of flowers somewhere near a window.
- Replace worn curtains with mini blinds/valance.
- Paint dull cabinets.
- Consider replacing dark countertops.
- Clean and organize pantry. Face all products to the front.
- Add a new soap holder.
- Add a bowl of imitation fruit if you cannot make sure the real fruit is replaced as it gets old and brown.
- Add a colorful valance above the windows.

- Add a couple of bar stools if there is a bar and no furniture.
- If there is a kitchen table or island, add a bowl of grapes. Drape a few outside the bowl for a less formal look.
- Add a couple of colorful placemats that blend in the kitchen and place in front of the barstools.
- A light placement that suggests an after school snack would be great here.
- If the seller will be available just before a showing and just after it ends, have the seller bake a cake or some cookies. Add to a plate with a pitcher of lemonade or iced tea for prospective buyers to enjoy. They will linger in the kitchen longer if there are light snacks available. But you want to make sure the kitchen is cleaned afterwards as they won't always be conscientious about this.
- If the cabinets are plain and ordinary, consider adding some decorative trim with molding for a more custom look. There are also companies that specialize in re-facing cabinets for an updated look.
- Change out the old hardware for new hardware. This is a very easy and inexpensive way to change the whole look and feel of a kitchen quickly.
- A light, neutral counter top has more universal appeal than a dark one and adds cheer to the kitchen.
- Few aromas arouse my homemaking urges better than the smell of a roast in the oven. A roast can take quite a while to bake, leaving plenty of time to let it's aroma fill the home..
- Make the seller a homemade brew of spices and water to keep in a container between showings. You just throw in a handful of spices such as nutmeg, cinnamon sticks, allspice, cloves and let them simmer on the stove after bringing to a boil.
- During hot summer months, cut lemons in a bowl add a fresh scent to the kitchen.
- Easiest of all, the aroma of fresh coffee appeals to most everyone, even non coffee drinkers like me.
- Store the dish draining rack out of sight.

- If the kitchen is large but poorly designed with inadequate counter space, rent or purchase a serving cart. Place it in a convenient spot and add a vase of fresh cut flowers to draw attention to it. The seller can take it with them afterwards or maybe even sell it to the new owners.
- Install an inexpensive hinged table top to increase the counter top. Make sure it is extended before buyers enter.
- Install a hanging pot rack over the stove, in a corner, over the island. Hang just a few pots so buyers know what it's for. Place some greenery and candles on top. Just a touch.
- Install a plastic grid system against the wall that has hooks to hold utensils.
- A Lazy Susan can be used for holding small items to keep drawers free of clutter.
- Anything goes to make the kitchen look larger, more organized and more spacious.
- Place small growing herbs in small decorative containers near the windows.
- Line the window sill with beautiful glass bottles in various colors to reflect light from the window.
- Hang a small grouping of wind chimes in front of or near the window.
- Hang a bird feeder outside the window. Small feathered visitors can add charm to the kitchen's ambience.
- Make a small kitchen look larger by painting all the cabinets and walls white. Hopefully the appliances are white too. Make the curtains white using light weight fabrics. Accessories should be colorful but used very sparingly.
- If the home has a breakfast area separate from the kitchen along with a formal dining room, make the dining room more formal in the place settings and make the breakfast nook or area more casual and fun.
- Even if there is no kitchen eating area, you can create one with a couple of unfinished stools painted with a bright color on top and placed in front of a counter. Place a magazine or newspaper in front of one stool with a coffee mug and placemat. Young parents like being able to feed the kids quickly and easily or linger over a second cup of coffee while reading the newspaper. Or maybe they would love a place to sit while making a grocery list or talking on the phone.

Bathrooms

Before Staging

After Staging

This counter would be more cleared off were it not for the fact that the owner was remaining in the residence and wanted some items to remain handy.

100

CONSOLIDATING

- Clear off the counters completely
- Store daily personal items out of sight in a decorative box or basket
- Remove all medicines and store at another location or in a safe, private place
- Remove all nail polish
- Face forward anything that is left in the medicine cabinet or cupboards
- Put cleaning supplies in a bucket

SANITIZING

- If shelves are old and stained, paint them or replace with glass shelves
- Clean all windows until they sparkle.
- Remove all water spots from walls and ceilings
- Launder or clean curtains and drapes. Replace if needed.
- Scrub the floor, wax and polish it
- Wipe down all woodwork and polish it
- For fresh fragrance, use products containing lemon
- Polish all chrome or brass fixtures until they shine. Clean the pipes under the sink as well, even if they are out of sight.
- Remove rust stains in the toilet, sink, shower or bathtub.
- Remove any mildew from tub and shower area.
- Thoroughly clean all grout. Use a grout whitener. Re-caulk if needed.
- Use a glass cleaner to scrub tile and mirrors.
- Replace shower curtain even if it looks ok.
- Remove all soap residue from shower doors. Clean the frame of rust or residue.
- Clean the toilet bowl with cleaners and sanitizer. Wipe down the exterior, from top to bottom of the entire toilet. Leave all lids down.

RESTORING

- Replace all switch plates or outlet covers.
- Replace old toilet seat cover.
- Replace cracked, stained or missing tiles.
- Repair grout and caulking.
- Check to make sure toilet and plumbing is working fine. Fix if necessary.
- Check for cracked or broken windows. Replace if needed.
- Check condition of blinds to make sure they work.
- Repair any cracks, smudges, chips, holes in walls or ceiling.
- If tub is chipped or stains won't lift, hire an enamel company to re-enamel the tub. It can be done in half a day.

DEPERSONALIZING

- Remove dated, overly busy or questionable wallpaper. Paint walls and ceiling white.
- Use neutral or white shower curtain and towels.
- Roll up towels guests can use and place in a basket on the vanity or floor.
- Remove all dirty clothes and keep in covered container near washing machine.

ENHANCEMENT DESIGN

- Use plush new towels and rugs to soften

- Show towels can be in a combination of neutral and one strong accent color
- Tie off towels with white raffia so that buyers don't use them
- Tri-fold towels and hang in layers on bars so the edges and seams do not show.
- Stack guest or hand towels neatly in basket; tie together
- Softly drape bath towel over tub
- Place small bouquet of flowers on vanity next to a decorative bottle or box
- Add new fabric shower curtain
- Highlight tub/vanity with colorful bath oils
- Add accessories: soap dish, vase, drinking glass
- Consider new towel racks or shelves
- Add pretty soaps in a dish for color and scent, but have some small hotel-like wrapped soap for guests to use. Fresh soaps should be placed for every new buyer that comes through, but you might want to just add a soap dispenser if the owner doesn't have one. Put extra soaps for the seller to use in a basket under the vanity if you don't use a dispenser.
- Add a green plant or two – live plants are the best, but you can also use artificial ones.
- Add a scented oil nightlight so there is light of some kind at all times.
- Leave small opening in window to let in fresh air.
- Place decorative dish with mints on the vanity.
- To create luxury feeling, purchase, make or borrow a two-paneled curtain and valance to place in front of shower curtain or doors. Tie back the curtain if bathroom is small.
- Place new bath mat over the tub that coordinates with the other colors.
- Replace a dated light fixture. Consider a vanity strip for more light.
- If towel racks don't match fixtures, replace them to be consistent (chrome, brass, wood).
- Add potpourri. Choose just one scent per room and keep it subtle. Some people suffer allergies so you want to be careful and not overdo the scents.
- Hang a lush fern by a window. Ferns thrive on the moisture.
- Place African violets or some other moisture hungry flowering plant on a window sill.
- Beach shells in a basket add a unique touch.
- Add a nice decorative picture to the wall near the toilet.
- Place artificial plants on each side of the toilet to fill the area and draw attention away from the fixture itself.
- Paint an old coat rack and hang towels from it if the bathroom is large enough to manage it.
- Add a magazine rack next to the toilet.

Bedrooms

CONSOLIDATING

- Remove half of the clothes and shoes and hats from the closets. Box them up and remove from the premises to another location.
- Face all clothing on hangers the same direction.
- Remove all wire hangers. Use only wood or plastic, all the same color.
- Remove extra furniture from the room.
- Remove half of the toys from the room. Box them up and place in a decorative trunk or chest, preferably out of sight.
- Remove all family photographs from dressers and walls.
- Remove contents from night stands or thin out and organize.
- Leave closet floors as bare as possible. Put shoes on racks. Place folded clothes, bags, hats in decorative boxes or bins on the shelves.

SANITIZING

- Dry clean or launder all comforters and bedspreads.
- Clean all windows until they sparkle.
- Clean carpeting or hard floors. Polish all wood floors.
- Clean any woodwork in the room; polish all doorknobs and tighten them.
- Clean all light fixtures and lamps.
- Check bed for odors. Air out mattresses and put fresh sheets on the bed.
- Wash or clean all pillow shams.
- Dust all surfaces of chests and tables.
- Remove all dirty clothes and place in hamper near washing machine - out of sight.
- Remove all old and dirty sneakers from the premises - they are always odor carriers.

RESTORING

- Replace soiled, stained or broken lamp shades.
- Repair or replace cracked or broken windows. Replace broken or cracked glass.
- Repair damaged frames and glass or wood doors
- Check ceiling for water stains, an indication of roof damage.
- Check closet sliding doors to make sure they roll smoothly and easily. Repair or replace as needed.
- Replace all switch plates or outlet covers with new ones.
- Check condition of headboard. Recover if necessary.

DEPERSONALIZING

- Remove overly busy or dated wallpaper. Paint walls white or light neutral color.
- Choose colors that are restful and peaceful.
- Remove distracting posters or art and all personalized photos.
- Place beautiful scenic posters that look relaxing on walls. They should be framed.
- Enlist teenagers to help in making their rooms presentable. Remove all posters with their cooperation after explaining the significance of temporary depersonalization.

Master Bedroom - Before Staging

The huge vertical drop on each side of the armoire to the chaise lounge chairs is much too severe. With no art on the walls, it really looks off.

Master Bedroom - After Staging By moving the armoire to the corner, it allows the matching chaise lounge chairs to be placed together, creating an intimate conversational area in the master bedroom. A tray with glasses and water pot make a nice enhancement touch. It doesn't take much to "suggest" various usages for a room.

ENHANCEMENT DESIGN

- To make room look as spacious as possible, remove king/queen sized beds (if possible) and replace with full size bed in master bedroom.
- Use twin size beds in other bedrooms to maximize look of spaciousness.
- Use same color on bed as the walls to eliminated cluttered look.
- Paint doors the same color as walls.
- Add a small secondary room in master bedroom to suggest other activities besides sleeping: a small desk, a sofa chair with table and lamp. Place an open book by a well-known author on the chair or table.
- Paint master bath the same color as bedroom to create the "bedroom suite" look.
- Leave bathroom doors open so buyers don't think it's a closet by mistake.
- Leave a few empty hangers in each closet to suggest there is plenty of space for more.
- Place potpourri or cedar chips in basket and hang on wall inside closets.
- Closet lights can be picked up from hardware store. Very important to light closets, especially walk-in types. For convenience, use battery-operated portable lights.
- Use under-bed storage containers for sellers to place last minute things left out by the family. Buyers rarely check under the bed.
- Fold back plush comforter or bedspread on the beds to show layers.
- Replace comforter or bedspread if it just isn't showing well.
- Top bed with decorative pillows and shams
- Add curtains/valances to rooms without them. Go delicate with sheers rather than heavy drapes.
- Add artwork for elegance - landscape scenes are best.
- Add mirror for spacious feeling so long as it is framed professionally with no chips or cracks. Try to place it across from a window.
- Stack some books on nightstand. Face the spines toward the front.
- Add vase and reading lamp next to a chair to suggest pleasure reading on a cold, rainy evening.
- Place area rug for additional color/texture, but only if it is very large and doesn't make the room look cluttered.
- Use table runners over a nightstand to add a touch of color or soften the hard edges.
- Add green plants as filler as needed.
- Leave a few colorful toys in children's rooms, neatly organized on shelves or filling a chest or trunk on the floor. Stuffed animals are great.
- Set up a small set of two chairs and table in a child's room. Place small tea set on table and some stuffed dolls on the chairs.
- Or set up a small art easel with a painting half done in a corner. Add a paint set on a small table nearby.

Halls and Stairs

CONSOLIDATING

- Remove all family photographs.
- Remove most of the wall art. Leave enough to suggest a place to hang art but remove any large groupings.

- If there are any alcoves or shelves in the area, remove everything. Place a single nice accessory there, like a large artistic vase.
- Paint all doors the same color as hall walls.

SANITIZING

- Check for smudges and clean.
- Clean all light fixtures.
- Shampoo carpeting.
- Wash and wax and polish all hard flooring surfaces.
- Clean any windows until they sparkle.
- Clean and polish the banister from top to bottom.
- Instruct seller to be on the watch for children's handprints on the lower part of walls.

RESTORING

- Check walls and ceiling for smudges, holes, cracks, nicks. Repair as needed. Paint as needed.
- Replace any floor sections that are overly worn, torn, broken or cracked.
- Check banister for sturdiness. Fix if needed.
- Safety is the first concern. Be sure lighting in staircase is **more** than sufficient. Check out this space on a gloomy day or in the evening.
- Check all runners and carpeting on stairs to make sure it is tacked down securely.
- Replace worn runners on the stair treads and risers. Since runners are not as wide as the stairs, make sure the surfaces on either side are in excellent condition.
- Replace all switch plates or outlet covers.

DEPERSONALIZING

- If a metal banister and if it's not that impressive, paint it the same color as the walls. It should be functional and not draw attention to itself.
- Wallpaper will make the stairs and hall look narrower. The best choice for this area is to paint the walls white or a soft neutral color.

ENHANCEMENT DESIGN

- Strategically hang a few pieces of framed art either going up the steps (if they are wide) or on a landing midway or at the top of the stairs and the bottom of the stairs.
- Hang art in stair-stepping fashion in the stair well itself, but not on the landing.
- Keep the stairs and halls free of art as much as possible in order to make them appear wider.
- Steps must be clutter free at ALL times.
- Enhance landings with a plant on a plant stand if there is room.
- Or this could be a great place for a grandfather clock.
- Do not place art on the walls going up the stairs if the staircase is narrow. Art will make it look even narrower.

Office/Den/Library

CONSOLIDATING

- Remove all papers, invoices, contracts, file folders and so forth from the top of desks. Store in safe, in file cabinets or behind cupboard doors.
- Remove all family photographs from desk or credenza or walls.
- Remove all paperback books that tend to be overly colorful and distracting.
- Remove paper jackets from hardbound books.
- Remove clothes and shoes, water bottles, stacks of papers, printer inks or whatever is laying around.
- Pull back heavy drapes and tie with coordinating raffia to open up the room.
- Arrange all books so that spines face forward. Group like kinds together on shelves. (Consider getting a copy of **Decor Secrets Revealed** for specific training on how to arrange shelves. See last chapter for details)

SANITIZING

- Clean all windows until they sparkle.
- Shampoo carpet and vacuum.
- Wash and polish all hard flooring surfaces.
- Clean all drapes, curtains or shutters.
- Clean all smudges and marks from walls.
- Turn off all equipment, such as computer, printer, fax machine. Clean all surfaces where equipment sits, especially under and around printer.
- Clean file cabinets and all shelves.
- Dust off or wipe off all books, plants, ornaments, mirrors, art work.
- Clean all lighting fixtures on ceiling, walls or tables.
- Clean out fireplace, if any.

RESTORING

- Check windows for cracks or broken glass. Replace if needed.
- Check walls for smudges, marks, holes, cracks or other damage. Repair and paint walls white or soft neutral color.
- Check condition of floors. Fix or replace as needed.
- Check lighting sources and repair or replace as needed.
- Replace all switch plates or outlet covers.

DEPERSONALIZING

- Remove dark dingy colors from room.
- Paint walls and doors white or a light, soft neutral color.
- Remove family photographs or bizarre artwork.
- Remove any books or accessories that might be controversial.
- Remove all diplomas, plaques and awards from walls and shelves.

ENHANCEMENT DESIGN

- Arrange all hard bound books together. Alter heights slightly. Break into small groupings on shelves.

- Arrange all soft cover books together, but preferably remove these and pack away in storage.
- Add a few plants to soften the hard edges of the shelves.
- Do not fill all shelves - leave some bare spaces to create impression of having more storage than needed.
- Clear off desk and hide personal papers, invoices, correspondence, pens, pencils, diplomas, award plaques, certificates of achievement, trophies. You don't want buyers to get distracted reading about your achievements and not look at the home.
- Remove portable safes.
- Lock filing cabinets.
- Have seller remove all firearms and ammunition from the premises.
- Place flowering plant near window, especially if it has a nice view.
- If room is dark and cozy, place 3 lamps in triangulation so there is plenty of light.
- Replace all bulbs with new ones.
- Remove anything that might be dangerous to children, like sharp letter openers and the like.
- Straighten all furniture, plump up cushions.
- Place logs in fireplace or in basket or metal bin on the hearth.
- Place one large scenic artwork over credenza or at focal point of room.
- Spread recent business magazines in fanned arrangement on coffee table, such as Forbes Magazine or Entrepreneur Magazine. These can suggest that the family that lives in this home will be financially successful. That's going to appeal to everyone.

Laundry

CONSOLIDATING

- Place all dirty laundry in enclosed container.
- Consolidate cleaning products into fewer containers, if possible.
- Group like kinds together and face them forward.

SANITIZING

- Wipe down the washer and dryer – inside as well as outside.
- Remove rust, touch up scratches.
- Clean windows until sparkling.
- Clean overhead light fixtures.
- Polish door handles and chrome or metal on washer/dryer.
- Vacuum carpeting/scrub and polish hard floors.
- Sweep around machines and vacuum behind them.
- Remove any cobwebs or dead bugs from the area.
- Wash curtains or wipe down blinds or shutters.

RESTORING

- Check out machines to make sure they work if they will be sold with the house.
- Check latches.
- Check for leaks and mold. If you find mold, a professional mold exterminator should be called in immediately.
- Check dryer for air flow through the exhaust hose.

DEPERSONALIZING

- Remove bright, busy wallpaper, if any. Paint the room white and ceiling too.

ENHANCEMENT DESIGN

- Add removable storage racks available at most hardware stores.
- Add sheer curtain to window
- Add laundry baskets that are big and decorative.
- Face laundry products outward; arrange neatly
- Consider new ironing board or cover
- Add green plants or silk flowers
- Place stack of clean towels on dryer
- Brighten corner with fun piece of art
- Make this room look like doing chores is easy and even pleasurable.
- If a large room, place a hobby project nearby to suggest other activities for the room.
- A shelf unit with potted plants, clay pots and some potting soil suggest a bonzai hobby.
- An old sewing machine on a small table with chair, with a piece of bright fabric laid across it, suggests a great sewing nook.
- A lemon scented nightlight is great for this room.
- Replace all light bulbs with new ones.

Basement/Attic

CONSOLIDATING

Not all homes have useful basements or attics, but if your seller's does, make plenty of good use of that selling advantage. People like to use them for storage areas and they can easily feel daunting to you. So attack one room at a time. The best way to remove a mountain is one shovel-full at a time. Now would be a good time to have a garage or yard sale, right?

- Box up items to be sold or stored.
- If some items are in a box already, have the seller sell the contents, donate them or put them in another storage container until they move.
- Sort what will remain and arrange any furniture or equipment in logical places.
- Use organizers to hang tools, sports equipment on the walls or from the ceiling.
- Sort and store all games, hobby items.
- Make the space as free of clutter and items, even furniture, as you can.

SANITIZING

- Basements and attics seem, at least in one's mind, to be more prone to attracting insects, cobwebs and the like. Use a vacuum or broom to make sure bugs and webs are removed completely. Call an exterminator for best results.
- Clean the floors thoroughly.
- Clean lighting fixtures.
- Replace all light bulbs.
- Replace all electrical outlet covers.
- Wash or remove all curtains. You want as much natural light to come in as possible.
- If there are any appliances or equipment, wipe them down and make them look as clean as possible: washer, dryer, water heater, water softener, furnace, fans, air conditioners.

- Polish and clean any wood paneling.
- Sweep old brick. Consider painting the brick white.

RESTORING

- Fix anything that visually needs repair.
- Make sure entrances are sturdy, including any steps or stairs.
- If walls are marred, scratched or dull, paint everything white or off-white. You always want a basement or attic to look sparkling clean.
- Have seller make sure all systems are serviced.
- Check exposed pipes for rust or leaks or damage. Have fixed if needed.
- Check windows and sills for leaks and damage. Repair if needed.
- Replace switch plates or outlet covers.

DEPERSONALIZING

- Remove all old family photographs, antiques, old trunks and chests, old clothing, things seller inherited.

ENHANCEMENT DESIGN

- Create just one vignette so the rooms don't look completely bare.
- An old rocking chair and small table suggests a place to read or rock the baby.
- An old truck, opened with a few toys spilling over the side suggests a play area for kids.
- An old wedding dress on a mannequin or dressmaker's form suggests a place to store heirlooms, family collectibles or a future sewing or hobby room.
- If there aren't any electrical outlets, use clip-on lights for added light to the space.
- Paint the old paneling to simulate a "washed" cottage look.
- A large beanbag chair on a braided rug with a small TV in the corner suggests a private TV and play area.
- A pool table or table tennis table in the middle, with cues and rackets on the walls will entice some buyers to see the space for more than a storage area.
- Even a work bench or sawhorse, a tool bin with neatly arranged tools, a place for nails, hooks and so forth can maker a buyer fall in love with the potential of the home.
- An upright piano dusted off, music pages on the bench, movie star posters on the walls can suggest the perfect teen hangout.

Garage

CONSOLIDATING

- Collect all tools into one place. Store in a bin if possible.
- Collect all paint cans together. Throw out the near empty cans.
- Put paint brushes, spackle, rollers and handles, masking tape in one labeled box.
- Collect all yard equipment into one area.
- Pack up in boxes and label all other garage contents. Remove to a storage bin or sell or donate prior to putting house on market.
- Remove any old cars.
- Remove all bikes, stored toys, boxed goods, athletic equipment.

SANITIZING

- Sweep the floor thoroughly, removing all debris.
- Clean off any grease, oil or stains from the concrete. You'll find good stain removers at the hardware store.
- Remove cobwebs. Clean out all bug droppings.
- Have exterminator treat this space for any pests, rodents, bugs.
- Wipe down any systems, such as washer, dryer, water heater, furnace, air conditioning.

RESTORING

- Check garage door opener. Fix or replace as needed.
- Check garage door hardware.
- Replace garage door if necessary.
- Oil moving parts such as hinges and springs to eliminate squeaks.

DEPERSONALIZING

- House your cars elsewhere.
- Remove spare tires, bicycles, storm windows, rakes, wheelbarrows, old paint and so forth.
- Remove pets, their food, their toys and their litter boxes.

ENHANCEMENT DESIGN

- Consider a new garage door with decorative windows at the top to let in more light.
- Add plenty of additional lights if garage is dark. This makes it look larger too.
- Hang certain remaining items on the walls to keep off the floors (tools, bicycles, etc.).
- An empty garage is ideal because it will look much bigger than one with items stored in it.
- Box up items that will stay or put in large barrels at the back of the garage.
- If some stains won't come up, consider painting the garage floor. Cement paint can be purchased at home improvement stores.

Porch/Deck/Patio/Backyard

CONSOLIDATING

- Pick up all toys and place in large baskets or barrels.
- Remove garden tools and equipment and store in garage or elsewhere.
- Remove garden pots, bags of mulch, fertilizer, poisons, plant food or watering cans.
- Remove excess items from balconies, decks, porches.
- Contain or remove all pet litter boxes, beds, toys. It's best to move pets elsewhere, but if not possible, any areas that pets occupy must be clean and neat.
- Remove all debris, such as: bottles, cans, wood, firewood, extra tiles, limbs and branches, old appliances, leaves, cuttings, rocks, bricks, stones (use them or dump them), old planter boxes, carpet fragments, stored keepsakes, old bikes, carts, skates, skis, newspapers, magazines, books, lighting fixtures or non-functioning cars.

SANITIZING

- Mow and edge the lawn.
- Clean flower beds and remove weeds.

- Remove all weeds between stepping stones.
- Sweep or hose off cement, brick, tile, stones.
- Clean and seal the deck.
- Clean all lawn furniture, grills, spa, spa equipment, pool and pool equipment.
- Hose off portable canopy, gazebo, tool shed, tree houses, play areas.
- Rake and bag all fallen leaves.
- Trim bushes and shrubs.
- Hose down screens.
- Wipe off all railings.

RESTORING

- Repair any loose boards on the deck.
- Repair and replace screens, especially if pets have damaged them.
- Repair or replace broken or chipped tiles.
- Check the spa and pool equipment to make sure it is working properly and safely.
- Tighten railings.
- Remove twigs, branches, wood piles, old tires, debris of any kind from back or side yards.
- Toss out old trash bins and replace with new ones with lids.
- Repair lighting fixtures and put in new bulbs.
- Prune trees. None should look over-grown.
- If pool or spa needs serious repair, have seller hire a specialist for this.

DEPERSONALIZING

- Neutralize any colors that are questionable.

ENHANCEMENT DESIGN

- Add a sun dial for an interesting conversation piece.
- Arrange lawn furniture to suggest an outdoor barbecue or picnic.
- Bring out the grill. Arrange tongs, fork and knife as if ready to start cooking.
- Pull out or borrow a croquet set or badminton set and set it up.
- Use clay pots with planted annuals to add color. Group them on the deck or patio.
- Place bowl of artificial fruit on the outdoor table.
- Add a large pot of flowers on the steps that lead back into the house.
- Stain or paint the picnic table if it looks old and dingy.
- In snow country, make a snowman holding a welcoming sign.
- Place a number of solar lights around in strategic places.
- Add strings of white lights to trees or bushes to give depth to area after dark, plus it's a very elegant and romantic touch (more to come).
- Place a new welcome mat near the back door as well as the front.
- Paint dog house or backyard shed.
- Paint fence.

Night Enhancement

ENHANCEMENT DESIGN

- Add plenty of solar lights to make home look enchanting after dusk.

- Add strings of white lights on trees and bushes especially in cold climates or near holidays.
- Up-lights behind foliage near the home will create interesting shadows and make the home look taller and more sophisticated.
- Take pictures at night and print out on paper for buyers to pick up as they leave. Offer this as an additional service to the seller or as a bonus.

Special Finishing Touches

I've given you a long list of enhancement tips you can use for every part of the house. But here are a few extra little gems you're not likely to discover from any other source. Remember, the key to getting good referrals, that will help you sustain your business after your current project ends, may often rest on the smallest detail that you provided that was unexpected, charming and touching to the seller in some manner.

- Place a tray, with an open book, glasses and a teapot or bud vase on the master bed. It shouts "intimacy".
- Leave a long stemmed red rose, tied with ribbon and a thank you note in the master bathroom for the seller to discover later.
- Create some welcome notes for the prospective buyers in some of the rooms. Use calligraphy and glue them to stiff cards. Place the cards on a plate stand. Each card could state some loving activity the seller has enjoyed by living in that home.
- Leave perfume scents in unexpected places: a drawer, a cupboard, the laundry basket. Buy some sachets with potpourri, or make your own. Tie off with a ribbon and attach your business card.
- Show up unexpectedly after the project has ended with a bouquet of red roses for the seller. Use it as an excuse to just drop by and check up on them. It will be appreciated and gives you a way to create a strong bond for those all important referrals. That's a great time to ask for a written testimonial.
- Take some evergreens from your yard and a piece of bark or some cinnamon sticks and tie together with raffia and wrap in foil paper. Attach a thank you note on it and leave on the seller's car or somewhere outside to be found afterwards.
- Take a roll of 3" wide ribbon. With gold metal marking pen, write "Sanitized" in large decorative lettering. Tape ribbon onto toilet seats to show buyers that the toilet has been sanitized (like you see in some fine hotels).
- Use your own creativity to leave special remembrances or treats for your client to find after you're gone.

Home Staging Tricks of the Trade

When you encounter dramatic alcoves, place something simple and dramatic in the space to draw the eye and suggest what can be done with these types of architectural elements within the home.

Tie up the bathroom towels to keep buyers from using them. Place alternative towels in the area for them to use. This will keep your baths looking good during showings.

Two matching occasional chairs have been placed in front of the patio doors to draw attention to the great view. This is a very easy way to enhance a view, especially if the colors of the chairs stand out from the rest of the room. They then sort of form an anchor, drawing the eye in the direction you want it to go.

Keep the arrangements simple yet appealing to the eye. Here some white flowers from the garden where pulled into the décor. Simple - even elegant.

Look how organized this barn is. Granted, you may never do a barn, but take the idea of how organized it is and use it for the client's you serve.

Check out how attractive this bedroom setting looks. You don't have to have a lot of fluff and stuff everywhere. If the pillows are dramatic enough, a little goes a long way.

One of the most effective ways to build unity into a display is by repetition. While you would want to simply the display when you stage from what you see here, can you see that the repetition creates a nice feeling of unity. By grouping like kinds together, you not only bring a harmonious calm to the space but you attract more attention to the architectural feature that this built-in display unit affords.

Homeowners rarely have plants that you can use effectively to stage a home. But look what you can do by just laying a couple of hard bound books on their side and placing a few accessories nearby to create an attractive table display. Look for things in the home that blend with the color palette and use those to create simple arrangements of interest.

Here's a wine cellar that has been meticulously arranged. Even though there are a lot of items in the room, it's amazingly clutter free because everything has a place and everything is in its place.

Beautiful flowers from the back yard have been picked and placed in a nice arrangement on the table. When you create table settings, only put out enough dishes for one or two place settings. All you need to do is "suggest" the idea of a dinner party. Don't set it up for an actual one. A few plates with colorful napkins help to dress up a kitchen counter or island as well. A simple arrangement of a wine bottle and grapes give the area a focal point. It doesn't take much to create the impression of casual or formal dining.

On the exterior, make sure all walkways are free of debris and clutter. Trim back the shrubs and flower beds so that they are as neat and attractive as possible. If you're cutting off flowers, use them inside to decorate tables.

Buyers will look into your client's walk-in closets, so you also have to make sure this area looks neat and orderly. You could arrange pants or skirts in an artful display. The repetition of the same type of items helps to create unity.

Stacks of clear plastic bins with labels made on a label maker help to identify items easily and quickly.

Buyers will also pull out drawers in chests. Some can get really snoopy. So you'll want to organize these areas too, or eliminate as much from the drawers as you can.

114

Raid the refrigerator and pull out some fruit to create a nice table arrangement. The best staging solutions are ones that are free. Notice how simply but attractive the shelf unit has been arranged.

When you have an open pantry or open shelves (and even when you don't), put all of the products toward the front of the shelf and face them forward so that the labels are all readable. It's a little finishing touch that makes all the difference. Buyers will open the kitchen cupboards so these areas need to be arranged as neatly as possible.

Don't forget to add a touch of interest in the hall. Keep it simple but this console helps to emphasize other decorating usages for an otherwise bland part of the house.

If you see heavy drapes, think about removing them altogether. Keep the area as light and airy as possible. Here there is just too much going on to be an effectively staged home.

I love porches. What a fantastic grouping of chairs. Wouldn't you jump to buy this house just to get such a porch.

A basketful of lemons placed on an attractive platter make a very inexpensive and unusual centerpiece. What fun! Perhaps your homeowner has fruit trees on their property that can provide some colorful fruit to help stage a dining room or coffee table.

Have the outdoor trees trimmed to tidy up the exterior. Then pull off the twig branches until you've stripped down some of the limbs. Lay these down the center of a table for a very unusual centerpiece. Think outside the box and figure out free ways to utilize things that would normally be discarded to create the ambience you need.

 Don't neglect the exterior. It's easy to focus so entirely on the inside of the home that you forget to attend to the back yard or porch or deck. A simple arrangement of outdoor furniture helps bring this porch to life and takes away from the old wrought iron railing.

Every owner isn't going to have attractive outdoor furniture. You can rent this or even purchase some to use from home to home. If you purchase furniture to use in your projects, use neutral colors so they will be more versatile.

Place an open book of music on a piano to suggest learning to play the piano or some other instrument. This helps to suggest other usages for a space rather than merely pa seating arrangement. People will start talking about how they can use the home for their lifestyle when you help the seller give multiple usage options by the way you arrange the rooms.

I have to admit that all of my purses are jammed onto shelves in my closet. What if you display some of these types of items on hooks attached to a closet wall?

 A colorful throw tossed casually over a chair adds color to a space without adding clutter. It also suggests casual living so that a prospective buyer doesn't feel uptight and can better visualize their family living in the home.

If your client has a view that is not necessarily as attractive as you would like, pull the shades down part way to focus a buyer's attention on the part of the view that is attractive. You can even create an artistic look by using a different height for one of the shades from the other two.

116

Just as it's important to face your groceries and books in the same direction, so too your client's shirts. Arrange and display them by color family. Repetition of color is one of the best unifying concepts you can apply to your decorating.

If your client's home looks sparsely decorated outside, add extra colorful flowering beds to make it more attractive. It will be well worth the effort. If you don't want to do it yourself, hire a landscaper to add some finishing touches.

The two prints on the wall (right) with the 3 bowls below help fill this space without it looking overdone. It might appear a little empty if you were doing a redesign for a client who planned to live there permanently, but for a staged home it's just right.

Here is another example of a tight, simple arrangement. You don't have to fill all of the shelves. Just give the feeling by placing a few items on the shelf unit. The simplicity of 4 prints hung in a contemporary arrangement above is just enough to make the space charmingly inviting.

A vase of fresh flowers and an exquisite hand towel are all that are needed to make this bathroom look lovely and take on some charm. What is nicer than fresh cut flowers?

A trio of stylized pottery. A hard bound book. A small vase of flowers. A coordinating throw. Nothing especially expensive. Easy to do. The essence of staging a house with just a few finishing touches turns it instantly into a home.

Arrange bookshelves with like kinds. Try to put hard bound books together. Try not to mix soft cover books in with them. Vary the heights. Try to fill at least 2/3rds of the available height in the shelf as you see here. Add variety by laying some books flat and stacking them.

A small wicker loveseat is just what this balcony needed to draw attention to the great view. The yellow thongs on the floor suggest casual relaxation. Beautiful.

Remove the greenery on the windows and doors if you run across it. It just clutters the room which is what you don't want to do.

Remember to keep the arrangements simple and clean for best results. Books stacked on their side on the coffee table are a nice easy touch. Most homeowners have books. Try to use only hard bound books and take off the dust jackets.

Have the homeowner turn all the lights on when dusk starts as many buyers will do a drive by after work just to see what the property looks like at night. Could you resist buying a home that looks this beautiful at night?

Tidy up the exterior too. Use potted plants near the front door to soften and make it more attractive. You want to draw the attention to any area of the home that is most beautiful, but usually the front door is the architectural focal point. Draw the eye there first, then fill out the rest of the exterior with good design.

Potted plants can be brought in and most buyers recognize that potted plants will not be part of the purchase. Dressing up a coffee table can be as simple as a bowl of colorful balls or fruit. Just be sure the colors blend in the room. Red or black are always good colors to add to any room you're arranging.

Most home buyers don't have a pool table. If the home you are staging has one, try to have it removed and show other options for the room. Buyers will be better able to relate without it and you don't want buyers getting sidetracked and playing a game while in the home. But if you can't remove the pool table, then dress up the table. Set out the balls as if starting a game. Lay one cue on the table on the other side for balance.

Keep the counters as free of clutter as possible.

See how elegant this contemporary home has been arranged. But watch out for pictures that are not hung level. Before you leave a home that you've staged, make sure all pictures are hung at the right heights and that they are level. Adjust as necessary. You can buy packages of felt squares or circles that have adhesive on the back. Tuck one near the corner of a picture at the bottom and press against the wall to hold the picture level, especially if the wall has a door that is always being opened or shut. You don't want buyers passing through the home to knock a picture ajar. Most adhesives will not harm the wall.

The decorative mural art over the front door is beautiful but probably not appropriate to leave when one is trying to sell a home. It is very "country" and chances are most buyers will not be decorating in that style. Best to remove it to appeal to the broadest number of potential buyers as you can.

Just because a home has been staged already by the owner or an agent, doesn't mean it will be successfully sold.

There is a market for tackling these types of properties and improving on the staging to help the home finally sell.

Keep track of the homes going up for sale in your area. Visit their open house showings. Keep tabs on them. Contact the agent if the home stays on the market for a long time.

Here is an example of a staged property that did not sell. A new stager was hired to improve on the presentation and here are the results of what was changed. As you can see, the home has a little more sizzle now than before and this can make all the difference in the world in helping buyers fall in love with the home.

Colorful Staging Ideas Report

To see these staging pictures in color,

you can download the following report from my website.

Go to:

http://www.decorate-redecorate.com/StagingIdeas.doc

Cleaning Aids

Disinfecting Wipes are helpful in getting rid of bacteria. Use them to clean counters. Choose ones with an EPA label, as these are the ones that have been proven to actually eliminate bacteria, fungi and viruses. To keep them from drying out, store the container upside down.

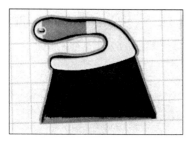

Baking Soda is a natural scouring powder that will neutralize acids and bases. It is good for eliminating odors as well. Make sure it is 100% pure sodium bicarbonate. Place in client's refrigerator to eliminate odors.

Rubber Gloves will protect your skin from harmful chemicals or other agents you will run across. Pick a size that allows the glove to breathe but still tight enough to allow you to use freely and easily. If they are too big, they are floppy and hard to use. If too snug, they are hard to get off. Those with a foam lining will absorb interior dampness better than the cotton ones.

Scrub Brush A hand scrub brush comes in handy when you really want to get aggressive cleaning. They are great for using on rough surfaces too. Use them on the tubs and showers to

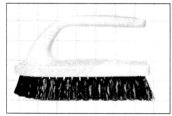

help remove soap scum rings. The kind with heavy duty nylon bristles are the least likely to scratch surfaces. Buy the ones with the handle to keep your hands removed from chemicals and cleaning products.

Hand Broom You'll want to have a regular broom on hand to sweep large areas, but the hand broom and dust pan is great for quick tasks or hard to reach areas. Look for the ones with nylon bristles, a comfortable handle and a clip-on dust pan. A good item to loan or rent to owners so they can easily keep up with tiny, last minute messes you don't want around just before an open house or a surprise visitor.

Spray Bottle The all purpose spray bottle with hot or cold water (or a cleaning solution) is indispensable. Spritz the area and wipe with a clean sponge or paper towel. You can even put carpet stain removal solutions in one. Stock up on several to have handy but be sure you label them accurately. Follow the manufacturer's cleaning instructions on any cleaning product you're using.

Dry and Wet Sponges The cellulose foam-latex sponge has tiny pores that pick up soot, dust and pet hair from upholstery and lampshades and remove scuff marks from walls when left dry. The 3x6 inch size is ideal. Wet sponges can be used for most cleaning projects when you need liquid cleaners.

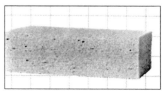

Squeegee You're likely to find you need to clean glass windows, glass table tops and shower doors. Since you don't want to leave streaks, a squeegee will help a lot. Use it on mirrors too. The best ones are brass or stainless-steel. Be sure to have a microfiber cloth handy and wipe the squeegee with the cloth after every pass.

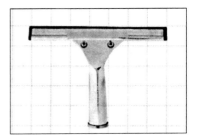

Toothbrush Never underestimate the value of your common toothbrush when it comes to cleaning. It's great for reaching tight, skinny places you can't reach in any other way. The tracks of sliding glass doors, the bases of faucets are two ideal places for toothbrush technology. Use a soft-bristle brush, whether electric or manual.

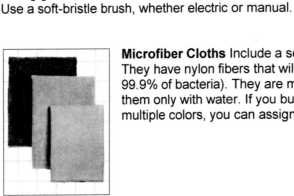

Microfiber Cloths Include a selection of these handy cloths. They have nylon fibers that will lift and trap dirt (and remove 99.9% of bacteria). They are machine washable and you use them only with water. If you buy them by the package with multiple colors, you can assign a task to each color.

Caddy For easy transport, buy a small caddy that has a place for each of the tools you will use the most. You can always have more tools in your vehicle that are larger or seldom needed, but the common ones you'll want to be able to carry easily from room to room.

Other Items Other items you might also find handy include: a microfiber duster, a mild abrasive cleaner, vinegar, dishwashing liquid and an all-purpose cleaner.

A Final Check List for Sellers to Address

- Check all the plugs and switches in the home and outside to make sure they are all functioning properly.
- Check all plumbing to see if there are any drips or leaks. Let the water run for 5 minutes full blast to properly test the pipes.
- Flush each of the toilets several times in succession.
- To find noticeable wall imperfections, take a dim light at night that casts shadows and look at the walls at an angle.
- Turn on the heat, even in 90 degree weather, to check the heating system.
- Turn on the air conditioning too and check it, even if it's 5 degrees with howling wind.
- Check appliances, chimneys, fireplaces, roof, sprinkler systems.
- Door on refrigerator should close on it's own. If balanced it will do it.
- Look for spots that painters might have missed. Look for dripped paint. Make sure seller has touch up paint on hand.

Removal and Storage

Once all of the items being removed from the premises are congregated, boxed and labeled, they can be taken to a storage unit, a relative's home or wherever the seller has decided to put them temporarily. I suggest you leave the transport of the items completely up to the seller, who can hire a moving company or can rent a van if needed. Don't take on this type of liability. Keep your business simple and involve yourself only in the things you really want to do.

Furniture Rentals

So now we get to the part of the business that tends to scare many people. Perhaps you're one of them. Dealing with complex contracts makes most of us nervous. I'm one of those people who love to keep my business very simple and uncomplicated. I also work very hard to minimize my risks. You should too. For that reason, I highly recommend that all rental contracts be a transaction strictly between the seller and the rental company. But there are stagers who do handle the rentals themselves and love the extra money. For me it isn't worth the liability and hassle. But it's your business. Do what you want.

At the end of this manual, you'll find some samples of the type of information a renter of furniture might expect to have to provide to a rental company.

You'll also find a listing of some typical package deals that you might find if you visited a furniture rental company. Most furniture rental companies will offer you a way to rent furniture that you pick out yourself so you can customize it to the actual home's needs and/or the seller's budget.

Usually the package deals are offered at a savings (but only if you need every piece in the package). They may or may not offer flexibility in the package program. So whether or not you want to be a "middleman" between the seller and the furniture rental company or not, you need to visit a few of them, introduce yourself, tell them about your business and begin to create a relationship with them. Don't wait until you have a client needing furniture to build a relationship with the rental company. Get yourself set up in advance.

If you need resources for renting furniture, check your local yellow pages for companies. You can also visit www.aaronrents.com or www.rentacenter.com online. A quick search on your favorite browser should pop up other companies to consider as well.

If you're going to act as the manager/agent of the rental, you'll need to go in advance and provide all of the information they will require of you so they have it on hand. They will naturally want to do a credit and background check on you, because you are actually their client, not the home owner or the real estate agent. It's sort of like registering your business with a trade showroom as a re-designer. Get your account set up first, privately, then when you have a need of the service it's ready to go immediately.

Ask the rental company if they presently work with other home stagers. If they don't, you need to show or tell them what you do. If they already work with stagers, ask them what discount they offer to the stager. Discounts may vary from one rental company to another. You'll want to set up accounts with more than one if you can.

If your services as an adviser will be needed by the home seller to visit the rental agency, be sure to charge the home owner for your time and expertise. Don't let the owner use you without getting something for your time. By all means, make the rental company both deliver and pick up the furniture and accessories. You do not want the transportation liability to fall on you. Just make sure it's part of any agreement.

Choose furniture and accessories that are relatively neutral. Don't go for the bright red sofa and chairs, no matter how pretty they look on the showroom floor. Most people won't be able to relate to such strong colors. You want the furnishings to be fairly bland, actually. Believe me, if you place them in the right places, the rooms will look spectacular even though neutralized.

Offering 11 Other Services

Besides the typical fare of consolidating, de-cluttering, cleaning, organizing, repairing and placing furniture and accessories, there are other services you can offer the home owner to add to your bottom line. Here are a few ideas and you'll think of some on your own as you get more immersed in the business.

Floor Plans

When a buyer walks through the front door, it would be very nice to provide them with a floor plan of the home, preferably drawn to scale. If you're good at taking measurements and drawing on grid paper, why not offer this as an additional service to the home seller. You can easily make one up and have them copied. Make sure to include your business name and phone number somewhere so that people can contact you for your services if they wish. You can buy pads of grid paper at your local office supply store for this purpose. The lines on the grid paper are usually printed in light blue which should drop out when copied giving you a really clean drawing. Make up a sample of you own home to use to show your client.

House Records

Offer to organize all of the home owner's house records into a handy organizer. Many people don't have the time or the motivation to organize all their important documents, receipts and relevant papers and would love someone who is already working with them in other areas to do that for them.

Color Consultation Services

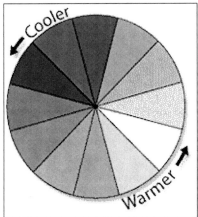

You may be working with a home owner who wants to do much, or most, or all of the work themselves but isn't sure how to go about picking colors to properly neutralize the home prior to market. In exchange for an hourly fee, offer to give your clients a color consult. Use the color key system discussed in **Decor Secrets Revealed** or **Rearrange It** to help you select the perfect colors that will blend with their furnishings. Remember, there are warm neutrals and there are cool neutrals. It's better if the proper neutrals are picked. Interior designers often use **Color Boards**, where they mount samples and swatches for a proposed room. By overlapping your samples in one place on a board, you can easily give a client a great visual of how all the finishes, colors and textures will work in the room.

Redesign Services at New Residence

If you're not planning on also offering a redesign services as part of your business, you should definitely reconsider. Interior redesign and home staging are so closely related you should definitely offer both services to maximize your profit potential. Naturally the goals of each business regarding design are different and you should clearly understand that difference. But many of the techniques, concepts, strategies and tactics are exactly the same. One business will support the other one, and vice versa. Often your home seller is moving into another local residence and will really appreciate your help making their furnishings look terrific in the new residence. So be sure to let your home owner and agent know that you also offer redesign services.

Yard/Garage Sale Organization and Management

I am so busy and have collected so much stuff over the years, I really need to have a garage sale and unload a good deal of it. But I just don't have the time and don't want to make the time for such a task. I would love to have someone just do it all for me - organize it, manage it, supervise it, then dismantle it all. Yard sales can be very rewarding financially and really help get rid of lots of stuff, but they involve a lot of work. Mention to the home seller and agent that you also offer this service.

You'll need to be on top of such things as: sorting, pricing, tagging, advertising, set up, selling, security and tear down, repacking and labeling. There's a lot of work. But if you price yourself by the hour, you could come away with some nice dollars at the end. Use this service as a spring board to a full blown staging service.

Painting Services

Just about anyone can paint walls but if you're a really messy person you might want to bypass this service. However, if you like to get grungy and you love to change colors, this will appeal to you. Lots of home owners hate to paint or have never done it, so you might consider doing this yourself rather than hiring a painting contractor. I would only recommend this service, however, for the interior. Let a professional painter do the exteriors and any vaulted walls and ceilings. They can do it much faster, safer and probably for less money than you would want to charge. You don't want to be climbing way up high and risking life and limb. But many walls in a home can be painted by standing on a chair or step stool. These are the walls I am comfortable painting.

To properly prepare walls for paint, you'll need: spackle, painter's tape (for masking) and lots of drop cloths, an assortment of brushes, rollers and roller element. Repair the wall first, then prime it, then paint it. Walla. Extra profit for you.

Wallpapering Services

Removing and hanging wallpaper is a lot of work too. Again it's one of those chores that people may or may not want to do themselves. The more that don't, the better for you if you want to tackle it. You do need to know what you're doing, however, because removing wallpaper can be tricky depending on the type of paper, the type of glue and the surface of the wall. Many manufacturers promise easy removal, but that doesn't always happen. It can be a very exhaustive ordeal, so be sure to quote a range or stipulate in advance what will happen if you run into unexpected removal problems.

My sister bought a previously owned home recently. She hired her daughter and son-in-law to remove the wallpaper. I don't know how long it had been up, but they slaved away for a full day to remove a short section. Eventually my sister's husband said, "Forget that! I'm just going to paint over the rest of it!" I don't advocate that, but maybe I'd change my mind had it happened to me.

If in doubt, you can always bring in a couple of professional wallpapering companies to give a quote on the job. Then decide, based on what they say and their estimates, whether you want to offer the service or not in that particular home yourself. You may elect to do some and not do others. Hey, you're the boss.

Sorting, Packing and Labeling Services

Some home owners may only want to you provide certain aspects of all the tasks that need to be done. This is not a very creative part of the job, but must be done by someone - why not you - for a fee of course! As I stated earlier, this job requires someone who is not emotionally attached to the possessions, but also someone who is empathetic to the feelings of the owner. You might need to be ruthless about getting rid of some items but tender about other things. So it takes class and diplomacy to assist a home owner in freeing themselves of stuff they've had for years and really don't need any longer.

Open House Supervision Services

Once the house goes on the market, let the homeowner and agent know that if they would like someone to be present to act as security, conduct tours, hand out refreshments and so on at the Open House that you would be available on an hourly basis. In a seller's market when lots of buyers are out going to open house previews, they just might like an extra person knowledgeable about the property to be available. Naturally all questions regarding price and so on would be handled by the agent only.

Accessory Purchasing Services

I've just been hired to work with a stockbroker who has recently completed building a multi-million dollar property in Long Beach. She had worked with a very high priced snobbish interior designer/architect, who eventually saw fit to want to charge her $10,000 just to come to her community and select a single vase. She had grown increasingly disenchanted with him anyway because he was looking to place his own signature style on the home rather than working to bring out her style and taste.

After firing him, she brought in a local interior designer to give her a two-hour consultation regarding the many art and accessory pieces she already owned. She needed someone to come in and place her art and accessories. The woman who came did give her a couple of good ideas and left. Later she submitted a quote for $40,000 to return and place her accessories and she also wanted 20% commission on whatever was purchased. The client was mortified to say the least.

Now she has hired me to do the job for a fraction of what the others wanted to charge her, including my time to go shopping on her behalf or with her or to just advise her so she can shop on her own. Offering a purchasing service can be very rewarding, but you must be careful to be fair. Just because some client obviously had a great deal of money is no excuse to try to gouge them. Make sure you adequately predict the time involvement of shopping, but keep in mind that it's one of those ambiguous intangible benefits. Price your services at a reasonable rate.

Neighborhood Improvement Advocate Services

One of the strongest selling assets your home seller may have is location - location - location. However, as good as that is for some sellers, it might be just the opposite for your next property. People are definitely concerned about location and which neighborhood a home is in. If a neighbor's home across the street is a mess, it will definitely affect property values for all the homes in the immediate vicinity. Addressing issues with a neighbor can really be tricky. Hard feelings can develop. Check out the neighborhood on your next property.

If the property isn't on the market yet, and there is a messy home nearby, offer to work on behalf of all the neighbors to remedy the situation. This will take people skills and a good deal of diplomacy, but it will be worth the effort. Perhaps you can get several neighbors to split your fee and let you take the steps to improve the neighborhood for everyone.

Perhaps the unkempt home needs the grass mowed, the house repainted on the front or some other type of repair. By approaching the homeowner of the problem property with an **offer of help** rather than a criticism, progress can be made to improve the quality of the neighborhood.

Perhaps the City needs to be contacted regarding the repair of roads, the removal of graffiti, the flooding of certain intersections or other issues that negatively impact certain neighborhoods. Often the people who live in the neighborhood either ignore the problems or believe that nothing can be done about "city hall". This is not true. It it is something that requires commitment and action. By offering such a valuable service to homeowners, you might well position yourself in a league of your own when it comes to competing with other home stagers. Think about it. Plus if other homeowners in the neighborhood ever need a stager or re-designer, you have an inside track.

A Word About Certification

One of the values of going through my certification process is you have a chance to have your initial portfolio of work (your before and after pictures) critiqued so you can make sure you have properly understood the concepts of furniture arrangement. Here is an example where a student was staging an empty home. There was a fireplace in the corner of the room that was in an awkward place. Not being sure how to manage a difficult room like this, she decided to feature the view from the windows and ignore the fireplace altogether (Can you see it behind the loveseat in the corner?).

When she submitted her portfolio to me for review, however, I suggested she re-arrange the furniture to include the fireplace and suggested how that should be done.

Below you can see the corrected arrangement and how much better the room is featured for buyers, who can now see how they could arrange their own furniture effectively in the room. The arrangement still features the great view, but it also features the unique fireplace and gives a whole added dimension to the room.

While certification isn't essential for success, it is one effective way to make sure your learning process has been correctly interpreted and applied. This stager learned a lot by going through the process and will, no doubt, go on to achieve her dreams.

I believe wholeheartedly that it is important for a certification candidate to prove they have the proper knowledge and concepts and be able to prove they can apply those concepts out in the "real world". In many cases there is no accountability for knowledge and talent required and some people are going out and starting businesses without a real clue regarding the proper techniques.

Shoddy work gives everyone in the industry a poor reputation. To keep my certified stagers from making these mistakes and failing long term in their business, I require they pass an exam and submit a portfolio for approval before granting them my coveted designation. Many also get certified in redesign at the same time. This makes the CSS designation one of the most difficult to achieve, but it also makes it one of the most prestigious designations in the industry, if I do say so myself. When you stop to think that your future business may depend on this, can you afford to rely solely on your opinion or your interpretation of what you've learned? For some the talent comes naturally. But for most, it is an acquired talent. A review process is then very, very helpful.

Chapter Four

Marketing Tactics and Strategies

The best way to generate leads is to acquire a lead generating mindset at all times. A successful consultant, or any entrepreneur for that matter, is someone who will look for leads almost anytime and anywhere. It's a matter of focus and awareness. Make the most of every opportunity. Look for opportunities. Act on them. You'll be amazed at the sources for leads you will garner that go beyond the ones I will discuss here if you are focused and your antenna is up.

If you are constantly looking for new business and referrals, you will help keep yourself from falling into an up and down sales cycle. It's important to be generating leads continuously, not just between projects.

Tickler Files

The method you choose must be something that is comfortable for you. It really doesn't matter what method you use, so long as you have some way to store leads and follow up on them in a consistent manner. Some people prefer working on the computer; some people prefer working the old fashioned way. I like not having to be at the computer so much so I keep mine in a card system on my desk.

Some consultants enter a lead onto a sheet of paper and then gather as much information as possible. Choose the most promising ones each month and note on your sheets the most likely date to pursue them.

I prefer a 4x6 file box that has two sets of dividers minimum but you can do it on your computer too. The first set of dividers are numbered 1-31 for the days of the month (daily dividers). I place my leads on file cards that are 4x6. One lead per card. The leads that I want to follow up on that month are placed behind the day of the month that I plan to make contact.

The second set of dividers are labeled for the months of the year (monthly dividers). Those leads that are not ready for follow up until later in the year are placed behind the month that I plan on making contact. At the beginning of each month, I take all the cards behind that month's card and redistribute them to the daily dividers (the ones from 1-31).

If you want, you could even add more dividers to the back of the box that are labeled according to year. In early January of each year, take the cards behind the upcoming year and redistributed them to the monthly dividers, placing the leads for January behind the daily dividers.

This is the easiest method I have ever found of storing the original lead information, then keeping me focused on making contact in some way at the appropriate time. I guarantee that if you do not have a lead tracking system in place that you will miss out on a lot of business you could have had. If you prefer to use your computer, you can purchase software for it or even use Microsoft Excel or some equivalent software program.

People don't always say "yes" to you right away. Most people need time to get to know you a little and this requires an effort on your part to establish some kind of repetitive contact (be careful not to annoy them). When you have a good lead follow up system, you don't have to shuffle through your leads constantly trying to figure out what to do next. It's organized and it works.

You can buy all of the supplies for a good tickler file at your local office supply store. The file boxes come in plastic or metal. The dividers come pre-packaged and pre-numbered and with the months of the year already printed on them. You can also buy blank dividers. I suggest 4x6 card stock for each individual lead. You can buy these plain or lined, white or colored.

Satisfied Clients

You've probably heard it said, "The best client is one that has been referred to you." Well, I don't know how true that is, but referrals can and will be very important to your business. Your clients can become one of your most valuable sources for leads. Most salespeople will tell you that developing referrals is their best marketing technique. There is nothing quite like the third party endorsement of a satisfied client. It is valuable advertising for you and costs you nothing. If you do your job well, most clients will be happy to enthusiastically recommend your services to others.

History has shown us that, by fulfilling the client's expectation of a quality product and good service, you will be fulfilling the number one reason why many of America's top companies are where they are today. The number one formula for success is, "Put the customer first."

Some of your projects will be quick and almost effortless. Others will require much more careful consideration and planning. It can be difficult to predict which projects will need more of your time. So when you encounter a home that is more complex than you anticipated and takes longer to pull together, rather than feeling a bit resentful and trying to think of ways to cut corners or leave before the client is fully satisfied, view it as an investment in your overall marketing efforts. The extra work and time will build goodwill toward future projects.

Consider it an on-going learning process as well. From this experience you will hopefully learn how to ask more probing questions or predict your real costs and time commitment on the front end so that you will be better able to quote the project more realistically. Try to anticipate as much as possible the things that can delay your work or things that could possibly go wrong.

There will be times when you get surprises. You just have to roll with the punches, so to speak. There will be other times when the project will come together quicker than you anticipated and it seems to all even out in the end.

Challenges will happen to you. But just take it in stride because it happens to everyone now and again. There are many ventures in life that are far more risky and complicated. As time goes by and you gain more experience, you'll get better at knowing what to expect and properly preparing for it.

But back to the subject of referrals. Third party endorsements are not only very effective, but can create an endless chain. But you aren't likely to get referrals unless you keep your name before your satisfied clients in some way.

Here is a brief check list of strategies you can use to create an endless chain of referrals:

- Follow up with visits to the client
- Propose new services that might interest them
- Send thank you notes and presents
- Over time, develop a personal relationship if you can
- Leave brochures and business cards with them before you leave
- Ask for and acknowledge referrals - you have to ask, your clients just don't automatically think to give them to you
- Attend parties - host parties
- Send annual notes
- Put your identification and contact information on everything you give or send out

Don't be afraid to ask for referrals. People who have been sold on your services will usually be enthusiastic about recommending you to others. If they are reluctant, chances are you don't have a truly satisfied client and you might want to find out why. If there is something wrong, hopefully you can correct it and turn them into a satisfied client. If not, at least you'll know what to avoid in the future. However, there are some people who just don't want to be responsible for recommending anyone ever. Sometimes they just want to take the credit themselves and not admit they got help. There's nothing you can do to change their mind, so don't try. There are plenty of people who will be glad to refer your services. Concentrate on those clients.

Centers of Influence

Centers of influence are people who are probably not your clients but could be. They are typically people who know people - lots of people. They are in a position to contact lots of people on your behalf, or write a letter of recommendation on your behalf that you can send out yourself. Hopefully they are knowledgeable about your services, perhaps in a related profession, such as an architect, a CEO of a furniture store, a CEO of a moving company, owners of real estate companies, highly successful real estate agents. A referral from a center of influence is an excellent way to develop new leads. Make a list of all of the people you know who just seem to know everyone. This is a good place to start. Contact them and ask for a 5 minute meeting to explain what you are going to be offering. People like to be thought of as mentors. If they can help, they usually will want to do so, because "centers of influence" are referred to as "people-people".

If your center of influence is a close contact, perhaps a lunch date would be most appropriate. If you don't feel a brief meeting is appropriate, send them a letter and let them know about your service. Don't look to these people to become clients. See them rather as referrers that may be critical to the success of your business.

Scouts

Many people can serve as "advance men" without any effort on their part. These are professionals in noncompetitive fields who service homeowners or real estate agents, or even furniture rental and moving companies. Think about all of the service people who provide goods and services to homeowners. Here is a brief list: landscapers, maid services, mailmen, tree trimmers, babysitters, plumbers, electricians and so forth. These are people that may receive advance notice that someone is going to sell their home and move. Their recommendations to the homeowner, who already trusts them, can be very valuable to you.

131

Leads Sources

Leads Clubs are groups of salespeople from all fields and industry groups that meet regularly to share leads. Usually they get together for breakfast once a week. As they get to know you and the services you offer, they will consciously remember you as they go about their daily routines. People who attend leads club breakfasts or other types of gatherings know that if they want to receive referrals themselves, they need to be giving out referrals. You will need to be looking always for referrals that you can pass along to others in the group as well. Depending on the type of business you are in, leads clubs can be very profitable or can be a waste of time and energy. Before joining one and paying your membership fee, visit a few times and see if the type of people who are attending are people who are in businesses that deal with homeowners or real estate agents and brokers. If the majority of people work in the corporate world, it might not be the best club for you to join.

Yellow Pages

Check out the "Real Estate" section of your local yellow pages. See who is advertising and if any of the ads offer a home staging service. Many agents still don't know about staging and some offer the service themselves. But before you jump in and buy a display ad of any type, look to see how many companies are running display ads. If there aren't very many ads, it means that the yellow pages are not pulling that well. If there are a lot of display ads, you have stiff competition in the category, but the category must be pretty responsive, otherwise your competitors would not be paying out huge amounts of money to advertise there. So this can be a "catch 22". My advise is to work at building your business first through as many "free" methods as you can before you contract for an ad that you have to pay for all year long whether it is good for your business or not.

I do not recommend advertising in any yellow page directory that is not the main directory for the area you want to reach. And nowadays it even makes more sense to advertise in the online directories instead. My husband's business gets far more inquiries from his online ad than from the offline directory. You also do not want to advertise in any Business to Business directory. Keep all ads directly solely at your target market - homeowners!

Web Sites

If you want to be considered professional in the New Millennium you must have a web site. More and more, people are expecting to find your company on the internet. It doesn't matter if it is a small web site or not. The point is you really need to have one. As competition increases, it becomes more important than ever. We now offer semi-custom brochure websites to get your business instantly branded and help you get your message out. We will also link to your website from our International Directories to help drive prospects to your door. (We offer brochure websites in a domain name of your choosing in our Diamond Deluxe and Diamond Ruby Courses, giving you a quick start up. You provide the copy, we provide the site and will host it for a year for you as part of your course fee.)

If you want to create a website yourself, here are my suggestions. I wanted to have complete and instant control over my web sites, so I took a 6 month class at my local community college in web site design. It was one of the best decisions I ever made. There are a lot of software programs that have been developed which will help you create your own web site and do much of the work for you, however, a good knowledge of HTML (the code language for creating most web pages) is very, very useful. I have a software program called FrontPage 2003, but I've noticed on many occasions that it injects weird codes from time to time and then my pages don't display properly. Without a strong knowledge of HTML, I would never have been able to figure out what was wrong and correct the problem. I wholeheartedly recommend everyone take a class in HTML. You don't need all of the other training, like JAVA, but you do need to know HTML.

The reason I strongly advocate knowledge of HTML is that I have seen a lot of very poorly designed and constructed web sites put up by "decorators" and "interior designers". You only have a few seconds to impress a visitor to your site. If the site pages are poorly designed, do you honestly think a visitor is going to feel impressed with your skills in the real world? If you're in the business of interior design, you need to have a web site that is nicely designed. I'm not talking about some of those million dollar web sites. Your site might only have 8-10 pages. That's fine. Just make the pages attractive visually. This in itself will go a long way in establishing silently that you know what you're doing when it comes to decorating.

A web site is also great because you can show full color pictures of homes that you have done. Get permission from your clients to show before and after pictures. This will give your business enormous credibility. HTML knowledge will again be a great asset because you can post the pictures yourself and change them instantly whenever you want.

The best quality pictures you will get for your web site are the ones you will take with a digital camera. If you don't have one and can't afford one, see if you can borrow one for your appointments. The benefit of a digital picture is that they are virtually "free" to take and you can easily adjust the color and lighting to enhance them if you need to do so. You can display them immediately and don't have any processing and developing fees to pay. Nor do you have to buy film. The one draw back is that they create bigger files due to the better quality. Bigger files take longer to download on people's computers and many people won't wait long enough to see them.

The other way to acquire before and after pictures of the homes you rearrange or stage is with a non-digital camera. Make sure you have one that will take good quality pictures, particularly in low light situations. To protect yourself, always carry a tripod in your car. Concentrate the majority of your pictures on different angles of the home "before" you rearrange it. Why? Because once you have started work on a room, you will never be able to go back and get more "before" pictures. You could, in a pinch, go back to a client's home to get more "after" pictures (or even to make changes), but you can never recapture the home as it was when you first arrived.

More than once I have been disappointed with the quality of my "before" pictures and had no way to redo them. A few times I forgot to take pictures altogether. Since you don't know at the time you take them what the full extent of their use will be to you later, try to get as many "before" pictures as you can.

The benefit of having photo prints of the homes you have done is that you can then scan these pictures. Scanned pictures usually create smaller files which may not have the quality of digital photos, but will download much faster onto people's computers. What good are pictures of your former projects if no one sees them?

Whether you take your pictures with a digital camera or a traditional camera, you will want to also create a portfolio of your projects. Periodically a potential client or a referrer will want to see examples of work you have done in the past. Having a professional portfolio of your work will be very impressive. It's a nice keepsake for you as well. After you get really going in your business, you're going to start to forget projects from a long time ago. Your scrapbook will serve as an excellent reminder whenever you need it to.

If you just don't have the time or want to take the time to learn HTML and web site design and you have the money, then consider hiring a professional to create a web site for you. But before you take that step, check out their work thoroughly, compare prices (as there is a huge difference in pricing out in the marketplace) and get everything in writing. It's also a very good idea to put all of your ideas down on paper first so that you can give your web developer a real clear picture of just what you want.

If you want to be taken seriously, you should also register your own domain name and have your web site hosted by an Internet Service Provider. Select the ".com" address. Do not fall for putting your site into an "internet mall". Have your own ".com" address and use the email address that comes with your domain as your business email address. In this way, potential clients will not be able to differentiate a small home-based business from a large, commercial brick and mortar business. This gives you, as a start-up home stager, an even playing field.

It costs a lot less money to launch and sustain a web site than it does to have a yellow page ad. Use your yellow page listing as a place to list your web site. Interested potential clients can then visit your site and really get a good feel for what you offer. It's a lot cheaper and more effective than printing off an expensive brochure to which you also have to add in the expense of mailing. We have also created a discussion forum to allow you a way to chat with other stagers and re-designers all across the globe and support you in an on-going manner. Periodically check back on the website as we are growing and developing and there is almost always something new to help you grow and sustain your business.

I could go on and on about web site development and design, but this is not really the book for that. It requires a book all of its own. By the way, the textbook I used in my HTML class is called: "Creating Web Pages with HTML" by Patrick Carey. You should be able to purchase it over the Internet, but if not you might contact the bookstores at your local colleges to see if they can get it for you. I'm sure there are many other books equally good, but this one has really been helpful to me.

One last thing on website development. Try to concentrate your whole presentation on the "benefits" your potential clients will derive. Don't confuse "features" with "benefits". Human nature is the same everywhere. People are mainly interested in "what's in it for them". So the more you can translate your service into statements of how it will "help" them or how they will "feel", the more successfully you will turn prospects into clients.

Personal Observations

Take every opportunity and make the most of it. If you are always in an "opportunity mode", you'll be quite amazed at the number of opportunities that will actually arise - even just going to and from the market or your bank or your child's school. Be willing to talk about your business everywhere to everyone. Talk about what you do at the gym, on the airplane, at a product show, at a social event or civic event. Always have some business cards handy to give out.

Set a goal of collecting a minimum of 5 business cards from other people when you are in a social event. The moment you accept someone else's card, you're free to hand them yours. The moment you have exchanged business cards, there is an implied permission to call them. These people automatically become part of your network and can be good sources of referrals, if you follow up.

Any activity that puts you in contact with homeowners or real estate agents will be good for your business. Get involved in community activities of interest to you or members of your family. Look at your personal style and formulate a business marketing strategy that suits your style.

Personally, I'm very comfortable speaking in public or teaching a class or seminar. But I am not comfortable with chatting at social functions and would never include a cocktail party as part of my marketing plan. But you might be just the opposite. Try to stretch yourself outside your comfort zone from time to time, but concentrate your marketing efforts in the manner and ways that suit your personal style.

New Buyer's Lists

If you are also offering redesign services, depending on where you live, you might consider subscribing to a list composed of new homeowners. These are lists compiled by businesses who are in the profession of creating all types of lists. You would want to zero in on a specialized list of homeowners in a certain locale, who own homes in a certain price range. They can be new owners or established dwellers, so long as they are in the income bracket that can afford a service such as redesign.

Before buying a huge number of names and addresses, you should run small tests to see if the list is "clean" and current and to get a feeling for your marketing strategies on how to approach the owners. Never jump into any marketing strategy without testing it first. Again, when starting out, try to use the "free" strategies first. You may never need to purchase lists and leads and pay for expensive advertising if you work the other methods diligently and effectively.

Moving Companies

Just as real estate agents and brokers are in touch with homeowners who are in transition, so are moving companies. Visit the moving companies closest to you and try to establish some rapport with the owner or salespeople. Explain your services, tell them about your web site, offer to refer business to them as you run across people. Perhaps the moving company will be happy to hand out your brochure or flyer to everyone who rents a moving van or hires their service. You could offer a special price to anyone who contacts you for service as a result of being referred by their moving company. This is an excellent way for the moving company to generate more good will and be well remembered favorably after you do an outstanding job of staging the home of one of their clients.

Other Methods

Encourage referrals from other types of companies: home furnishing retailers, painting and wallpapering businesses, home decorating centers, builders, fabric centers, floor covering retailers, window treatment retailers. Place classified ads in local and regional newspapers and magazines. Rent a booth at home furnishings and real estate industry shows. I talk quite a bit about doing shows and setting up for speaking engagements in **Advanced Redesign** (See Chapter Six for details).

Getting the Appointment

You Make the Contact

I totally hate it, as a homeowner myself, when I get calls from salespeople. If I hate being bothered by sales pitches over the phone, I can imagine other people feel the same way. I do not recommend making cold calls to homeowners. If you do, you need a really thick skin! You will find a lot of rejection and you may even encounter people who will be irritated with you.

Under no circumstances should you resort to a computer to dial your phone numbers for you. You will just generate negative reactions and your business cannot afford to start off making ill will all over the area.

The only people I ever call by telephone are people who have called me to request a return phone call, people who have been referred to me by people they know and trust, or business people with whom I would like to interact for the purposes of gaining or giving referrals.

But it's your business and you can handle it any way you please. I'm just saying that a negative response will travel a lot farther by word of mouth than a positive response. So try to treat homeowners the way you would like to be treated. Then your good reputation will precede you and you never have to be concerned about overcoming a negative reputation.

The Prospect Contacts You

When a prospect contacts you, try to find out as soon as possible how they found out about you. This is important because you're going to want to track your marketing methods in some way to know which strategies are good and which ones need to be dropped. So I am trained to ask very early in the conversation about where and how they heard about me.

If you are a member of our International Staging and Redesign Directory (hosted on our server) and you are contacted by phone or email by someone asking about your services, be careful about what information you give out until you are convinced it is a legitimate inquiry. The best way to do that is by asking pertinent questions about them, what they are seeking and where they are located.

Before you get to the point where people are calling you, however, you should spend some time in advance of thinking through the kinds of things you wish to say to a prospect over the phone. Paramount to your thinking should be your USP. A USP is your "unique selling proposition". It needs to be specific and have a clear benefit that you are offering to your prospects.

You need to think carefully about your fee structure and have a clear picture of what you will charge for your service, how much the charge will be altered by the distance you have to travel, whether you have a minimum charge, flat rate or hourly fee, how long you anticipate a project will take. Naturally this will vary from home to home. You'll be able to quote a fee for consultations, but you won't be able to quote a fee for doing a full-scale staging of a home until after you have been to the home and researched it. In due time you might be able to gauge some kind of average figure, but you really should never give a quote over the phone, except for mere consultation services.

The reason you need to have all of this information well thought out in advance is that you are surely going to be asked specific questions. You do not want to hesitate with your answers. If you are hesitant, the prospect is going to get hesitant as well and you will surely lose the appointment. Hesitation makes you appear unprofessional and silently suggests you either don't know what you're doing or that you are creating a special price or stipulation just for the caller.

So predetermine as much as you can what your answers will be to the questions you will undoubtedly be asked.

Here are some of the typical questions that prospects ask:

- Can you tell me what your service is all about?

- How long does it take?
- What do you charge?
- What is your experience or expertise?

If you find yourself really being pressed for some kind of ballpark figure, ask the person what the home is selling for. Ask them for the square footage of the home and how long the owner has lived in the home. Find out what the major decorating colors are in the home. Experience will eventually help you. The longer a person has lived in a home, the more junk and stuff they will have collected. That's going to mean that you're likely to have a big job of sorting and packing to do. The longer they have lived in the home, the more repairs it will likely need. The longer they have lived in the home the more dated the furnishings and decorating will be. Knowing in advance what colors the home is will give a clue as to whether you'll have a big job neutralizing the dwelling or not. The square footage of the home will tell you the size of the home. Naturally larger homes will require more work than smaller dwellings. And finally, the asking price of the home may give you a clue as to how well-maintained the home might be, but not always.

At any rate, these are clues that might guide you in what you would say. In a situation where you are being pressed, give out a possible range in price and let the asking price act as some sort of guide. An asking price of $200,000 might yield a fee in the neighborhood of $2000 at 1%; a $500,000 asking price might yield $5,000 at 1% and a $1,000,000 asking price might yield $10,000. Whether 1% seems low or high to you will depend on you and where you live and what the competition is charging. So don't latch on to it automatically. You really need to get into the business and get a feeling for what the market will bear in your part of the country, but more importantly, you need to know what your talent and knowledge is worth to you.

Most of the time a prospect's priority questions will relate to what you charge (whether they ask the question right away or not). The beauty of being self employed is that you can charge whatever you want to charge. But it should be affordable and competitive. If you charge too little, the prospect might think you're not really a professional. If you charge too much, they just won't see the value or might not be able to afford that much. So you need to be affordable, yet professional. This can be tricky and you may have to experiment for a while until you find a fair price that is acceptable to you and to your typical clients.

If the prospect tells you that they want to think about it or that they have to discuss the matter with a spouse or their real estate agent or additional person, chances are they either cannot afford your price or you have failed to get them to understand the value and benefit of having you serve them. It could also mean that you have failed to convince them that you are uniquely qualified to handle the project no matter what.

I'm not a pushy salesperson. I hate it when people get pushy with me and I refuse to do that to others. I can tell you from experience, however, that if someone doesn't set an appointment for you to come to their home or give you contact information to their agent, you're probably not going to get them at all. People just don't call back and they use the excuse of talking to someone as a reason for getting off the phone.

But that doesn't change how I respond to them. No matter what they tell me, I'm always pleasant, I always try to be as informative and helpful as I can be, and I treat them as I would want to be treated. You must understand that people do not want to say, "Well, I can't afford you." No one likes to say "no". So they say "maybe" instead. A "maybe" is nothing more than a disguised "no".

Don't fret! There are probably thousands of people selling their homes all around you and you can only manage to do one property at a time anyway. If you are persistent and consistent, you'll eventually get it going and build your business. If the person who cannot afford your services takes a pass, they might know other people who would love to hear about your services. If you are kind, friendly, enthusiastic and helpful, no matter what their response is, it will come back to you in the future. Entire businesses have been built off of the referrals from just one or two people - and they don't have to be clients to refer you.

Business Stationery

As soon as you are ready to get this business off the ground, and even if you've been doing it already for a period of time, you ought to announce your business to the people you know. You can throw a **Grand Opening Party** and invite everyone you can think of to come and help you celebrate your business. For those of you who want a simple route to getting the word out, sending out an announcement postcard is an effective means of communication. It forces you to keep the message short and sweet and to the point. It also doesn't cost as much to send out a postcard mailing as it does a brochure or flyer. But if you like working with brochures, they are an excellent addition to your marketing portfolio.

Direct Mail

Business that your direct mail flyers, letters and brochures generate is bonus business. You can build a successful business without them, but they will enhance your business if you have them. They will help you set out your credentials and help you identify what is unique about you, thus separating you from your competition. You can mail them out or hand them out. They are all seeds that you are planting in your local area. Any one of them can result in a referral that you may or may not know anything about.

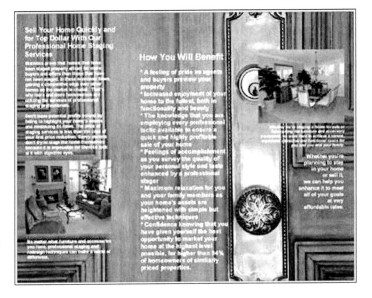

I suggest that you set aside a small portion from every project you do to cover the cost of developing your marketing strategies, no matter what form they take. The old saying, "It takes money to make money" isn't true in every situation, but you do need to be prepared to reinvest a portion of your earnings back into your business to help it grow.

For more help in planning and developing direct mail pieces, flyers, letters and brochures, consult your local library. There are a lot of good books on marketing strategies. Take time each week to continue to educate yourself in the area of marketing. It will pay off for you in the future, if not immediately. I have also listed some good references and resources at the end of this manual.

When sending a letter, don't try to pitch your whole service or product in the letter. Briefly introduce yourself, briefly state some quick benefits and features, and invite them to contact you (unless you have a way to follow up yourself). Save the "sales pitch" for the first appointment or at least the first phone call where the client will be able to pick up on your friendly voice and enthusiasm. It's impossible to convey those feelings in a letter. So don't try to do anything more in a letter than peak their interest.

Here is part of a sample introductory letter:

> "Dear _____,
>
> I noticed the other day that you just put your house on the market. Knowing that most homeowners who list their property seek to sell it as soon as possible, I thought you might be interested in knowing about my home staging service which has been extremely helpful to other sellers, getting them a quick sale for a much higher price. " . . . .
> Then you go on to briefly explain some other benefits.

OR

"I couldn't help but notice over the last two months that your home is still on the market. I thought you might be interested to know that I specialize in preparing a home to sell very quickly and for top dollar. If you or your agent are frustrated with the amount of offers you have received, I know I can help get you the results you want and deserve....." Then go on to give an example where you have helped another home seller.

OR

> "Dear _____,
>
> I noticed the other day that you are new to the area and I want to especially welcome you to the neighborhood. I know a lot of people who move into a new home and bring their furnishings from a previous home to use in the new space. Sometimes that's really difficult to do.
>
> I thought you might be interested to know that I specialize in helping people adapt the older furnishings and accessories to the new space by providing a very affordable professional room arrangement service." . . . . then go on from there.

You get the idea.

Keep the letter simple and straight forward. Remember that it should be laden with benefits and how you can make life better for them quickly and easily.

At the end of the letter say something like,

> "I would like the opportunity to discuss your marketing plans for your home with your or your real estate agent.
>
> "Please give me a call at _____ and I will be happy to explain how I can help you. You can also visit my web site at www._____.com to get more information at your convenience."

Remember, don't try to cover too much ground in your letter. Peak their interest, give them multiple ways to get more information and thank them for considering your services for themselves or for passing the information along to someone else they know.

Business Cards

If you don't use your personal name in your business name, then you will need to choose another name to call your business. This is called a DBA, which stands for "Doing Business As". I will discuss how to set up a DBA later, but for now I just want you to think about choosing a name for your business that is descriptive of what you are offering.

A lot of businesses choose names that are so non-descriptive or confusing or cute, they are poor marketing choices. The best names are the ones that tell people instantly something about what your company specializes in, are easy to pronounce, and are easy to remember. That way your name itself is a mini billboard working for you wherever people see it.

I once drove by a business named "Tuesday Mornings". Well, it was sort of easy to remember and did create momentary curiosity, but not enough to cause me to stop and investigate. I had absolutely no clue at the time what they offered. The name told me nothing. So it's no wonder that they are struggling to stay in business. "Tuesday Home Discounts" would have probably caused me to make a u-turn and drop in for a visit.

So stay away from vague, non-descript names that don't tell anyone at a glance something about what you do.

Phone Discussions

There will be some people you will never reach. There are tons of businesses floating around out there that will never interest me at all, even if their product or service were free. So there's room for everyone and something for everyone. You just need to figure out how to reach your target market. In the home staging business, your target market will probably be homes selling for $200,000 on up (in rural areas primarily) and $450,000+ (in metro areas primarily), especially ones that are in less desirable neighborhoods or being sold by people who need to make a quick sale and are willing to spend some money to make that happen.

Be wary of doing anything free for anyone. Even though I spent hours of my time and dramatically improved the homes of people I donated services to, half of the people who received the service for free were the least grateful "clients" I have ever had. There is something about human nature that makes us devalue what we get for free. Therefore, don't do it unless you are brand new in the business and just do one or two homes to "practice on". You can offer to do the homes of close friends or family if you want to so you can get some practice and get some good before and after pictures to use, but once you have a few projects under your belt, charge for the service after that and if someone isn't willing to pay, they don't deserve you.

There are people who will be happy to pay for the service out there. You just have to get the word out in a consistent and persistent manner. Don't give up if it's slow at first.

I've also found that if someone can't get a good idea of what you can do for them over the phone or by looking at your web site, you're probably never going to convince them (or their spouse) anyway. Your strongest ally will probably be the real estate agent and that's why developing a strong relationship with agents is so vital to a successful business.

Beware of the prospect who will pretend to be interested to get you to their home. Their secret agenda is to pick your brain while you are there, send you away without a project and then use the ideas that you gave them for free. This happens. Never agree to do a consultation without payment. If someone isn't willing to pay you a fee of some kind for your time and expertise, they will never hire you. So don't think you can turn them once you are there. This type of person is not your target market.

Confirmation Call

After you make an appointment, it's a very good idea to call the client/agent the day before to reconfirm the appointment. Yes, it's an opportunity for the client to back out of the appointment altogether, but better for them to back out than for you to travel to their home only to have them gone. That's a complete waste of your time.

You also want to re-convey to the client that you will keep the appointment and that you operate on a professional level.

It's also a good time to ask any questions that you want to ask that you may have neglected to ask when the appointment was set. You can also use this time to restate what you plan to do and remind the client of anything you want them to do prior to your visit.

Regarding Cancellations

I've never, never had any one cancel and offer me money anyway. Never! I've had my share of cancellations though. I think you'll shoot yourself in the foot if you insist up front on a cancellation fee, personally. You might scare away someone that would have booked otherwise. But it all depends on how much of a cancellation problem you have. If it happens all the time, then you might want to protect yourself. If it seldom happens, don't worry about it.

I personally have never had a cancellation fee if they call me before I leave home. Now if I got to their home and they weren't there, I'd be really put off, which is why I always confirm appointments the day before. You will, of course, want to insert a cancellation fee if you are putting together a time consuming proposal for a client, you've invested several hours researching the home in the belief that you would manage the entire staging, and then after a good deal of work the client backs out. In a situation like this, it is customary to get paid for the work you did to the point of cancellation. This is another reason why it's so good to get plenty of pictures and have forms that you use to help you document your recommendations. Should you need to take someone to small claims court to get payment for services, all of these documents will prove to the judge that a meeting of the minds did exist and that you are owed the money for your services to that point. Once again, put everything in writing.

Should you receive a cancellation notice after expending time and energy on a project, you need to tell them that if they should wish to cancel, there will be a penalty and explain why. If they simply postpone and set up for the following week, I would not penalize them. I try to walk in their shoes because unexpected things do come up. You can't go wrong by not charging them, but adding them to your mailing, etc. they may still become your client at a later date and in the meantime speak highly of you because you didn't penalize them.

I once thought I needed to sell my home and hired an agent who happened to live in my block to represent me. He did a walk thru of my home and began preparations to sell it. Soon after I changed my mind and decided to stay in the home. I'm sure he was disappointed to lose the listing, but he never charged me for any of his services. I would have paid him if he had presented me a bill, but he never did. I appreciated that and would gladly have given him my business in the future and plenty of referrals, however, he eventually moved away and changed profession, becoming an attorney.

Just the other day, I went to pick up our car from a dealership where we had turned it over for repair. When I got the report back from them, it was ridiculously high and we decided to pull the car and take it to our regular mechanic. We only took it to a dealership because my husband thought there was a computer problem.

When I went to pick it up, they wanted $120, at which I balked. The man came in and told me they always charge for diagnostics whether you have them do the work or not, that all dealerships do that. Well, I had expected to pay something, but not $120. So I told him that then he should have mentioned that to us at the outset and told us how much the diagnostics would be. He didn't and, therefore, there was no verbal contract with us to pay for diagnostics. There was nothing in their written contract as well. He tried to find something in writing and couldn't. So then he offered to lower it to $80 and that's where we ultimately settled though I argued for $60. I can understand giving them some money for their trouble, but $120 was too much. I got my car and left. However, it left a bad impression which you don't want to do. Be fair with people and they will usually be fair with you. I've never taken my car there again for repair work.

So the bottom line is this. How much negative talk do you want floating around about you and your business, even if you have a right to be compensated? You have to make that call. People will always, always spread bad news faster and farther than good news. And they will probably embellish the bad news and downplay the good news. But by the same token, you want to minimize your damages as much as possible. So I think you should keep the problem in mind, put nothing in writing, and judge each case individually. If your client is somewhat hesitant to book the appointment, then mention the cancellation fee. If they are very excited and enthusiastic about having you come, don't mention it because if they cancel, more than likely they will re-schedule anyway.

In the real estate market, expect anything. It always helps me to remind myself that my business is in God's hands, and that He knew there was going to be a cancellation and He was not surprised by it. And since my business all belongs to Him anyway, what would He want me to do about the cancellation and my unexpected free time? So I always have a Plan B if Plan A gets cancelled. You should too.

Your Personal Aura

Consultant Etiquette

There are a few rules of proper etiquette which you should abide by. Always remember that you are going to someone's home, their private space. No matter how long someone has lived in their home, they attach special feelings to their home, their furniture, their accessories and their family members. There are some rules of etiquette that you should abide by.

BE ON TIME - Just as you value your time, your client values hers (or his). Be considerate and arrive on time. Do not arrive early, unless you have indicated in advance that you might be early. I hate for someone to come to my home before I am ready to receive them, so don't do it to someone else. If you arrive early, sit in your vehicle and wait until the appropriate time to ring the doorbell. The homeowner will be grateful.

DO NOT PARK IN THEIR DRIVEWAY - A person's driveway is their private space. Do not invade this space. Even though they don't say anything, they will prefer for you to park on the street.

When I make an appointment, I always inquire about parking. This is from my years of working as a corporate art consultant where I was dealing with high rise buildings and usually limited parking places where I had to pay for parking. So I always want to ask about where to park.

Even if the homeowner tells me to just park in their driveway, I never do unless there just isn't any where else to park. Why? Because I never know if someone else in the family is going to arrive home and become irritated at someone parked in their space or what they perceive to be their space.

Where you park is especially important if your vehicle leaks oil (or anything else). You definitely do not want your vehicle to spew out something on their driveway. So make a habit of parking on the street. Parking is usually not a problem at most homes.

COMPLIMENT THE HOMEOWNER IMMEDIATELY - I don't care if you have just walked into the most awful house you have ever been in. If you look for it, there will always, always be something that you can genuinely compliment the homeowner for - even if it is not the home. Compliment them on the easy directions they gave you, the neighborhood, the front garden, the entry, the colors they have decided to decorate with, her hair, the family -- I don't care what it is regarding, find some way to compliment the owner. Be genuine, however. They will know if you are being phony. Try to be as specific with your compliment as possible. It will have more meaning if you are specific. I can live on a good compliment for a month. So can other people. So quickly look for one or more things you can comment on and greet the client with a huge smile. More on this later.

ASK FOR PERMISSION – Wherever you go in the house, ask permission first. This is a person's private dwelling. Do not presume that you can go any where you please. Be particularly sensitive to going into the person's bedroom or private bath. Once you have completed the seller led tour of the home you can ease up because you will be expected to look over the entire home. But don't just start walking around on your own.

HANDLE THINGS CAREFULLY AND GRACEFULLY - You are going to be working with the personal possessions of your client. You are going to be involved in moving furniture and accessories. You definitely do not want to damage anything. Some of the furnishings are going to be heavy, some are going to be delicate.

I have never broken a client's possession, partly by being extremely patient and careful of what I am doing. But there's always the first time waiting to happen. Breaking something can have a drastic affect on your entire relationship with this client. Be careful. I will discuss a liability waiver form you need to have them sign later in this training.

First Impressions

Someone once said, "I can tell the second I meet someone whether I want to do business with them. The rest of the time with them is spent justifying my first impulse." Whether you realize it or not, we all gather first impressions and once gathered, they are hard to change. That's why you want to create a good first impression.

Your wardrobe and personal image are primary key elements toward creating rapport with the client when you arrive at the home. Up until that time, you have conversed over the phone, you may have sent them literature, they may have visited your web site. Each time they have seen something generated by you they have added information to their list of impressions.

Normally I would be advising you to wear business-like attire, but that may be somewhat adjusted depending on whether you're just doing a consultation or whether you are expected to jump in immediately and begin the process of staging the home. It would probably be better to arrive in comfortable, more casual clothing. I don't mean jeans or sweats. But you probably don't want to wear a dress or suit. So it makes great sense to arrive in more casual attire that makes it possible for you to do the work you are hired to do.

I recommend slightly loose fitting attire, not overly baggy, but loose enough to be comfortable - clothing that will allow you to bend easily, reach easily, push and pull easily. A nice pant suit with low heels would be quite appropriate.

I recommend comfortable shoes that tie on. You don't want to worry about a shoe coming off while you are moving something or carrying something. You certainly don't want to trip over a stray shoe, but nor do you want to trip over shoelaces. So it's a good idea to double knot your laces. I like to wear shoes with plenty of cushioning. In any appointment, you can figure in advance that you're going to be on your feet most of the time, so you definitely want your shoes to be well padded and as comfortable as possible. (Memory Foam insoles work great.)

After introducing myself and giving out my opening compliments and stating how glad I am to be there, I always look for an out of the way place to store my case or purse.

So within 60 seconds I am ready to begin. I don't like to waste my client's time (nor mine), so I arrive prepared to begin immediately.

Gaining Control

Now this can be a tricky part. Even though this is my client's home, and in essence I am a guest while there, I am also the consultant with the expertise, so it is important to take leadership with regard to what is to happen next.

I prefer to ask the client if I might give them an idea of how I work with **most clients**. They may be very happy to know this information and appreciate having a structure to predict what will happen next. Most will be very willing to follow any sequence you set up for them to follow. Most will be very cooperative unless there is some kind of time pressure they are having. By discussing right away how you wish to proceed, you can find out any time constraints that might exist and adapt as necessary. Since I discuss what to do first in another section, I will not discuss it here, except to say that you are the person who needs to set the agenda and sequence that makes sense to you.

Getting Client's Feedback

Through the process of consulting and staging your client's home, you should be doing three things:

1) Finding ways to continually affirm your client on their choices of furnishings and accessories, their sense of style or whatever you can, and making them feel supported and appreciated;

2) Explaining what you are doing and why, enlisting their help so they feel a part of the process (assuming they want to be part of the process);

3) Periodically checking with them to see if they feel comfortable with the changes you are making, asking for their input as well.

If you have done all of these things simultaneously and effectively, you should complete the whole process with a very happy client. If you sense along the way that there is a problem and they are not voicing their concerns, readjust immediately so that the client is happy. After all, even though you are striving to give them the best possible outcome, it's still their home and they still need to feel comfortable with what you are doing. Often a brief explanation is all that is needed.

Collecting the Fee

I will discuss a little later in another segment what you should charge for a full staging project, but for now this would be the point in your consultation-only project where you would collect the fee that your client has already agreed to pay if all you were hired to do is consult with them. I have never had problems collecting my fee at the end. I always make it a point to give them more than I have promised to give, so getting paid has never been difficult.

Make sure before you begin just how much time the client has available. Many times they will have some other appointment to go to later in the day, or for some reason need you to be done by a certain time. Always make sure you know how much time you have and keep track of the time as you go.

When I have completed the project, most clients are immediately going for their checkbooks to pay the fee. However, if they don't bring it up, I simply pull out my invoice and other forms, and I never even have to bring the subject up. Be sure to have some official invoices printed up, either on your home computer or at a print shop, because you want to act professional at all times. Never give a client a little store bought receipt from a booklet you got at the office supply store with your name stamped on it at the top. This is not going to get any respect. You're a professional consultant, not a day laborer.

Have the amount of the consultation written on the invoice, along with the client's name, address and phone, and email address (assuming they have one). If they pay you by check, record the check amount and the check number on the invoice. Give the client a copy of the invoice and retain one for your own records. If you receive cash, note that it was cash and write the amount given to you on the invoice before you give them a copy. Make all notations on the invoice in INK.

If I am ever given cash, I also place my initials by the amount given to me and request that the client initial the amount as well. This way, should there ever be any problem arise, you both have stipulated to the exact amount of cash you received.

Never leave without getting paid! Never let a client "con" you into letting them pay you later, write you a post-dated check, or promise to send you a check in the mail. None of this! I've never had a client try it, but there can always be a first time. So I just want to go on record and tell you that you should never accept any terms other than payment on demand in full at the completion of any consultation-only appointment.

The Referral and Testimonial Form

Now, this is the perfect and the only perfect time to ask for a brief testimonial (in writing) and one or two referrals. If you think you can call them back later to get this, or send them something in the mail to fill out and return to you, you will most likely get nothing at all.

You must make the testimonial and referral gathering a part of the payment process. I have found it effective to even mention at the time that I set the appointment, that I will come and do the consultation, after which I will give them an invoice for payment and ask them for a brief testimonial and a couple of referrals, since I build my business mostly by word of mouth.

Be sure to add the "word of mouth" phrase. It definitely helps. By telling them in advance that I expect to get a couple of referrals they then have no excuse when I do ask for them. It also gives them some time to think about one or two people why might be selling their home (or moving into a new space where my redesign services would be most helpful).

If you have let them know ahead of time that this is part of the final process, you should not have any problem getting them to sit down for a brief moment and give you what you want.

I have an official form that first asks for a testimonial. It should only take them a minute to give you a few sentences about how they feel about the service you have just rendered to them. Getting a testimonial is important because you can add it to your marketing materials and to your web site. New prospects are always interested in how other people have found your service to benefit them.

You might even ask them to comment on how they feel they have "benefited" from the consultation. Remember, people aren't going to hire you because they like you or even because they think you are good. They ARE going to hire you because they believe you have something to offer that will BENEFIT them.

Don't ask for a bunch of referrals. Give them a place on the same "form", below the testimonial, to give you the contact information of 2-3 people whom they know whom they feel would be interested in hearing about your services. Tell them that you're looking for people who are planning to sell their homes or who have had their home on the market for some time without success.

Assure them that you will simply make an offer to them and will not badger them in any way. Since your client has just experienced the professional manner in which you have conducted yourself with them, and have experienced first hand the benefits of what you can do, you should find it quite easy to get them to give you a name or two. If they don't know anyone in that situation at the time, that's ok. If you stay in touch with them later, you might get referrals eventually. Staying in touch is what most business people fail to do, however.

If they claim, after your explanation of the type of person you are looking for, someone with equally good taste, that they just don't know anyone to pass you on to, then there isn't too much you can do at that point. Thank them and give them some business cards and ask them to pass them on to anyone in the future they feel could benefit by hearing what you do. Then in a month, consider re-contacting them to see if they have thought of anyone since you left that might appreciate hearing about your service.

A wise home enhancement specialist will have several referral gathering systems in place. Referrals can be very powerful and sustain you in business if you constantly seek them and have procedures in place that help you remember to ask for them. You must constantly ASK for referrals. Most people will not remember you. And even if they did, they often forget what they did with your contact information and couldn't pass you on if they wanted to. This is another reason why it is important to periodically make contact with past clients. It serves, not only as a reminder to them that you are still in business and eager to help people, but if they have misplaced or thrown out any previous literature from you, they now have your contact information handy again.

Work very hard to have that Testimonial and Referral Form all filled out by your client before you leave the consultation. If you don't, the likelihood of getting it later is slim to none.

Taking the "After" Pictures

While the client is busy writing your check and filling out your Testimonial/Referral Form, you should go ahead and begin taking your "after" pictures, assuming you have actually been involved in staging the home. You don't want to stand or sit watching your client write on your form. It may make them nervous and a little irritated.

Besides you are done now and you want to wrap things up as quickly as possible and let them get on with the process of selling their home. So take your digital or traditional camera and try to find angles to re-shoot the rooms that are as similar to the "before" shots as possible. This can be tricky.

You want to have pictures of the same walls as the "before" shots, but at the same time you also want to shoot the room from a point of view where the arrangement can be easily seen and from an angle where the arrangements look best. So I suggest that you take as many pictures as you can, because you're not going to know until later, when you have both the "before" and "after" shots lined up together, which ones can be combined to give other people the best feeling for the staging solutions you were able to achieve for your client.

These pictures aren't just for your later enjoyment. These pictures are to be used effectively in your advertising and marketing strategies to prove to other prospects that you have, indeed, made a major, significant improvement on the overall ambience of the rooms you have staged. Your prospective clients in the future are going to carefully scrutinize these "before" and "after" pictures to see if you know what you're doing and to see if your staging ideas are going to most likely be worth the consultation fee or the full service fee. If they cannot see the value in the photos, you will most likely not see them become a client.

It's hard for a lot of people to visualize what you might do for them. If they were able to visualize, most likely they would be doing it themselves and not considering your services in the first place (unless they just don't have the time or motivation). So while you want to wrap things up at this point, don't be in such a hurry that you fail to take good "after" pictures. Your business depends on this.

If you have a video camera, you might also want to take some video shots of the room before and after the consultation. Having a video tape of homes you have done could be very handy in your marketing efforts, particularly if you enjoy speaking in public or conducting seminars. This is also an option.

No matter what method you use, however, get plenty of distance shots and close ups. They will all be worth the effort and will definitely help you garner more clients.

Advising Clients on Making New Purchases

Whether the client needs to purchase anything new will depend on a number of factors. It first depends on how much of their furnishings you were actually able to utilize, whether the home was empty to begin with, and whether something really, really important just doesn't exist in the dwelling. Never try to sell a client on buying additional furnishings (or even renting some) unless they truly, truly need to do so. They will spot any attempts to profit from the situation and that will not be good business.

I always preferred to keep my business simple and a client would have to drag me kicking and screaming (well, almost) before I would consent to shop for them or even go with them. I much prefer to simply make recommendations and turn them loose to shop on their own. But you may feel differently and love to shop so much you want to provide this type of service. I prefer to simply tell them what I recommend for a certain spot, what size, what shape, what color, what height. The only drawback is that they don't always do what you ask them to do. So there may be some items concerning which you will definitely want to participate in the purchase decision, but apart from that it's not worth your involvement. It's a judgment call.

Leaving Business Cards

Always carry a supply of business cards with you. Make sure you leave a few with all your clients at the end of a consultation. Stick cards in the mail with bills you pay that go to local addresses. You never know whose opening the mail on the other end that might be interested or able to pass your card along.

I know of an attorney who would eat at a restaurant and never fail to leave the restaurant without passing out his business card to every customer there. I've never been bold enough to do that, but it worked for him. Let's face it - you never know when you might need an attorney. The same is actually true for this business - you just never know when someone will put their home on the market.

Some people leave business cards in mail boxes, on car windows, at door steps. I don't know how effective this would be, but if you're seriously low on funds to get the word out any other way, it is another option. One good client can pay for a huge supply of business cards. I would be wary of leaving anything larger. People get irritated at flyers, but it is a rare person who would get irritated by a business card. I have yard care people leave me their business cards all the time. An occasional real estate agent farming my neighborhood will leave a note pad or flyer. More rare now than in years past.

I have received a huge assortment of business cards stuck on my door, or left on my driveway in front of my home. Most get tossed in the trash, but I have kept some in a special drawer that are of interest to me. I do always look at the card. That is what you want to remember. I think I'm a pretty typical homeowner, so I consider doing the things that do not offend me and I do not do any marketing strategies that do offend me. Again, do unto others what you would have them do unto you.

Make sure that the design of your business card is well done. Remember, people will judge your staging ability by everything you put out there. If I see a stager whose card is poorly designed and ill planned, it tells me right away everything I need to know. This is not the place to cut corners, so if you don't feel competent to create a really nice calling card, hire a professional to create one for you. The same thing is true for your letterhead, envelopes, invoices and such. Your materials are an extension of you -- make sure they "speak" well of you.

The Thank You Note

After every consultation or staging project, make sure you send a personal thank you note to your client. This is very important and you wouldn't believe how many businesses fail in this area. It is especially important for a consultant to send thank you notes. It shows your professionalism, it's just common courtesy, and it gives you another opportunity to communicate anything you may have forgotten, communicate anything you have thought of since you left the home, and serves as a reminder of your services.

If you offer additional products or services, which I always advise, you should know that 80% of your business in the future will most likely come from past clients, if you stay in touch. They have already experienced your service once and trust you. So it's always much easier and less costly to sell additional products and services to your past clients than it is to find new clients.

At any rate, I invariably think of things I want to further suggest to my clients while I'm driving back to my office. So not only do they get a nice thank you card from me, but I slip in a letter with all of the other ideas I want to share with them at the same time. This is my way of giving them "more" than I promised. When you do that you are always remembered more favorably.

The thank you note is also a very appropriate place to remind them and reinforce how you appreciated working with them, to wish them your best in selling the home, to again compliment them in some way, and to state how enjoyable it was for you to work hand in hand with them to achieve the final result. Make sure they feel part of the "team".

If there were any misunderstandings during the consultation or project, this is another opportunity you have to clarify your position and reassure them of your continued appreciation of them, not only as a client, but as a valued "friend".

Thank you notes are so rarely sent, this one activity can mean the difference between on-going referrals and future business and none at all. Even if it brought you no benefit at all, I would still advise you to send a thank you note. It's just something that well mannered service-oriented people should do. Later I'll tell you about the service I use to send out all my cards. It's great. Once the home sells, send your client a "congratulations" card and remind them gently how much you'd appreciate their referrals.

Reminders of Your Other Services or Products

All too often we assume that people understand our businesses -- the full scope of our products and services. The fact of the matter is, people don't. They can't be expected to know what you really offer.

We are all people who are focused on our own worlds. What we think and do is largely only important to us. So don't neglect to make sure you inform your clients, in some way, over a period of time about other products and services you have that might be of interest to them or someone they know.

This is called "spaced repetition". This is one of the founding principles of marketing. Get the message out repeatedly to the same market in some kind of spaced period of time. It takes time to build a relationship of trust.

So don't lose heart and think that just because you got the message out one time and you didn't get the response you wanted that your efforts were in vain. It is one part of a much larger picture.

When you first meet someone, you don't go out for lunch immediately, as a rule. No, you usually get to know someone over time, and eventually as a closer relationship starts to build, then you possibly do lunch. Well, the same principle applies to your marketing in an even more important manner.

People want to do business with people they feel they know and trust. All of your marketing efforts should have one goal. Get to know them! Let them get to know you! Help them trust you!

You get to know them by being interested, genuinely interested, in them. If you're with a prospect and you're doing all the talking, you're not going to get the "sale". People really only value the things they say, not what you say. So getting them to talk about themselves, their home, their family, their activities and so forth -- these are all ways in which you come to understand them and show them that you care about them first.

Letting them get to know you must follow in a slower process. Letting them get to know you can happen easily by slipping something into the conversation from time to time that genuinely applies to what the client is saying. Experienced consultants never have to officially notify people of their accomplishments. It is gently woven very carefully into their conversation as they are focused on listening and gathering information from other people. Experienced consultants usually find that at the end of discussing a client's wishes and needs, they never have to "present their case" at all. The client has already become familiar with their expertise and experience just from some brief examples woven into the consultant's responses to comments or questions which the client has asked.

How to Win Friends and Influence People

I wholeheartedly recommend you get a copy of the classic, long time bestseller, "How to Win Friends and Influence People" by Dale Carnegie. It is an excellent book and will serve you well whether you're in business for yourself, whether you work for someone else and whether or not you work at all. I guarantee that this book will be one of the very best marketing books and personal growth books you will ever read. It is out in paperback and runs about $6.

Regardless of that, here, briefly, are some important concepts to remember and use. Building trust and relationship takes time.

- Develop keen "listening skills".
- Keep your own words to a minimum.
- Show pictures whenever possible.
- Remain positive and confident at all times.
- Don't brag.
- Give more than you promise and promise a lot.
- Back everything you promise by a risk free guarantee (more about this later).
- Thank them afterwards.
- Affirm them positively whenever genuinely possible.

These are just a few of the ways, in a nutshell, prospects will come to feel they "know" you and "trust" you. Then they will do business with you.

Charging for Your Services

Selecting the Right Fee

Is there a standard way to charge for your consulting services? No. It's really up to you and what the market will bear in your area. But here are some guidelines to help you decide what is best for you.

- Look at your marketing area
- Decide what your time and experience are worth
- Research the market rate in your area
- Learn the psychology of charging for your services
- Know and embrace business ethics

High end clients are accustomed to a fee-based structure for services they purchase. But in the middle range, you're going to find that some prospects are wary of paying anyone for their time and expertise. They are more accustomed to paying strictly for "products". You may have to tailor your fees for each client in order to optimize your success.

But before you settle on what works for you, keep in mind that what you do with one client will directly affect business you get in the future that relates back to your first clients. To illustrate, I did a redesign for a client who passed me on to a friend. The original redesign was offered during a slow time of year at a discount. When the friend called me, she expected to receive the same discounted price the referring client had received. But it was no longer a slow time of year. I had to decide whether to give her the same discount her friend had received. If I had not been happy to do that, I would have had a disgruntled client in some manner. She would have forever felt she didn't get as good a deal as her friend, no matter what I did for her. So remember that what you do for one person affects other people. I occasionally have trainees who want me to do something special for them that I don't do for other people. My answer is "no". If I'm not going to do something for everyone, I don't do it for anyone. But again, this is your business, and you will have to make those calls for yourself.

DECIDE WHAT YOUR ANNUAL INCOME SHOULD BE YOUR FIRST YEAR

I don't know what the income level should be in your region of the country much less what you feel you need to make vs. what you want to make. It does vary depending on where you live. Obviously, it's bound to be less in your first couple of years from what it has a potential to become.

So the first thing you need to do is be realistic of what you feel would be a reasonable income in your first year. Notice that I wrote "reasonable income". Don't try to overpay yourself; but don't underpay yourself either. Try to be as realistic as possible.

Take the figure you arrive at and divide it by 52 (the number of weeks in a year). Then divide that figure by 5 (days of the week) and divide that figure by 8 (number of working hours in a day). Now you will have the hourly rate of that initial figure.

Now triple that figure. This is the lowest figure you should charge.

Remember that your consulting rate must be a lot higher than the figure you initially got after the math, because of the overhead of your business and because you're not going to book every hour.

Your fee should be close to the hourly fee that other stagers in your area charge, but only if you have fairly comparable expertise and experience. Remember that a prospect will usually get more than one bid.

BE COMFORTABLE WITH WHAT YOU CHARGE

You have to have a comfort zone. So the best rate is also the one you feel comfortable charging. In the beginning, you'll find yourself probably offering to work for less just to get some actual clients under your belt, get the photos and experience to build your marketing portfolio and confidence. You can always raise your fee as you go.

Keep this in mind. Decide what scale of client you really want to have. If your fees are too steep, some middle range clients won't be able to afford your services. On the other hand, if your fees are too low, the more discerning prospects, who really CAN afford your service, will think you are not sophisticated or experienced enough for them.

So it boils down to this: Make sure you have done a good job of showing your prospects all of the benefits they will receive for this somewhat "intangible" service. Charge the highest fee you feel you are worth; but be comfortable in what you charge.

You may have to test the market a bit before you settle into something consistent. Testing is also a good marketing habit to develop.

OFFER A BONUS OR SPECIAL PRICE FOR EXTRA ADDED VALUE

More and more often, people expect to get a little extra. Everyone likes to feel they have gotten a "deal" that others haven't received. So you might find it very beneficial to always offer a "special" rate. I do this very simply by saying, "I normally charge $_____ for my consultations in your area, but I'm running a special right now and I'll work with you for $_____ if you book the appointment today. Otherwise I'll have to charge my normal rate. When would be the best day for you?"

Offer a special rate but put a time limit on it. This will make the prospect happy but help you immensely to get them to book the appointment right then. The more time that passes between your conversation and a decision, the less likely you will be in booking this prospect at all.

It is human nature to put off making a decision. If they don't decide to hire you right then, they will almost never book you. People just don't think things over and then act. So whatever you can say over the phone when you first discuss your consultation fee is most likely going to be the best (or only) chance you will have to convert this person into a client.

A "special fee" for acting immediately can make the difference.

ETHICS OF A CONSULTANT

Whatever you decide to charge, it is essential that you make *full disclosure to your client*. Your client has a right to know in advance exactly what you intend to charge and how much time you anticipate the consultation taking (I'm only speaking about consultations, not full blown staging services).

I give my client prospects a *special rate*, and I have a *minimum* I will accept before I book anyone. I tell them all of this up front.

I assure them that my charges will not exceed what I quote them, no matter how long it takes me to make my recommendations. Then I leave it to them to decide if they can afford my services. I want them to be able to make an informed decision. I don't like unhappy clients. They don't do me one bit of good. It's another reason why I don't like hourly rates and prefer a flat fee for consultation services. Hourly rates add an element of uncertainty into my client's thoughts and I don't want them to feel uneasy. I've been doing this business long enough to know before I walk out the door roughly how long it's going to take me. You will get to that point yourself in time.

Quoting Your Fees

Never let a client suggest to you what they feel you should charge. No way. No one knows the value of what you bring to the equation except you. Never let anyone else determine how much you are worth. Never. Employers determine an employee's worth to them – you are your own employee, so you must determine your own worth.

If someone were to suggest to me that I charge them the same or lower rate than they can find elsewhere, I tell them "Best wishes. Go there." Actually that has never happened to me. But that is what I would tell them if it did happen.

We're not talking about a *product* here. We're talking about the unique creativity, gained over time and trial and error – this is what **you** bring to the project - not someone else. Don't ever let anyone compare you with any one else. What someone else charges is merely a loose guideline and bears little on your value in the final analysis. Some consultants will undercharge on the front end in the hopes of getting more on the backend. Well, there's nothing wrong with that approach. It's done all the time in business. But you never want to hide what you're doing or go back on your word in any way.

I've never had a client try to define my worth, per se. But I have had them try to negotiate a better deal from time to time. One lady wanted me to travel an hour each way and didn't want to pay extra for my travel time. I held my ground and she ultimately agreed to my price. When I got to her home, I discovered she and her husband were quite wealthy (he was a top writer in the TV industry). How she had the nerve to challenge my rate was beyond me, but she did. Don't be surprised if your toughest negotiators are your wealthier prospects. Maybe that's how they got to be wealthy.

My time is worth money whether I'm sitting on the freeway or in their home. And in addition to that, I have wear and tear on my car and gasoline expense. So you have to factor all these aspects into the equation before you throw out a figure or before you discount your fees in any way. Don't let people take advantage of you.

Not only do you have to weigh the distance, but the time of day you're going to be traveling. I live in Southern California where the traffic is horrendous during peak periods. If a client can only meet with me at a time when I know I will be in heavy traffic as I travel to the appointment or return, I always factor this extra time into my quote. So should you.

Other Expenses

Here is a brief list of typical expenses you will definitely have to factor into your business. There will be others, no doubt, but you can definitely expect to pay for the following:

- Phone
- Liability and auto insurance
- Gasoline
- Vehicle mileage
- Tires
- Postage
- Printing
- Staging supplies and props
- Marketing materials
- Arrangement and moving tools
- Web site fees
- Advertising
- Record keeping materials
- Film and processing (unless you go digital)
- Office supplies
- Books, audio tapes, videos for on-going education
- Legal fees
-

- Bank fees
- Merchant account fees (optional)
- A computer (optional)
- Self employment taxes
- Health insurance (optional)

When you stop to think of the massive costs involved in running most businesses, this business requires very little overhead. That's one of the reasons that make it such an attractive profession. As I've stated earlier, there is also very little risk. I like that.

There is virtually no product to be inventoried other than your props. Nothing you have to send. You can literally hold all of your tools of the trade in a case or two. You can be mobile in minutes. You can make every minute count by listening to audio tapes while you travel that will help you market your business more effectively, or help you communicate better.

You work strictly by appointment, so if you have another job or a family, you can schedule your appointments when YOU are able to do them. Most of the time it doesn't even feel like work.

And you are paid a very nice fee for services. On top of that you'll probably meet some very nice and interesting people who will spark creativity within you that you didn't know you had. What can be better than that?

Your Professional Guarantee

Not all consultants offer a personal guarantee. I think you are foolish if you don't. But it's your call.

I offer the ultimate guarantee! Why? Because people just won't take you up on it and it sure removes their perceived *risk* on the front end.

I offer to refund the entire consultation fee, up to 100%, if my client is not happy. So it is virtually risk free for the home owner and/or agent.

But trust me, you really don't have to worry about people taking advantage of the guarantee. I've never had a client refuse to pay my consultation fee.

So it's really not something to be concerned about, that is as long as you do a good job. And since you really don't have to worry about it, why not make your guarantee really, really strong? You have everything to gain and nothing to lose - nothing.

In a worst case scenario the only thing you are out is your time and gasoline. Can you survive that? Of course you can.

This is called *risk reversal*. It's a very powerful marketing concept. You offer to take all of the risk upon yourself, leaving your clients with no risk whatsoever. It's much easier for them to say "Yes!" and schedule a consultation. And that is the goal. Besides, it's just good business.

Becoming a Temporary "Buyer"

Pricing seems to always be a concern of clients and prospects. This is to be expected. And the lower the income bracket, the more pricing issues is a concern. When sellers are eager to put the home on the market, they quite naturally are reluctant to spend more money to get it ready to sell. And they often don't realize that they are shooting themselves in the foot on price if they do not stage the property properly.

For this reason, you will need to educate your prospect on the benefits and the necessity of staging the property. I have recently been involved in helping my business partner purchase property. We have been out looking for a couple of weeks so far, trying to narrow down the field and really determine just what he wants.

He has not found one house so far that has all of the features he wants. Maybe he'll have to settle for less, but he won't arrive at that decision until or unless he feels he has seen everything there is to see. I have been fascinated with the emotional and mental changes he has undergone.

In the end, while price is an issue, there have been many positive homes we have visited and a host of negative ones. Of the 20+ properties we have previewed thus far, roughly half are empty and half are occupied. Only about 3-4 have been staged in any kind of appealing manner. Even when the agent knows about the concept of staging, staging has not been part of the program.

I have the ability to see a home's potential and look past the clutter and badly chosen décor, but even I have been greatly affected by the cosmetics (or lack thereof) of a home. I can tell you for a fact that he nearly purchased a home that had been freshly renovated and beautifully staged, even though it was not exactly what he wanted.

A good night's sleep brought a more analytical evaluation come morning, but the beauty of the staged property was definitely alluring.

Compare that to the homes that had more of the features he wanted but had red paint in the kitchen, or prison gray counter tops or broken steps leading to the front door. As a buyer, you really tend to focus on what's wrong, even though it might be something minor.

Going through a real life search for property with my partner has rejuvenated my focus so that I will be a better stager for my own clients. I recommend highly trying to place yourself in the same mode of a buyer from time to time. Call up a friend who is looking for a home to buy and ask if you can join them when looking at property. This will be a great experience for you, especially if you've never purchased a home yourself or if it has been some while ago.

Goals of Good Interior Design Services

UTILITY - Your first goal should be *utility*. This means that the space you design should be effective and serve the primary purpose of the space. Your rooms should be designed to be useful, comfortable and efficient. But don't carry it overboard. Being too efficient can also be boring and cold. Make the usefulness of a room your primary goal, but don't make it the only goal.

ECONOMICAL - Your second goal should be *economy*. I'm not just referring to your client's budget, but to the saving of human resources, materials and the environment. For an example, a gourmet cook will want a totally efficient, large kitchen. I, myself, hate to cook, so I get by with a small kitchen that has low maintenance. Instead of rushing out to buy a new gadget when an old one needs repair, tell your client to conserve and get the old one fixed. Many times they are made better anyway. Make an overall plan of your client's needs, so that they don't wind up making costly mistakes and buy unneeded items.

You can also conserve within the environment, not just for the sake of ecology, but for budgeting as well. Example: wooden objects have a long life generally speaking and can be refinished many times. When discarded, they will be absorbed back into the environment, whereas plastic or metal will not. Give old objects new life by repairing them, fixing them up and giving them a new purpose. Use your imagination.

BEAUTY - Ahhh, we all want things to be beautiful. Beauty enriches the senses, lifts the spirit and gives pleasure to the eye. It is personal. It is subjective. It expresses your taste. Always seek ways to make your home more inviting and pleasing to the eye. Sometimes it means adding something more. Sometimes it means reducing what you have. Seek beauty as a third goal. Remember, that just because a client has something in a room when you arrive, it does not have to remain in the room necessarily.

CHARACTER - How much time, money and effort you are willing to invest will dictate how personalized your client's home becomes. The client can gut their space and rebuild it according to their specifications. Or they can simply throw on a fresh coat of paint to an existing element. It's totally up to them.

Your ability to create character in their home will surface naturally. It is an extension of them, and that's the way it should be. Even if they do nothing, that is still an extension of them, their family and their lifestyle. Make it their special and unique space. Give it their personality. Be daring. (Staging, as we've discussed, is just the opposite of this.)

CLIMATE - Where a client lives is going to factor into your decisions. It will affect the materials they choose, the colors, the textures, the surfaces, the complexity. For instance, in a warm or hot climate, they'll want to choose "cool" colors, simple and uncluttered spaces that make them feel cooler. However, in a cold, damp climate, they'll be opting for warmth and feeling snug. So you'll most likely be looking at warm colors, plush carpeting and rich woods, with lots of furnishings to make them feel comfortable in their cozy, inviting home.

LOCATION - A high rise condominium with a panoramic view of the city will most certainly affect your decisions as well as theirs regarding materials compared to a country home nestled in trees by the side of a lake.

MOBILITY - I've lived in my home for nearly 30 years and don't plan to move. Therefore my decisions regarding decorating will be very different from someone who doesn't plan to stay in one place very long. Whether your client is anticipating a job relocation, a marriage, a divorce or a graduation, with the hopes of turning a quick profit, or whether they just know that they will want something bigger and better in the near future, you're goals and expectations will greatly be affected. So plan accordingly.

HOUSEHOLD - Your client's age and the ages of their family members are also considerations in your decision-making. Don't just plan their home for today, but keep the future in mind too. Remember that their little ones are people too, and plan for their comfort and function as well. Keep everyone's privacy issues as a factor and remember how each member of the family interacts with the others. Allow everyone to have a private space where they can express their own individual personality.

LIFESTYLE - Another major consideration in decorating their home is their lifestyle. Are they a single person, spending most of their time away? Do they have a large family that likes to spend a lot of time at home? How much do they entertain? How large are their parties? Do they work from their home? These and many more lifestyle considerations should be taken into account before you arrange a home, and certainly when they are adding more furnishings to the home.

PSYCHOLOGY - Are they claustrophobic? Do they feel confined in small spaces, anxious? Does anyone in their family feel that way? Are they agoraphobic, overwhelmed in a large, open space? Is anyone in their family that way? An agoraphobic person needs a snug, smaller space to feel safe. The claustrophobic needs just the opposite. Rooms that will be used heavily by many members of the household should be larger, with higher ceilings and openness. Private spaces should be smaller with lower ceilings and fewer windows. Arrange their furnishings in the home to fit the psychological makeup of their family.

All in all, your goals should be to create a beautiful environment that is totally functional for the family that lives in the space.

Chapter Five

Managing Your Business

When you are first starting out, survival is the goal. It is more important than success. If I equated it with a sport, survival is equivalent to staying on the field, playing the game, learning the rules and developing your skills and reputation.

So to help guide you in a start up process that is orderly and makes sense, here are some steps you might consider following:

- Decide on the legal structure of your business
- Select your business name
- If a fictitious name, register it and publish it in a legal newspaper
- Develop a solid business plan so you know where you're going
- Obtain the necessary permits and licenses required by your state, city and country
- Obtain your business insurance
- Open a business bank account
- Get a business telephone
- If not conducting your business from your home, acquire a business address
- Acquire the appropriate tools and supplies and props
- Create your marketing materials
- Create a web site

All of this assumes you have the entrepreneurial skills, the design skills and the desire to dedicate yourself to building a consulting business of this nature.

Selecting Legal Structure

Your first decision here is to decide what legal form of business is best for you. There are three major types of businesses: a sole proprietorship where you (and your spouse, if you have one) own the business; a partnership (where you co-own the business with someone other than a spouse); or a corporation (where the stockholders own the business). A corporation provides the most write-offs and provides you with liability protection personally. Many people elect to set up a Limited Liability Corporation (LLC) because of the liability protection.

I am not an attorney nor am I a tax consultant. These decisions are best left to professionals and you should consult one if you are not sure what is best for you.

Each business form has its advantages and disadvantages. Some have to do with taxes; some have to do with the general operations of the business; some are control issues; some are liability issues and so forth. Get inexpensive legal help by joining such organizations as www.PrepaidLegal.Com. For a manageable, low-cost monthly fee, you can get local legal help (or discounted help) in structuring all of the legal forms and in dealing with any other issues you might need help concerning.

Check at your local library for good source books. Here are a couple of suggestions: *Small Time Operator* by Bernard Kamaroff; *Running a One-Person Business* by Claude Whitmyer, Salli Rasberry and Michael Phillips.

Selecting a Business Name

Selecting a business name is an important part of your marketing strategy. At the end of this manual we have provided an extensive list of possible names you could use. The first thing you must decide is whether you wish to use your name as part of your business name or whether you wish to use a DBA. DBA means "doing business as". It is a fictitious name and, therefore, must be registered legally.

Using your own name as your business name, such as Mary Smith's Home Staging, is good in the sense that people will find it easy to remember your name. But in the future you may have hired other consultants or wish to sell the business. It is harder to sell the business and pass on the goodwill you have developed if you use your personal name as part of your business name.

Clearly the name you pick should state in some way *what* your business is about and it should be easy to pronounce and easy to understand over the phone. Shy away from difficult spellings, names that can easily be confused with other businesses, names that may suggest your business does something it does not. In an age where we are overloaded with information, the easier your business name is to say and remember, the better.

Know what your plans and dreams for the future are. You don't want to pick a name that is solely staging specific if you have definite plans to offer other services down the road. Think about the short term, but plan for the long term as well.

Check to see what the procedures are in your state or county or province for doing business under a fictitious name. In California, I have to first register the proposed name with a state government agency at the courthouse (Fictitious Business Name Department) to make sure no other business with that name exists in the county. There is a fee for registering the name of around $10-15.

Once the name has been accepted by the court registrant, I must then advertise a statement in a legal newspaper for a period of 4 weeks. This legal notice states the names of the owners of the company, their residence addresses, the name and address of the business, and what type of business it is. Check your local phone book for the names of newspapers in your area that publish DBA statements or you'll probably run into some of them at the court house. They charge a fee as well, usually somewhere in the $40-50 range, but it may vary.

To make it simple, many newspapers will handle the registration of your DBA name and automatically publish the statement too for a fee of around $50. You can even find them online. They can handle the whole process quickly and by computer. This is great because it eliminates a trip to the courthouse. You will want to have two extra names available just in case your first choice is not available.

Once the DBA has been processed and the name approved and you have proof that you have submitted the name to a legal newspaper for publishing, you will be able to open a bank account in the name of your DBA.

I venture that most states have similar requirements, but since they are not all likely to be the same, you should inquire first to make sure you have taken every step necessary to set up your business' name.

Licenses You Will Need

There are several licenses or accounts that you will probably need.

CITY BUSINESS LICENSE

Not all cities require you to have a license for a home based business. Mine does. You need to call your city hall to inquire about this. In my city I not only need to pay a yearly license fee, but I am required to keep my business limited to only one room in my home (and it cannot be my garage). I am also prevented from posting any signs about my business on my property and I cannot have any clients coming to my home.

Your city or town may have similar regulations so you need to find out first what those are, so that you are in compliance.

RESALE LICENSE

Not all consultants need to have a resale license. Generally you must charge tax on products that you sell. If you are only selling a service (your time and expertise), you probably will not be required to have a resale license. To make sure of your requirements, however, you should check with your local State Board of Equalization.

In California, a consultant must charge sales tax on their consulting fees that are attached to the sale of a product. I have a resale license because I do far more than staging, redesign and training.

If you do get a sales tax license, you will be required to fill out quarterly or yearly reports and send in all sales tax collected each reporting period. If your business is very small, they sometimes require a report only at the end of the year. It's best to check with a local accountant to make sure or talk directly with someone at the State Board.

There is usually a deposit that you are required to pay which the Board will hold for 3 years in a savings account to guarantee that you pay your taxes. This fee is in part based on the amount of sales you anticipate making in your first year, so if you are asked to speculate on how much business you will be doing, keep the figure very low to reduce the fee you might have to pay.

FEDERAL IDENTIFICATION NUMBER

All businesses are required to identify themselves on forms and licenses by one of two numbers: either your Social Security Number (SSN) if you set up a sole proprietorship or a Federal Employer Identification Number (EIN) if you set up a corporation.

If you decided to set your business up as a sole proprietorship, you will need your SSN until such time as you hire employees. At that point you will need to have an EIN. If you do not plan to have employees at the start, file Form SS-4 with the IRS. There is no fee. Do not file for an EIN until you know you're hiring employees, otherwise the IRS will automatically send you quarterly and a year-end payroll tax return that you must fill out even though you don't have any employees. Don't put yourself through that until or unless you have to.

A partnership or a corporation must have federal and/or state EIN numbers whether they have employees or not.

Payroll

If you do have employees, or you have started your business as a corporation and you are receiving a salary as an employee of the corporation, I recommend you hire a payroll service to handle the processing of all of the checks and reporting all of the payroll taxes to the appropriate governmental agencies.

Payroll is a time consuming and confusing task that is best left to the professionals to handle for you. Don't let yourself get bogged down with it. Your time and energy are going to be much better deployed in concentrating your focus on marketing your business and servicing clients.

Check your local phone book for a good accounting/payroll service with a competitive rate. It is money well spent. Be sure to shop around. There is quite a bit of difference in the rates of payroll services. Be sure you know what their services include and what they do not. A lot of banks recommend ADP for payroll. I found them to be overpriced for my area and a Mom & Pop service gave me more for less.

Mission Statement and Business Plan

Develop a mission statement for your business that is really specific. To really define it properly, write it down. In order to get where you want to go, you have to know in advance where you want to go, otherwise you're going to end up somewhere else.

You not only need to know where you want your business to go, you need to have a plan of how you're going to get where you want to go. It's wise to write all of this down, review it periodically, make necessary adjustments as you need to.

Think about the following elements that should be part of all this:

- the purpose of your business
- what special niche or target audience you want for your services
- what secondary markets there are for your business to fill
- how you will describe your service and promote it
- what the most compelling benefits are for your clients
- what is the most unique aspect that will separate you from your competitors (this is your unique selling proposition)
- what back end products or services you could offer to your clients
- how you could utilize the internet to your advantage
- what policies and procedures you will put into place

Write everything down. Then pull it all together in a one or two page document that is as concise as you can make it. Develop a one sentence statement that really describes what you do and it's major benefit to your target market. This is sometimes called an "elevator speech". Sometimes you only get a minute or less to tell someone about your services. Having a pre-planned summary statement that is powerful can be very, very useful. Make sure you develop one.

Start Up Budget

Your start up budget should be constructed as thoroughly as possible. The major reason most businesses fail is for lack of proper funding. Before making any major purchases, get quotes from two or three different sources. When you need to find an insurance broker, an attorney, an accountant, shop around.

If you have never been in business for yourself before, talk to your friends and relatives and ask for advice. Seek people who are successful, particularly if they own a business of their own. Most people will be happy to give you advice. They can steer you in the right direction for your locale to find the office supplies, equipment and other products you will need at the best prices.

Create a start up budget that is realistic. You will need to be well funded in the beginning to sustain you during the initial months.

Set up a budget that includes the following:

- *your start up costs:* initial investment, equipment needs: phone, typewriter, computer, answering machine or service, calculator; installation costs of any equipment; your marketing materials, any remodeling or decorating expenses, licenses and permits, legal and accounting set up charges, your accounting system, business checks and a cash cushion, cleaning supplies and props.
- *your operating expenses for 3-months minimum:* your monthly draw or salary, outside services, rent (if not in your home), telephone, utilities, office supplies and equipment, advertising (yellow pages, etc), debt finance charges, maintenance supplies, taxes, legal and accounting services, insurance, answering service, promotional expenses, entertainment and travel, training/professional seminars or conferences, out of pocket expenses, auto expenses and miscellaneous expenses.

To break down your start-up costs further, consider the following:

- *Marketing Expenses:* Stationery and printing, business logo design, portfolio and briefcase, marketing materials, wardrobe
- *Business Organization Expenses:* accounting fees, decorating and remodeling costs, cleaning supplies, tools of the trade, props, insurance, legal fees, license and permits, telephone installation, internet access costs
- *Operating Expenses of Your Office:* Office supplies, answering service, outside services, photocopying, maintenance supplies
- *Furniture and/or Equipment:* Desks, chairs, filing cabinets, typewriter, computer, telephone, fax, copy machine, tools of the trade
- *Other Expenses:* Gasoline, bridge tolls, auto repairs, client gifts, unexpected expenses, on-going training costs.

Creating Invoices

If you have a computer, your word processing program should come with some generic invoices and other types of forms that can be readily adapted for your usage. This is the route I would take. Do not pay a printer a costly fee to have NCR invoices printed off. You can do that kind of thing down the road when you are well established and doing a lot of invoicing on a regular basis. See our Forms at the end of this manual as many are all ready for you to photocopy and use immediately.

But in the beginning, you're going to be spending most of your time getting set up and marketing your services and spreading the word. You can easily print off a few invoices as you need them. They will look every bit as professional. If you don't have a computer to personalize your forms, then check with your local office supply company. Visual Organizer, Inc. was a company in the mid 1980's that published a book called, "Forms for Business". It was a compilation of all types of generic business forms. You only need to take a form, have your personal business information added to it, take it to a copy service, and have copies run off in any quantity you want.

Since most people have computers, or at least access to one, looking to your word processing software will still be your best source for ready made forms though I do supply a few in this training you might find useful.

Record Keeping

It's not difficult to keep track of your consulting time. All of the information will be recorded on your invoices. Ask your local office supply store for samples of either manual recordkeeping books or accounting software which is easy to operate.

Keep all your receipts for every expense related to your business. These will become very important when you prepare your tax return. I have file cabinets to house all of my invoices and receipts. I create folders for the types of expenses that are repetitive, like my phone bill. For the receipts that are non repetitive, I have a Miscellaneous folder to put them in.

Bank Account

If you have elected to use a fictitious business name rather than your own personal name, you will need to file a Fictitious Name Statement and publish it in a legal newspaper before you can open a business checking account. You do not need to wait until the business has been published all four weeks to get your account, but you will probably have to prove that the process as been started.

The bank you choose is entirely up to you. I do highly recommend that you have a separate business account so that the revenue you generate is not co-mingled with your personal money. It's just good business to keep things separated, especially if you are ever audited by the IRS. You will not appear to be a professional business person if your business income is mixed in with private income, and this is something the IRS doesn't like at all.

It is also much more difficult to tell at any given point just how well you are doing in your business if the records for the business and the bank account are not separate entities. The checks you will write to pay expenses are not going to be seen by your clients, so don't feel that you need to have a certain kind of check. Keep your expenses as low as possible by any means possible. But before you order checks, know what type of bookkeeping system you will be using. Order your checks accordingly.

If you have hired an accountant, be sure to check to see what system he or she thinks would be best for you. Many of the convenient one-write check systems, that use a combination of checks and ledger, have checks that must be ordered directly from an office supply company rather than from your bank.

If your office is computerized, consider getting one of the simple bookkeeping systems that will save you a lot of time, such as Quicken. Many are designed for both PCs and Macs. I use

Microsoft Word's Excel spreadsheets and a combination of other procedures to manage all of my business, but mine is far more complicated than yours will be at this point in time.

Pay all of your expenses with a business check or a business credit card, not your personal checks and credit cards. Should you ever get an audit by the IRS, the more organized and documented your business is, the easier the audit will go. For this reason, type the information on your checks instead of making them out by hand. It just gives a more professional image.

Business Telephone

Your telephone is your best friend. You cannot exist without this friend. As a consultant, you're going to be away from your phone often, hopefully, so you need an efficient system for receiving calls. At the very least you should have two incoming lines. Prospects and clients get really annoyed if they call and get a busy signal and you would be amazed how often you will get a phone call while you are on another line.

Use your secondary line for your outgoing calls, keeping your primary line open for incoming calls. If you can't afford a separate phone line, then use your private home line. But you should train every member of your family to answer the phone with your business name rather than "hello".

Decide whether you want to have an answering machine (which obviously lets people know that you have a home-based business) or a voice mail answering system or service (which makes your start up business appear to be more established).

ANSWERING MACHINE

If you choose an answering machine, make the message brief and current (unless you have one that allows your caller to press # to go directly to leaving you a message). The latter is nice since you can leave a more descriptive message about your services. The downside is that some people don't listen to the instruction about pressing # to bypass the longer message and they just hang up.

A sample short message might be:

"Hello, you've reached Mary Smith Home Staging. I'm either on the phone, staging a client's home or you are calling before or after business hours. Your call is very important to me. Please leave a message of any length when you hear the electronic tone, and I will get back to you as soon as possible. Thank you."

This is all the information you need to give. Don't tell them to "have a great day" or give your itinerary for the day or week. Make sure your answering machine will allow them to leave a long message if they choose. It's very annoying to be cut off in the middle of a message. Most people won't call back to continue where they left off.

Do be diligent about checking your messages and return phone calls in a timely manner.

ANSWERING SERVICE

I've personally never used an answering service. I'm sure there are good ones that will be reliable. Ask for references and be sure and call the references before you settle on one. Then periodically call yourself to see how the service is handling the calls. Check with your local phone service provider. They carry voice mail services that are very professional.

You may also opt to conduct business entirely with a cell phone. The more sophisticated services give you voice mail, as well as other nifty services. But be prepared to pay a lot more for your phone service this way. I much prefer a home answering service to operating from a cell phone. I wouldn't want to be disturbed at a client's home by my cell phone unless it's an important or emergency call from a family member.

Business Address

I highly recommend operating your business from home. First of all, it's really typical and not at all unusual for stagers and re-designers to have home based businesses. I doubt sincerely if any homeowner will care if your business is home based or not. I have operated a home based business from day one and the only thing that I cannot take advantage of is any "off the street" business I might pick up from some business signage. But then I don't have to pay out any high priced rent and my other expenses are much lower as well. I also don't have to sign any leases, pay out any deposits, provide insurance coverage that is mandated by a landlord, and so forth.

What I would avoid is using a post-office box as your address (like Mailboxes Etc). It not only does not look professional, but it could create doubt in the mind of your prospects about doing business with you. People want the reassurance that they can actually "find" you in person if they need to and that cannot be done if you are promoting a PO box address. I don't know about other states, but in California if you use a mail box address, you have to designate your PMB number, which tells people instantly that it is a mail box address other than the US postal service.

So either select an actual business location and rent space or set up your business in your home. Always check with the local city governmental offices to make sure you understand any zoning laws and license requirements.

If you just don't want to host the business in your home, you could also consider renting an office in a building where other small businesses join together to co-pay for the generic reception, telephone answering services and a conference room. These types of office set ups generally give you a nice, prestigious business address.

As a consultant, no matter what additional products and services you might choose to offer, you're really not going to have clients coming to your office unless you choose to. You're typically going to be going to the real estate agent's office or the homeowner's home. I have never found using my home address to be a problem. But it all boils down to what you are most comfortable setting up and what type of revenue you have to support yourself while you are building your business.

Marketing Materials

WEBSITES

Once you have developed a marketing plan, you then need to create and design your marketing materials. With the vast majority of people owning or having access to computers and the internet, a well-designed web site will be the best marketing "material" you could ever create, in my opinion. First, it is just so inexpensive compared to traditional marketing materials, like a color brochure or color flyer. And it can be changed on a moment's notice.

If you don't have a web site, I would advise you to create strong marketing materials that you have stored on a diskette, zip disc or CD, which you could hand out or mail to a prospect. It's still much less expensive than paying a printer. If you don't know HTML, consider purchasing a pre-designed web site. They are kind of generic but will give you something pretty sharp visually. You just plug in the appropriate images and text using software that the host provider gives you. As time has gone on, the developers of quick website design have gotten more sophisticated and versatile and now offer more options. A template can cost as little as $15. Free domain hosting is available but it comes with advertisements which you cannot control and hinder credibility.

To make good decisions, people have to be able to visualize themselves enjoying the benefits of your service. Here is the prime example of "a picture is worth a thousand words". Be generous with pictures or graphics though watch out for slower download time.

Every time you want to feature a service or product, try to demonstrate it in some way. This is qualified, however, for a web site. Graphics take a long time to download and many people still have slow modems though that is gradually changing as high speed becomes more affordable and easier to acquire. On a web site try to keep your graphics to a minimum per page with files as small as possible.

Always strive to keep your materials current and in good condition. This is another good reason for having a web site to recommend to prospects. You can update a web site instantly if you know HTML or use a software program like FrontPage. You can't do that with a printed brochure, so the commitment to what you want on a brochure or flyer has to be images and text that are more generic and that you can "live with" for a longer period of time.

BROCHURES

If you do have a brochure printed up (or have a CD or disc), you could use them as an "interest sparker" before you have ever talked to a prospect, or once you have set an appointment, send one to reinforce the good and wise decision your new prospect has just made.

Here is a brief list of some of the ingredients you should consider including in your brochure. Keep the brochure short and to the point.

- Your business logo
- Brief statement describing your company: your business' reputation, your standards of quality, your credentials
- The range of services you provide: focus on the key benefits first, then the features
- Brief description of how you work and how you charge for services
- The scope of your business: the size, location and cities where you have worked
- Your staff and resources: your credentials and your experience that is relevant
- A list of some of your clients
- An encouragement for them to contact you or a "call to action"

Don't try to include everything. Use it as a "teaser", a door opener, a brief image or quality statement. (We have tri-fold brochures now available for purchase if you like.)

Keep your paragraphs short. Use 10 pt or larger type size. People over 50 generally cannot read small type. Don't use overly excessive feminine colors like pink or powder blue. Make it as classy as you can.

Don't overcompensate in your brochure because you feel your credentials aren't strong or you don't have many clients yet. Eventually your list of clients will speak for you anyway.

Don't include a history of your company. The prospect really doesn't care about your history. They just want to know who you are today and what you can do for them in the immediate future.

Don't include any long, boring, tedious resumes with data that is totally irrelevant to what you do now. As you write the copy, ask yourself this question after each sentence: "So what?" If you don't have a good answer, eliminate the statement or rewrite it.

Remove all design jargon. Write and talk as if the person was just a friend. Don't try to impress anyone with your verbiage. I once had an employee who had a great command of the English language and she took every opportunity to use as many 4 syllable words in the same sentence as she could. Her speech was belabored, boring and suggested she had a haughty attitude. She was unsuccessful and I had to let her go. Just be your everyday self. People will like you better and you'll get more work, I guarantee it.

So be sure to avoid insider design terminology which only other professionals would understand. In your business you're primarily not talking with professional people but with homeowners, so use words the layman will understand.

Keep your copy from being overly promotional or arrogant, but do write copy that is confident, thorough and informative. Don't promise anything you can't deliver. Don't make false claims.

LETTERHEAD

Since your letterhead is something that a prospect may see first, or something a client will see last (if you use it for your thank you note), it is an extension of you, therefore important. Make it business-like. Don't use colored paper (unless a soft gray or tan), and avoid real flashy type. Try to give it a "corporate image".

One Day Decorating Specialists
Home Staging/Redesign Business Courses

I help my human partner decorate homes for humans and their cats or to start staging/redesign businesses of their own.

BUSINESS CARDS

This is your mini-brochure. If it stands out and incorporates a mention of your main service, people won't be quite as apt to throw it away or forget you. Keep your cards handy and give them out generously. We offer custom business cards as part of our Diamond Deluxe & Ruby Combo Courses, along with a generous supply of custom announcement postcards but there are also numerous places locally where you can have these products created and printed for you.

One of my favorite business cards is the one I created for my cat, Gadget (see example). Gadget likes to get on my desk every day and lay on top of whatever papers I've got, putting his paws on my hands while I'm using my keyboard. He's actually a nuisance, but a loveable one at that. So I gave him a position of Marketing Mascot and he has his own business card, which I often hand out to people instead of my own card. Everyone always laughs at it and reads the entire card, keeping it because of its novelty. You can bet they're going to show the card to other people as well. Gadget even has his own email account: gadget@decorate-redecorate.com. If you write him, he'll answer you back. I'm telling you about him because you can really use humor in your marketing attempts to great advantage.

166

Business Insurance

When setting up your business insurance, I have found it helpful to work with a broker. Discuss the service you will be providing with your broker who should be most helpful in finding you the coverage you need at the best premium.

Most consultants need several types of insurance coverage: personal liability, general liability, disability coverage and automobile coverage. Coverage premiums will vary according to what you do, where you live and the types of places you will be entering to provide your services.

General liability covers all your office contents, equipment and business personal property while providing general liability in case someone is injured on your property. Discuss these issues with the broker because some coverage may already be adequately covered in your homeowner's policy. Usually a standard homeowner's policy will not cover anything related to business, however. And your standard auto policy will usually not cover anything related to business either.

It's also a good idea to protect yourself in the event a client sues you. Even if the lawsuit is frivolous, there are costs associated with defending yourself. A good insurance policy should protect you and pay for any damages that might be awarded against you and your attorney fees as well. If you don't have a contact, you might try www.insurezone.com, a national company.

Disability insurance will cover you in case you are temporarily or permanently injured and are unable to work. Far more people wind up with a disability of some kind than are killed in accidents, so it might be very smart to consider insurance of this nature, particularly if you are relying on the income from this business as primary revenue for you and your family.

If you hire employees, some states will require you to carry Workers Compensation Insurance, so many stagers and re-designers find it more beneficial to use independent contractors for services instead. Just make sure that the contractors you affiliate with carry their own liability insurance and that if they have employees, that they also carry Workers Compensation Insurance if your state requires it.

Again, I'm not an insurance agent or broker. Please discuss these issues with a professional that provides such services and then make an informed decision as to what is right for you and that will fit into your business budget.

Business Automobile

As I just stated above, your personal automobile insurance will not cover any products inside that are used for business. So unless you also acquire business coverage, just know that you carry business tools, accessories or other products at your own risk.

If you use a vehicle for business that is solely used for business purposes, you can deduct all of the expenses for tax purposes, or you can choose to take a mileage deduction for the total miles driven in the year.

However, if you use the vehicle for both business and personal trips, then you can only deduct the portion of your expenses or mileage in your tax return that relates to business trips.

No matter what, save every receipt you get for expenses related to your automobile. In addition to that, buy an automobile record book from your office supply store that will help you register every trip you make. You will be able to enter the date, destination and purpose, your starting odometer reading and your ending reading. In case you get an audit from the IRS, you may need to produce this record of trips to prove you have a legitimate deduction.

Technically, you are not allowed to deduct mileage of your first trip of the day and your last trip of the day (it equates to "commuting" mileage). If you have a home based business, the first trip and the last trip would equate to the mileage of someone who goes to a particular place to work. If you visit the bank first (which is ideally close to home), that can be your commuting mileage "to work" and if you visit some other business close to home on your way back, the mileage from that business establishment to your home is considered your commuting mileage "from work". This is just a small tip of how to maximize your deductible mileage. It may not seem like much of a deal at first, but you'd be surprised how much it adds up over the course of a whole year.

Tax Preparation

This is such a vast subject and a very important one, that I advise you to consult a tax specialist right from the start. Having said that, let me then say that you want to really become focused on looking at every expense as a possible tax deduction. Get a clear understanding of what will be deductible and what will not.

But don't get so focused on the fact that something is tax deductible and spend, spend, spend. Ultimately it's still money out of your pocket, so use common sense and discernment before jumping into any expenses that are truly not mandatory. Little things can eat up your profit very quickly and then you might get discouraged.

Be as organized as you possibly can. Save all receipts and try to enter them in a bookkeeping system that is easy to use and understand. Consider hiring a tax specialist to prepare your tax returns, at least in the beginning, if you've never done a business tax return.

Sole proprietors will file a Schedule C along with their personal federal tax return. Corporations will have to file a separate corporate tax return. Partners will file their own tax returns based on their percentage of the business profit and the type of partnership set up.

Know what your profit and loss statement shows before the end of December so that you can pay off additional expenses before the end of the year, if you need to reduce your taxable income.

There are several excellent software programs that you can purchase that will assist you in filling out your tax returns, if you chose to do them yourself. H & R Block makes a good one called "Tax Cut" and there are others. These programs will not only help ensure that you deduct every expense you are entitled to deduct, but they also will carry forward all of the pertinent data from one year to another and this makes filing your tax returns a breeze, sort of. Doing taxes is never a breeze!

Property Management Companies

PROPERTY MANAGEMENT companies are a great resource for you to bond with locally. You can write articles for newspapers and magazines, but you can also write articles for community newsletters and even advertise your services in them. A local property management company can put you in touch with any in your local community

Get your local property management companies to include your brochure. Give them a percentage of your business that results. Property Management companies often hear of homes going on the market very early in the process and can be valuable resources for you.

MORTGAGE LENDERS are anxious to close the deal no matter what. Since many deals are contingent on the sale of one home before settling on another, lenders are another great resource to tap into. Develop relationships with some of your local bankers and get them to share your contact information with other realtors, management firms, relocation service providers, title companies and other people in "the business" as well as the home sellers.

Think about others who may be an extension of the selling team; appraisers, home inspectors, repairman, etc. All of these individuals have the ability to plant the seed and get you in front of potential clients.

Dealing with Vacant Homes

About Vacant Homes

Always test your pricing. It needs to earn you a respectable income, be competitive and affordable.

Selection of furnishings will be made in keeping with your client's home's style and color palette and budget needs. Areas of most concern will be their Entry, Living Room, Family Room, Kitchen, Baths and Master Bedroom. Attention will also be given to the front and back exteriors.

As we have done, it's also good for you to have a growing inventory of accessories which includes a wide variety of home decorating pieces. Rental rates will vary according to style, value and number of pieces rented. Luxury homes will require upscale pieces that are larger and more artistic or distinctive. Elsewhere I've provided a list of typical accessories you should consider acquiring.

Typical Prices You Might Charge

Square Footage	Consultation (add $35 for detailed Report)	Re-Design	Furnishings Loan	Rentals for Vacant Homes
Less than 2000	$250	$75.00 per hr.	$100 - $1500	$1750 - $4000+
2001 - 2500	$250	$75.00 per hr.	$100 - $1750	$2750 - $4500+
2501 - 3000	$250	$75.00 per hr.	$100 - $2000	$3250 - $5000+
3001 - 3500	$300	$100.00 per hr.	$100 - $2250	$3750 - $5500+
3501 - 4000	$300	$100.00 per hr.	$100 - $2500	$4250 - $6000+
4001 - 4500	$350	$100.00 per hr.	$100 - $2750	$4750 - $6500+
4501 - 5000	$350	$100.00 per hr.	$100 - $3000	$5250 - $7000+
5001+	$450+	$125.00 per hr.	$100 - $3250+	$5750 - $7500+

*Prices subject to change without notice.

NOTE: Nothing is concrete. Nothing is written in stone. Let this be a guide but you must know that you have to evaluate everything based on what part of the country you live in, your competition, and what you feel you deserve to get. That could affect your pricing up or down.

When tempted to discount services, remember that if you don't value your time, effort and expertise, no one else with either. The respect for the value of what you provide starts with YOU.

Seller's Brochure or Door Hanger

Are you a "Motivated Seller"?

1. Homeowner name_____

2. Address_____

3. Telephone numbers_____

4. Email address_____

5. How long have you lived in your house? _____

6. What is the age of your house? _____

7. Describe any recent upgrades (including approximate cost and date) you have made to your house.

8. Is your house currently on the market? If yes:

- When was it listed?
- Who is the listing agent?
- What is the list price?

12. Is anyone currently living in your house? If so, how many? _____

13. If your house is unoccupied? Are there any pieces of furniture or personal belongings inside?

14. In your opinion, is your house in "market ready" condition? If not, what do you think needs to be done to prepare your house for sale?

15. Are you willing to put any personal items, furniture or accessories into storage while your house in on the market?

16. Is there anything in your house you must have immediately?

17. Is there anything in your house you are anxious to eliminate totally?

18. What is your budget for preparing your house for sale?

- $500 or less
- $500.-$1500.
- $1500.-$3000.
- $3000 or more

19. How did you hear about us?

20. How do you think we can help you with a quick and profitable sale of your house?

21. Can we help you settle in and decorate your new home?

To find out who the seller is, go to the public records at the tax assessor's office with the address of any house you see on the market. Get the tax map number, and then look up the owner's name and address. This is time consuming, but accurate. Then send a direct mail piece to the seller.

Some stagers have found good results from sending fully developed brochures directly to developers. Developers are owners and sellers at the same time. One good account like this can be worth gold to you.

You can also place an ad in the real estate section of the local papers. Anyone who is selling is going to be looking there. When a homeowner is considering putting their house on the market it is one of the 1st places they look to check prices for houses in their neighborhood.

Here's a good example of an ad you might try:

WARNING:

BEFORE YOU LIST YOUR HOME, HAVE IT EVALUATED BY A HOME STAGING SPECIALIST

ONLY 6% OF THE SELLING POPULATION KNOWS HOW TO GET TOP DOLLAR FOR THEIR HOME

CALL_____

Publicity and Advertising

Publicity and advertising are very closely related and often confused to mean the same thing. They both deal with how the public views your image. However, publicity and advertising are different. Publicity is generally exposure you are able to get for your business which you do not have to pay for: articles in the newspaper or magazines, interviews at radio or TV stations. Publicity is fantastic, not only because it is free and reaches a wide audience, but because it is viewed by the consumer as a *third party endorsement*. People tend not to view it as an advertisement and, therefore, put more credence in the information.

Advertising is more suspect because of the self-serving motives behind the ad and because there is a tendency to believe that claims by the advertiser are inflated or even bogus. People tend to take claims made through publicity as being fact and reliable. That's the power of *third party endorsement*, or at least the appearance of such.

Press Releases

Second only to word of mouth recommendations from clients, the best marketing tool for your business is a newspaper or magazine article featuring you or your services. It can be very persuasive.

People continue to be curious about what is written *about* others. Most people don't know that many of the articles that they read in newspapers or magazines were written by the person the article is featuring and not by a staff writer. They assume the latter. Impressions lodge in the reader's brain but they may not remember how or where they heard about you. The result is that a sense of familiarity with you arises long before they meet you or speak to you. And since confidence in you and your service is a necessary ingredient before they will do business with you, *third party endorsements* aid that process.

Whenever you have something new, or you are "tweaking" an older, traditional concept, the press should be interested. This is called "soft news". Whenever I send off press releases, I always write them as if someone had interviewed me. I use the third person pronouns, include quotes, and always include my contact information in some way in the first paragraph. I have found that media people like it when they don't have to write the article from scratch, and if they aren't going to print all of what I write, I certainly don't want my contact information to get edited out of the piece.

There are many good books on the subject of gaining publicity - web sites as well, where you can pick up free tips and strategies, download eBooks or whatever you need to help you write effective newsworthy articles.

Always remember that a good article will answer the following questions in the first paragraph: who, what, where, when, why and should also have a headline that peaks a reader's curiosity. A compelling headline is vital because most people don't "read" articles - they skim headlines.

How to Do a Press Release

Here are some tips for preparing a Press Release.

1) Make sure that the information you are reporting is newsworthy. If you believe the information would interest you if it was about someone else, then it is newsworthy.

2) Get your contact information stated clearly and fully. Reporters and editors work on non-traditional schedules and don't have time to be searching for how to contact you. So be sure to include such information as: your name, address, business phone, fax, after hour numbers, your cell phone, pager and your web site, if you have one. Don't let your news release get trashed because they couldn't contact you.

3) Create a compelling headline that summarizes the newsworthy event you are announcing.

4) Don't hype your article. Avoid adjectives that are puffed up and fluff. Editors see right through that. Give them the facts and don't go on and on.

5) Be sure your press release is sent to the right department or editor whose readership or viewers are specifically interested in your type of product or service.

6) It's always best to type it, double spaced, but if you can't then print it neatly. Make sure your spelling is correct.

7) At the top of the page, put the phrase "For Immediate Release" with your contact information below. This will tell an editor that they can use the release at any time they choose.

8) Make your headline in large, bold, easy to read lettering. But don't make it so large that it is glaring. Don't use a fancy font. The type of lettering in this Primer is perfect and easy to read.

9) Begin your opening paragraph with the city and state of your business. Editors want to know where the article originated from and this is called a "dateline".

10) Try to keep the news release to one page, but if you go over, center a "#" sign or the word "MORE" at the bottom of the first page so that it is obvious there is another page.

11) Do not go over two pages for best results.

12) On the second page, place the page number and the first two or three words of your headline in the upper left corner and repeat your contact information. Should your second page get separated from the first page, your contact information will still be in tact.

13) Don't split a paragraph in half and have some on one page and the rest on another page. Re-space it so that complete paragraphs are all on one page.

14) At the end of the news release, let the editor know that it is the end by placing three "#" signs in a row, centered on the page. Example: # # #

BIOGRAPHICAL INFORMATION AND PHOTOS

You should also create a one or two page biographical sheet about yourself and your business. You send this out to media people when you are requesting them to do a feature article about you. Have available two black and white photos of yourself. The first should be a 5x7 head and shoulder shot. The other should be an 8x10 shot of you in someone's home, perhaps in the process of moving furniture or painting or repairing something or boxing up stuff. You can include one of these photographs with your press material whenever it is appropriate.

Remember, the real value of promotional articles is not so much when they appear or where they appear, but the reprints you will be able to use afterwards to send out to prospects or to other media people you want to interest. Press people are just as accepting as the general public. They will assume you are an authority in your field if you submit evidence of previous publicity about yourself.

You can research publications at your local library in the *Gale Directory of Publications,* an annual guide to periodicals.

Thirty-Two Ways to Create Free Press News

1. Tie in with news events of the day.
2. Work with another publicity person.
3. Tie in with a newspaper or other medium on a mutual project.
4. Conduct a poll or survey.
5. Issue a report.
6. Arrange an interview with a celebrity.
7. Take part in a controversy.
8. Arrange for a testimonial.
9. Arrange a speech.
10. Make an analysis or prediction.
11. Form and announce names for committees.
12. Hold an election.
13. Announce an appointment.
14. Celebrate an anniversary.
15. Issue a summary of facts.

16. Tie in with a holiday.
17. Make a trip.
18. Present an award.
19. Hold a contest.
20. Pass a resolution.
21. Appear before public bodies.
22. Stage a special event.
23. Write a letter.
24. Release a letter you received.
25. Adapt national reports and surveys for local use.
26. Stage a debate.
27. Tie into a well-known week or day.
28. Honor an institution.
29. Organize a tour.
30. Inspect a project.
31. Issue a commendation.
32. Issue a protest.

From Wilcox, Ault and Agee, Public Relations: Strategies & Tactics, 3rd ed. (1992), p. 274. With permission. You can complete our certification and send out an announcement to local media.

Press Release Web Sites

Here are some web sites that you can visit if you are interested in having a Press Release submittal service help you reach a large online audience. Please investigate their services carefully to make sure you understand what they offer and what they do not offer. Be wary of any one who promises your submissions are guaranteed. These services do not control editors and journalists.

Gebbie Press	The MagazineBoy	Bacons Information
PR Newswire	Press Release	Oxbridge Media
The Paperboy	Network	Finder

Approaching Reporters

If you were a reporter and every day you had to hunt for a story or article, don't you think you'd like a little help from time to time? Where does a reporter go to find a story? Where do they find people? Send a brief notice to your local TV or radio station and tell them that you know a little about a certain topic and that if they are ever in a hard spot to find someone to interview on that topic after they have called around, to give you a call. Ask them to put it in their rolodex or blackberry or electronic notebook. Most media people have a database of local experts. You can telephone them or send them a letter. Just call the reporter up and tell him/her you are an expert in this area and you would welcome any questions the reporter might have for you.

Publicity Referral Services

Would you like to be on the lists of experts that media people reference every day from all over the country? These lists are called "Publicity Referral Services". One such referral service is the RTIR Magazine, otherwise known as Radio-TV Interview Report.

You can find the online version at http://www.RTIR.com. These are all people who can be contacted for interviews for all kinds of media on the topic of their expertise. By becoming a member (there is a fee), you can start getting media calls requesting interviews. It's easy and it works. Some of the New York Times' bestselling authors use this service.

Publicity Introduction Meetings

There are even meetings that you can pay to attend that will introduce you to media producers and editors at the highest levels? RTIR sponsors these types of events too. Think of it as a publicity networking meeting.

These top media people, producers and directors, are there to meet new people and hear your story. While they are pretty expensive to attend, whole careers and businesses have been launched by just one good contact.

Advertising

Advertising is probably never as effective as publicity, no matter what field you are in. It is particularly so for consultants, however. This is because when someone wants to find a consultant, they generally do not go to the yellow pages or to the newspaper or magazines to find one. They usually ask someone they know to advise them. For this reason, typical advertising is generally a waste of time and resources.

However, ads may be useful when you want to reach a special target audience. So if you are considering the use of traditional advertising methods, look for special interest magazines in the real estate market. But know that this form of advertising is very, very expensive and requires at least a two or three month lead time. That's a long time to wait for an ad to come out.

A small listing in the yellow pages where real estate agents advertise may be good, but a large ad will probably be a waste of money.

Word of Mouth

As I have stated earlier, word of mouth advertising and recommendations from clients who have benefited from your services is the most powerful and effective form of building any business, particularly that of a consultant. That is why it is so imperative that you learn and develop the habit of asking for referrals whenever possible and from as many people as possible.

Just as third party endorsements derived from publicity are beneficial to you, word of mouth from a third party endorsement is even more powerful. It is far more personal, as well. Be sure to ask all your clients for referrals. Do so immediately following your consultation, right there before you leave. Follow up in your thank you note with another reminder or request for referrals.

In a month or two, consider sending your clients some additional information that will help them further. It could be anything: an article you read that you think would be helpful; another suggestion for some other part of their home; a list of places to shop for unique accessories that would suit their taste and style; places to shop where they can get a bargain. It really doesn't matter what you send to them; it gives you an excuse to put your name and business in front of them. It shows you care about them *after* the consultation is over.

They may have met new people since you last had contact. They may have learned about someone new in the neighborhood or someone who just moved at work. You want them to remember you favorably for as long as you remain in business. Always give them something that will benefit them and they will remain your ally. You never know when the phone will ring and someone will tell you that they received your name from a former client.

Most of the time when this happens, the earlier client will have already told this prospect how much the consultation cost and so you can be pretty sure that if you suggest a similar price, the consultation fee will not be an issue.

Try to develop at least 5 different referral gathering procedures and work them faithfully. It may take awhile, but give it a chance. What else have you got to lose? And besides that, the best part is - it's practically or totally FREE.

Getting People to Call You!

Wouldn't it be nice if people just picked up the phone and called you and begged you to come do a consultation or staging service for them? I've had it happen, but the norm is that you have to pursue leads and referrals. This is especially true when you are just starting your business. That's the name of the game - no matter what business you are in. But let's take another approach, at least for discussion sake, and see if you find a fit for yourself.

Step 1. You've got to interrupt their thoughts

As a society we are so inundated with information overload that it is very easy to tune out important messages we might wish we were receiving. I'm ashamed to admit that there are times I'll be working and a co-worker, friend or family member will speak to me as they are leaving. I am so absorbed in what I am doing, I don't even "hear" them, much less acknowledge them. I've learned how to tune out background noises and fully focus on what I'm doing. Other people are the same way. So you've got to reach out and GRAB their attention.

You can do this by having:

- Bold, compelling headlines
- Unusual graphics or photos
- Unique opening statements
- Doing something outrageous or totally unexpected in your advertising

One savvy marketer runs ads in a pricey magazine. He grabs attention simply by running his ad up-side-down. This one little trick makes this 2x2 inch ad pull as well for him as a 1/4 page ad, which would cost immensely more. One of my marketing gurus sent out a magazine with a full page photo of him (and some buddies) with their faces superimposed over some sexy women dressed in bikinis. Now I wouldn't do that, but he got some results with the shock value and, I have to admit, he looked pretty silly with his beard on a curvy female body. I'm not advocating doing something that outrageous, but it takes more effort these days to attract attention due to the competition.

Years ago I wasn't getting anywhere sending press releases for my wall grouping book. Then I happened on the slogan, "101 Ways to Dress a Naked Wall". Wow! What a difference. I even used that little headline in my online pay-per-click advertising, but I changed it when I discovered I was getting all of the WRONG kind of visitors who were titillated by the word 'naked' in the subheading. So you do have to be careful. But the point is still valid. When you grab someone's attention, you have a chance to get your message thru.

Step 2. Make your content relevant to them

Relevant content is so important once you have their attention. I'm sure we have all been tricked by email spammers into opening an email because the subject category was intriguing, only to find that it was someone selling something which had nothing to do with the headline. So the content needs to be relevant to the headline and it needs to be helpful information.

It is also important that the content be relevant and of interest to your prospect. I have no interest in how to repair cars, so a headline that says, "How to Repair Your Car in 30 Minutes" will be of no value to me, no matter how good the training is.

But if I saw a headline that said, "How to Buy Furniture for Your Home at 75% Off Retail", I would probably be quite interested. And so would you, you know you would. So you see your message must be relevant and of interest to your prospect.

Step 3. Solve a problem through education

Education-Based Marketing is one of the most powerful marketing strategies available today. When you have grabbed their attention and the message is relevant to them, then is the perfect time to educate them and this will do a number of good things for you:

- It gives your prospect the REASON WHY they should care about what you're saying.
- It appeals to the prospect's emotional need to solve their problem. (People buy with their emotions - especially women)
- It positions you as the expert and someone to be trusted.

For instance, why do you think you find all those long, long sales letters on the internet? Mine are very, very long. The reason I use them is because they work! The more you tell, the more you sell. To be honest, this is one reason I create newsletters every month. While I really want to help my students become successful, I also want to be more successful myself. So I use education-based marketing concepts all the time.

Step 4. Then prove your solution really works

People today are so SKEPTICAL. We've all been duped at one time or another. It's not a good feeling and none of us like it. We've, therefore, come to be very wary of anyone pitching a message to us, no matter how genuinely good their product or service might be. Every marketing message tends to be taken with a grain of salt.

That's why it's vitally important to prove what you're saying is true. You can prove your truthfulness in a variety of ways: customer testimonials, findings from studies or surveys, quotes from experts, your "before and after" photos.

Think of yourself sitting in a court room, on trial to prove your case. Think of your prospects as the jury, listening with a wary eye to see if any part of your testimony is false. Are you proving your case in your marketing efforts? If you are not, you will most likely fail. People buy what they want and need, but they ONLY buy from people they feel they can trust. Showing PROOF of what you do, with before and after pictures, will encourage them to accept you as a trustworthy person and that you have the talent to back up your claims.

Step 5. Offer them additional help for their problem

Now that you have teased them and intrigued them, you must close the deal or offer by calling them to some kind of action. Here is where you would offer them something like a free report, a video, one of my CD slideshow presentations, free answers to questions and so forth.

However, bear this in mind. You want REAL prospects, people who are seriously interested. It does you little good to be sending out free reports, CDs or anything else to non-serious people. So to make sure your requests are really legitimate, you may want to decrease your response and increase the quality of prospects that come to you. In that event you can charge a small fee to make the next step.

Step 6. Make sure you know what you're doing

If you do not have a degree in interior design, then you really MUST get properly trained in standard interior design concepts and techniques. You will face a client now and then who quizzes you on why you are doing what you are doing, wanting to know the design concept behind your decisions. You may have a knack for knowing how to arrange things, but if you cannot back up your decisions with solid concepts, you will look and sound unprofessional. It's one thing to decorate for yourself. It's one thing to decorate for friends or relatives at no charge. But it's a whole other level to get paid to decorate or to stage.

When you are asked questions by a bona fide client, your answers should have authority. Studying our design training will ensure you that you have the proper concepts and theory under your belt. You'll have the right amount of training and can handle projects easily and quickly.

Online Advertising of Your Business

International Staging and Redesign Directory

We have an exclusive redesign/home staging directory on our website that gets a huge number of daily visitors and people searching for someone in their local area. You can list your business under your City and State category. Many trainees are getting business from their listings in the Directory and it's a lot easier to be found in the directory of a popular staging website than it is to get your own website up and ranking well.

Consider taking advantage of this additional marketing tool to reach prospective clients. This Directory is one of the fastest growing (and largest) professional directories on the internet – don't miss out. It's an excellent method for getting prospective clients to call you and it is working for you 24/7. Your competition may very well be listed already, so it is prudent to be found in the same place they are.

You don't need to worry about being dinged every year with a renewal fee either. Pay once and that's all you pay. (If you purchased this manual from our website, you may already be entered in the directory, depending on which level you purchased. Please check your city and state first before joining to see if you are already included.)

To register, visit: http://www.decorate-redecorate.com/directory/join.html

To preview the directory, visit: http://www.decorate-redecorate.com/directory/directory.html

NOTE: For Gold and Diamond Course trainees, we also have a 2nd directory located at http://homestaging4profit.com. You are listed in both directories.

Upgrading to a Staging and Redesign Course

We are often asked by readers how they can upgrade their training from this manual to one of our courses and whether they can receive any credit for the purchase of this manual. We are willing to upgrade any reader to a course. To inquire about upgrading to a certification course, here are some handy links.

TO SEE THE CURRENT COURSE OPTIONS, COMPONENTS AND PRICING

http://www.decorate-redecorate.com/home-staging-redesign.html

TO CONTACT US TO MANUALLY UPGRADE TO A COURSE

Write to support3@barbarajennings.com or call us at (714) 963-3071.

Generating Plenty of Referrals!

Referrals are the lifeblood of any small business and most certainly they are very important to a stager or re-designer. In fact, surveys show that the vast majority of all new customers, clients, and patients come from referrals. Why are referrals so powerful? Well, because the person that has been referred to you already has a degree of trust in you, simply because you were referred by someone they know. And trust is everything. No one will hire you to do anything if they do not trust you and like you. Successful stagers are likable people, as well as trustworthy people.

We all know that we should be getting more referrals so why then is it that the very best referral generating companies only produce a fraction of what they could be getting? Let's see why.

Why Most Businesses Aren't Getting Enough Referrals

You see, most small businesses get their referrals from customers. That's okay, but the truth is...some very good referrals should be coming from businesses that provide complimentary products and services.

Many of your referrals should be coming from complimentary businesses, in addition to current and past clients. This is such an important and vital concept, the savvy internet businesses use it all of the time, not only to get referral traffic, but to get better rankings from the search engines. It's called reciprocal linking on the internet.

It's much more difficult to set up a systemic referral program that brings in predictable and consistent results from customers. Word of mouth from my trainees and visitors is great when it happens. Thankfully there have been many, many trainees who have written me unsolicited testimonials. However, businesses that sell complimentary products and services can easily be motivated to consistently send you referrals....if you set up your referral systems correctly.

In reality, there's no end to the different types of joint venture referral relationships you can establish with complimentary businesses. Both you and those businesses are reaching the same target market with non-competing products and services. Do this short exercise and see what I mean.

Step 1

Take out a clean sheet of paper and draw a line down the middle of the paper.

Step 2

Now list all the "types" of businesses that provide complimentary products and services on the left side of the paper leaving spaces in between. For instance, for a stager or re-designer, some complimentary businesses might be: 1. a home painter, 2. a real estate agent 3. a landscaper 4. an accountant 5. a home insurance agent.

Step 3

Then on the right side of the paper, make a list of all the local businesses in your area that fall under each type of category. For instance, you might have five different painters in the area or 50 different real estate agents. List them all.

Step 4

Now take some time to think about what you could offer them in return for them sending you a referral. Use your imagination. If you really think about it you'll be able to come up with some great ideas.

Step 5

Lastly, it's time to go out and propose your referral systems ideas to your potential joint venture partners. What you'll find is that some just won't *get it*. They won't have the vision it takes to accept your proposal.

But you'll also find a lot of business owners that are hungry to grow their business and are happy to discuss the possibilities. You may even find they will be looking to get referrals from you in return. That way neither party needs to spend any money or exchange anything other than information. Those are the type of people that can potentially bring you large quantities of highly qualified referrals.

So what's stopping you?

Success doesn't just happen. You've got to make it happen. Sharpen your organizing, repairing, designing, decorating skills. Yes. Be trustworthy. Be likeable. All of that is very, very important. But you've got to get your products or services in front of people. They have to hear about you. They have to be presented with great reasons why they will benefit from your product or service.

If you fail to get the word out, you will fail and it won't matter how nice you are, how trustworthy you are or how much talent you have. It's a numbers game. For every "no" you get, you will be just that much closer to your next "yes".

And since we are in a very visual business, don't rely solely on your ability to verbalize what you do. 95% of people are **visual learners**. That means they have to **see** what you do, not just **hear** about it. So if you haven't yet ordered your slideshows (which will dramatically help you **show** people just what you can do and give them fantastic reasons why they need you) then you are losing out on money that could be falling into your pocket - guaranteed.

Your Seven-Step, One-Day Marketing Plan

I have noticed a similar attribute that is common in most entrepreneurs and business owners. Most are "do'ers" rather than "planners." In reality, being a do'er is perhaps the ultimate mark of a successful person. It's what makes entrepreneurs a rare breed. Rather than thinking or wishing, they get out there and make something happen.

But I have encountered many small business owners who get into trouble "doing" the wrong marketing activities the right way or "doing" the right marketing activities the wrong way. If you want to "do" the right marketing activities the right way you must start with a marketing plan.

You don't have to spend a fortune to create an effective marketing plan. In fact, you can create a successful marketing plan for your small business in just one day. To begin, don't worry about writing style or making a plan fancy. Just go get a pencil and paper and let's get started.

Step 1 – Understand Your Market and Competition

A big mistake that many small business owners make is to latch on to a cool product or service without first understanding the market and what it wants (not what it needs). If you try to sell something that people don't want, they won't buy it – it's that simple.

Try and find a market that is like a pond of hungry fish. A good market contains people who have dire wants that are being unmet, so much so that they will jump to buy your solution (product or service). People facing foreclosure or devalued property they need to sell are prime candidates for staging services. Unfortunately they are more reluctant to spend money to get help.

To get an understanding of your market you should ask yourself questions like:

- Are there segments in my market that are being underserved?
- Are the segments of my market for my product or service big enough to make money?
- How much share of that market do I need to capture, to just break even?
- Is there too much competition in the segment of my market to be competitive?
- What are the weaknesses in my competition's offering that I can capitalize on?
- Does my market want or value my unique competitive offering?

Step 2 – Understand Your Client

Knowing your client intimately is the first step to easy sales. Getting a good understanding of: (1) who your clients are, (2) what they want, and (3) what motivates them to buy, is a key to great marketing. This is why it makes sense, if you're a woman, that you sell a product or service that appeals to other women. And men should sell products and services that appeal to other men. Why? Because you're inherently going to already "know" something about your client, because you would be your own client if the product/service was presented to you by someone else. As a home stager you'll be able to appeal to both genders. Pretty terrific.

WHY PEOPLE BUY

There are two schools of thought on why people buy. Some believe you should only sell what people "need". Others says, sell what people "want". I believe in both. Don't confuse "wants" with "needs". People don't necessarily buy what they need until they need it, but they'll often buy what they want. For sake of argument, let's look at buying what you "want". Have you ever known someone that went to the store to buy a pair of pants that they needed and came back with a new shirt, sweater, and shoes too or instead of the pants? Or how about the everyday shopper who goes into the supermarket to buy some milk and eggs and comes out with a frozen pizza, cheese cake and other goodies. (You know you should never go to the market when you're hungry, right?)

People will buy what they want (even if they don't have the money), and they'll buy what they need when the need becomes really important. So they will do both, actually, but it does depend on the product or service. I need to get my teeth checked, but I tend to put it off. I hate dentists and I also believe it's going to cost a small fortune. However, I'll spring for a new handbag that catches my eye just about any day of the week. I don't need it, but girl, if I like it, I buy it. And no matter what the economy is doing, who ever heard of a lady going without her makeup?

DISSECTING YOUR PROSPECTS

To really get to know your prospects you'll need to ask yourself questions such as:

- How does my potential customer normally buy similar products (i.e. in a store, on the web, door-to-door)?
- Who is the primary buyer and the primary buying influencer in the purchasing process (i.e. husband or wife, real estate agent)?
- What kind of habits does my customer have? For instance, where do they get their information (i.e. television, newspapers or magazines)?
- What are my target customer's primary motivations for buying (i.e. look good, avoid pain, get rich, be healthy, be popular, sell home, redecorate, etc.)

Step 3 – Pick a Niche

If you say that your target customer is "everybody" then nobody will be your customer. The marketplace is jam packed with competition. You'll have more success jumping up and down in a small puddle than a big ocean. Carve out a specific niche and dominate that niche, then you might consider moving on to a second niche (but not before you've dominated the first one). Home staging is a very popular niche market, so you're already home free there. Interior redesign is a logical second niche.

You could be a "stager who specializes in affluent homes" or a "stager who specializes in senior citizen downsizing" or a "stager who specializes in staging empty homes in AnyTown, USA". You get the picture. I can't stress this point enough. There's nothing more destructive than to pick a niche that you can't communicate with or that costs you a ton of money to contact.

Step 4 – Develop Your Marketing Message

You marketing message not only tells your prospect what you do, but persuades them to become your client. You should develop two types of marketing messages. Your first marketing message should be short and to the point. Some may call this your elevator speech or your audio logo. It's your response to someone who asks you, "So, what do you do?"

The second type is your complete marketing message that will be included in all your marketing materials and promotions. To make your marketing message compelling and persuasive it should include the following elements:

1. An explanation of your target prospect's problem.
2. Proof that the problem is so important that it should be solved now, without delay.
3. An explanation about why you are the only person/business that can solve your prospects problem.
4. An explanation of the benefits people will receive from using your solution.
5. Examples and testimonials from customers you have helped with similar problems.
6. An explanation about prices, fees, and payment terms.
7. Your unconditional guarantee.

Step 5 – Determine Your Marketing Medium(s)

Remember, when I said that it's critical to choose a niche that you can easily contact? When you go to choose your marketing medium(s) you'll understand why that was sound advice.

Your marketing medium is the communication vehicle you use to deliver your marketing message. It's important to choose a marketing medium that gives you the highest return on your marketing dollar (ROMD). This means that you want to choose the medium that delivers your marketing message to the most niche prospects at the lowest possible cost.

The following is a smattering of tools you have at your disposal to get your message out:

Newspaper ads	Posters	Contests	Card decks	Seminars
Television ads	Signs	Sweepstakes	Door-to-door	Tele-classes
Radio ads	Banners	Trade shows	Yellow pages	Articles
Classified ads	Newsletters	Charity events	Networking	Infomercials
Billboards	Take-one boxes	Telemarketing	Magazine ads	Special events
Sales letters	Flyers	Email	Movie ads	Ezine ads
Postcards	Door hangers	Real Estate Agents	Media releases	Fax broadcasts
Brochures	Gift Certificates	Word-of-mouth	Websites	Sign picketing
Business cards	Catalogs	Air Blimps	Public speaking	Window displays
Social Networks	Google Ad Sense	SE Ad Words	Press Releases	Cell Phones

The trick is to match your message to your market using the right medium. It would do you no good to advertise your retirement community using a fast-paced, loud radio spot on a hip-hop radio station. This is a complete mismatch of the market, message, and medium. Success will come when there is a good match of these three elements.

Step 6 – Set Sales and Marketing Goals

Goals are critical to your success. A "wish" is a goal that hasn't been written down. If you haven't written your goals, you're still just wishing for success. When creating your goals use the SMART formula. Ensure that your goals are, (1) Sensible, (2) Measurable, (3) Achievable, (4) Realistic, and (5) Time specific.

Your goals should include financial elements such as annual sales revenue, gross profit, sales per person etc. However, they should also include non-financial elements such as projects sold, contracts signed, clients acquired, articles published, and so forth. Once you've set your goals, implement processes to internalize them such as reviewing them daily, updating them monthly and resetting them annually.

Step 7 – Develop Your Marketing Budget

Your marketing budget can be developed several ways depending on whether you want to be more exact or develop just a quick-and-dirty number. It's good to start out with a quick-and-dirty calculation and then to support it with further details.

First, if you have been in business for over a year and tracked your marketing-related expenditures you could easily calculate your "cost to acquire one customer" or "cost to sell one product" by dividing your annual sales and marketing costs by the number of units (or clients acquired) sold.

The next step is to take your cost to sell one unit or acquire one client and simply multiply it by your unit sales or client acquisition goal. The result of this simple computation will give you a rough estimate of what you need to invest to meet your sales goals for the next year.

Conclusion

There you have it, The Seven-Step, One-Day Marketing Plan. It's simple really. Of course you'll need to study up a bit more about your marketing medium(s) of choice, their appropriateness for your message, and their associated costs. But try not to make the development of your plan a laborious, drawn-out task.

My final word of advice is to make sure you set aside uninterrupted time to develop your marketing plan. It could very well be the most important document you will ever refer to.

5 Ways to Reach Your Niche Market

I've been asked by students to share some marketing mediums which have worked for consultants of all types of businesses when trying to reach their small niche market. This is one of the most common questions re-designers and stagers ask me. Here are 5 mediums you could successfully use to reach the niche market:

1. Public Speaking

Whenever you can speak in public you will naturally and easily posture yourself as an expert. People love to do business with experts - sometimes treat them like celebrities. Public speaking is a great way to reach many people for the same effort and time. There is a knack to doing it correctly but it is a very powerful way to get business.

2. Trade Magazines

Small classified ads in trade magazines can pay off nicely. You could place a small (2" x 2") ad.

The downside is that you usually have to wait for 2 months before the publication will display your ad and ads are very expensive with no way to test them in advance. The key to advertising successfully is to try to reach really targeted traffic, not general traffic. So never pick a magazine that is not primarily focused on decorating.

3. Pay-Per-Click Search Engines

PPC's are a way many people are generating traffic for a website. The results from paid "ads" are not as good as those from the free listings, but they can still pay off for you if you write good copy and make it as easy as possible for people to hire you. But you really have to monitor your ads closely so that you don't pay out a fortune for little payback. Success using the pay per click methods is a science all of its own and should be used with extreme caution. Sometimes competitors will methodically click on your ads to purposefully use up your budget. Yes, it happens.

4. Rented Lists

You can rent a targeted address for around $.05 - $.08 each. The secret to using rented lists is to NOT sell the recipients anything, but to get them to respond to a free report or an inexpensive gift that you can send to them with the real sales letter. The whole goal is to capture their mailing address so you can write to them over and over again. Make sure the list has been "cleaned" recently before you rent it.

5. Targeted Trade Shows and Conventions

You need to have some established credibility before you use this method. Event planners really want to know you'll be able to deliver the goods you promise and that you are not a staging amateur. Your space MUST look professional in every sense of the word and be "full" – otherwise people will walk by you and never stop to see what you are all about.

The Power of One

One of my all time favorite movies is called "The Power of One". If you haven't seen it, be sure to rent it from your local video store. It's an amazing story that takes place in South Africa during World War II. A waterfall is made up of billions and billions of tiny droplets. A single drop of water has very little power of its own. But put that drop with billions of other droplets - now you have power.

So what does this have to do with a staging business or re-design business? It's all about numbers, my friends. I'm not talking about putting ads in the newspaper or a target magazine here like I was above. Nope. I'm talking about the power of publicity.

A Live Case Study

Here's a good example of what I'm talking about...

Many years ago a New Jersey man named Paul Hartunian began studying publicity and trying to figure out a system to help him get all of the publicity he could ever want for his various business ventures. One day he was watching TV news and saw that they were ripping up the wooden walkway of the Brooklyn Bridge. He saw the phone number of the construction company, called them up and inquired about what they were going to do with the wood. "Throw it away," was the response. He offered the man $500 to deliver all of the wood to him. Before the wood was even delivered, Hartunian had a press release all written and ready to release.

The headline of the press release said, "New Jersey Man Sells the Brooklyn Bridge for $14.95". He faxed a bunch of releases to media contacts he had acquired and literally within minutes his phone started ringing off the hook.

To make a long story short, Hartunian sold thousands and thousands of small pieces of wood, along with a certificate of authenticity, to people who called him by the droves to buy one of the small wooden samples he made available. That initial press release then launched several successful decades of press releases all over the world on various products and services Mr. Hartunian sells and he has made a fortune.

You Can Do the Same Thing

It doesn't take a gimmick like pieces from a famous landmark to get news coverage. The best part about it is that it's always FREE and it will bring you far more potential clients than any kind of overt marketing.

Find out what is unique about you that would benefit someone else. The key is that whatever you write about must have a benefit to readers. Create a headline that grabs their attention. You only have a few seconds to get someone's attention. Make your article newsworthy by constantly asking yourself the question, "So what?"

Don't get bogged down in who you are or where you are or your background - none of that stuff is of much importance compared to what benefits the reader. Focus on the benefits the reader will derive. Benefits! Benefits! Benefits!

TESTIMONIAL
"My partner, Deborah, and I have been doing this for years and finally decided to get paid for it. We read your ebook and it has helped us launch a very successful redesign business. No one else in our area offers these services! It is really like getting paid to have fun! . . . With newspaper articles and speaking engagements, we have created a "buzz" in our area (previously untapped market) and are desperately trying to keep up with the calls. Thank you for all your help! - Lisette Dell'Apa"

Stay Organized

Being organized is very important in business. I can tolerate a small amount of mess, but if it gets pretty bad, I shut down mentally. I become useless. When my eyes started to lose focus and I had to resort to wearing reading glasses, it felt like I was spending half my day hunting for my glasses. This was infuriating. Being the organized soul that I am, it didn't take me long to figure out that I needed several pair, not just one. So I purchased a pair for each desk, a pair for my purse. And all I have to remember now is to leave the assigned glasses at their assigned "stations". Gone, for the most part, are my endless hunts for glasses.

Gearing Up for a Prosperous Business

Returning to the Basics

No matter what time of year it is now, you should begin your business with some well-thought-out goals. If you don't know where you're headed, you're going to wind up somewhere else. You need short term goals and you need long term goals. So here are some extra tips to guide you along the way.

It's not enough to say to yourself, "Well, I just want to do better." That's not a goal; it's just wishful thinking. To be effective, goals must be specific. They must cause you to have to stretch to achieve them, but they must be realistic and achievable.

One of my goals at the beginning of 2005 was to double my income from the previous year. I knew exactly how much I had made in 2006, so the goal of doubling that income was very specific. I didn't know how realistic it was, but I knew that the only possible way anyone could double their income from one year to the next was by being an entrepreneur.

In the years I worked for someone else (before I went into business for myself) I was never able to increase my income by 80% in a single year. But such lofty goals are totally possible when you are an entrepreneur. I did it – so can you.

When you consider the income potential we have as entrepreneurs, coupled with the freedom to be our own boss, work from home, set our own goals and hours, this is an amazing opportunity. But it all starts with having a plan for the year that is specific, detailed, easy to implement, easy to maintain. Because anyone who has ever been successful in any business will quickly tell you that it just doesn't *happen*. It takes work; it takes dedication; it takes focus.

You Must Have a Plan

Whenever I hear someone complain that their business isn't going well, my first thought is: "Well, what are you doing to promote your business? How many people have you talked to today?"

Years ago when I was first starting out as a corporate art consultant, a few years before I added re-design to my services, I began to do *cold calling*. This meant that I picked up the phone and made calls to strangers to drum up business. I was too inexperienced at the time to understand that cold calling is an extremely difficult way to promote a business. So I was easily discouraged.

When I commented on it to my partner, he asked me, "How many people did you talk to today?" I said, "Four." He burst out laughing. "Four??? You only talked to four people??? Barb, there are millions of people out there! You only talked to four??"

Ok, ok, stop laughing. I was a dope, I admit it.

The key to any successful adventure is the effective communication to others of what you have to offer that will benefit them. It's also a *numbers game*. Obviously the more people who hear or see what you have to offer, the greater chance of success you will have.

I've said it before. It bears repeating. People are only interested in what's in it for them. So if your message isn't getting out, and if it's not getting out in a manner that immediately tells them how they will benefit, all your hopes and dreams will go up in smoke instantly.

So what plan have you developed this year to market your business next year?

Essentials for a Basic Marketing Plan

- Put it in writing. Whatever you decide to do next year, put it in writing and put it up where you'll see it often as a reminder.
- As a reminder, assign a dollar amount to what you want to make for the entire year. Break it down into how much you must earn each month on average to achieve your goal.

Break that down further by dividing that amount by 4 so you know how much you need to average each week. Divide that by 5 so you know what your daily average should be.

- By knowing what your daily income average needs to be, what your weekly average needs to be, you will automatically have a constant mental reminder to help you gauge your efforts.
- Plan your daily, weekly, monthly schedule so that 80% of your time and effort is going into *promoting* your business, not *doing it*. I know, I know, I know. It's a lot more fun to DO it than to PROMOTE it. After all, doing it is creative. But you've got to recognize that the key to long term success is promotion.
- Put into play no less than 5 methods, that you do over and over again, to get referrals. Call people up. Write to them. Give them a little form to fill out. Don't ask for more than 2 names. Ask them to talk to the people first about you; then follow up with a phone call. Start sending them cards periodically for any reason whatsoever.
- Get 5 friends, co-workers, relatives to agree to invite people in for a mini staging seminar. Charge each person attending a small fee. It can be fun and profitable too.
- Sit down and think of newsworthy aspects about you and your business. Write up an article, always asking yourself the question, "Who cares?" When you have something written that will be very interesting or informative that people will care about, then you have a good press release. Send it out to all your local newspapers, TV stations, radio stations.
- Get your website launched if you haven't already.
- Have a license plate border made that promotes your business. They cost around $12-20. Your vehicle can promote you wherever you go, but you've got to get advertising on it first. If you don't mind more blatant advertising, have a magnetic sign made that can be attached to the doors on each side of your vehicle.
- Hand out business cards and brochures (or postcards) where ever you go.
- Contact churches, women's groups and associations and offer to be a speaker. Contact real estate agencies and brokers. Donate a couple of free consults as prizes. Set up a nice vignette that is decorative. It doesn't have to be elaborate. Put together a chair, some coordinating fabric, a framed picture, a little table, a lamp, some books. You hardly have to even mention your expertise: you've just shown them you know what you're doing.
- Start pulling together additional "back end" products and services to add to what you are offering. Clients love it when they see you are really serious about your business and that you have many things you can offer. It makes them feel more confident about you and it earns you more income too. At the end of this manual you will be presented with many more resources I offer that will help you. I'm showing you by example what you need to do in your own business if you want to capitalize on all the various ways you can build your business. So don't get mad at me for mentioning all these products. Learn from my example. They will help you. And I'm also showing you by example that I do the very thing I'm teaching you to do.
- Get yourself a large calendar and hang it in your kitchen. Stare at the blank spaces until it bugs you to death. Then begin to write each day on the calendar what you will do that day to promote your business. As the spaces begin to fill up with activity, you will know you're focused correctly on promoting your business. At the end of each week, each month you'll be able to see how much targeted activity you actually did. This by itself will encourage you and keep you moving in the right direction.
- Every time you get an appointment, land a press release, get a speaking engagement, make a sale, write it down on the calendar in large colored letters to separate it from the promotional activities.
- Every time you make money, take 10% for additional promotional efforts, 10% to save and spend 10% on yourself as a treat for a job well done.

Ok, did you notice that out of the list above, there's practically nothing on the list that doesn't involve the promotion of your business. And lest you think that you're being pushy, or too self-serving - think of this. You are doing your friends, family, co-workers, acquaintances a dis-service if you don't let them know what you can do for them. Everyone deserves to live comfortably. Everyone deserves to enjoy their home to the fullest. If they are selling their home, they deserve to get it sold in the shortest amount of time possible for the highest sales price. If you're an art consultant, everyone deserves to work in a space that is pleasing to the eye and pleasant to be in.

So if you're not sharing your talents and expertise with people, you are cheating them out of real tangible benefits that will improve their quality of life. And you'll be cheating yourself as well. So get up, get moving, start planning and then execute the plan. And may all your dreams and goals come true next year.

25 Organizational Steps

Organizing really can be as easy as A-B-C, you just have to set your mind to it. It is essential that you do this for the sake of your business, your family and your personal sanity.

Act Now While It's on Your Mind
Don't put it off until later. Later never seems to come. When you get an advertisement that interests you, if you lay it down to purchase later, you'll never do it, right? That is true for most of us in most things we do. So act upon something while it's in your hand or on your mind.

Break it Down Into Manageable Parts
Don't concentrate on the "whole", but break it apart into parts and focus on one part at a time. My elderly mother needed to pack for the hospital this week and just couldn't seem to focus on what to do until I reminded her it was real easy if she would set a date and time to complete and work on one small part of the process at a time.

Containerize Your Business
I personally don't care for see thru containers but they work for some people. I prefer to "hide" my clutter, papers, files. But I do take care to provide myself with a good desk, file drawers, shelves, boxes, baskets and so forth to place things into rather than having them strewn all around.

Delegate Some Chores to Others
Unless you work alone and live alone, you don't have to do everything all by yourself. Ask for help from family, friends, co-workers. You'd be amazed at how quickly a large task can be accomplished when everyone contributes just a little. You can always hire the services of an organizational specialist too. Make use of your computer, cell phone, answering machine, FAX and other equipment to streamline your procedures and processes. I have cut my support issues dramatically by putting detailed troubleshooting instructions on my website instead of answering each email on such subjects. So look for ways to cut down on time consuming details that could be handled more automatically.

Eliminate As Much Clutter as Possible
I can't think very well when my office gets overly messy as it does from time to time. So when that happens, I just stop everything I'm doing and de-clutter it. Take one day a week and devote to improving your work environment. You'll be amazed at how much better you function the rest of the week.

File It Away or Throw It Away
If you think you'll need it, file it in a logical place. If you aren't going to need it, throw it in the trash. Make the decision to do one or the other while the paper is in your hand. Don't let papers pile up on your desk until they become massive. The longer you wait, the less you will want to tackle the problem.

Give Things Away to Help Others
An old car I used to use for delivering art to clients sat in my driveway for years with the promise of my husband that he was going to fix it up and sell it. He never did. So a month ago I called a charity to come and get it. They will repair it and donate it to a needy family. I get a tax write-off, but more importantly it feels good to have done something to help someone else in need.

Home is Where You Choose
Everything needs a "home" of it's own. I found myself wandering around my office to find my glasses or my purse until I designated a special place to keep them. I religiously put them in that place and I have eliminated wasted time and frustration from my life.

Identify Everything With Labels
As my eyesight has diminished, I needed a way to make large, readable and printed labels. While you can make labels on your computer, I chose to purchase a small, inexpensive label maker. It's so easy to identify everything in a box, a binder, a file folder when you can make quick, professional looking labels.

Judge Your Priorities
To successfully build any business, you need to spend most of your time "marketing" it, not "managing" it. So this requires you to prioritize what you're doing. I have set hours and days that I work. During my prime time hours, I only allow myself to do things that lead either directly or indirectly to making more money. All other chores are reserved for non prime time hours.

Knowledge Works
There are many ways to organize your business and life. Visit your local office supply store and just roam the aisles looking for products that will help you keep all of your business papers in order. Choose the system that takes the least amount of time and that makes sense for you.

Lists Help You Stay on Task
I am always far more organized and productive each day when I determine at least the day ahead what I will do that day. I rarely approach my day without a clear idea of what I want to accomplish that day. Sure there are surprises, but you need to plan and organize your daily tasks. A daily "to do" list really helps. (I've included a form at the end of this manual for you.)

Motivation Gets It Done
To me it always feels great to be able to cross things off my list that I have accomplished. It provides additional motivation to keep going. To motivate yourself, see yourself doing the task, finishing the task and rewarding yourself afterwards. Give yourself a time limit and see if you can beat it - kind of like playing a game with yourself.

"No" Can Be Very Powerful
None of us like to say "no" to anyone, usually, but you have to learn when to say "yes" and when to say "no". You can't imagine the destructiveness of long term stress, so you need to keep your goals and tasks manageable.

Order Out of Chaos
When you know where everything is, because it is all in it's proper place, you eliminate stress from your life. Seek to live an orderly life and run an orderly business. You will reduce your forgetfulness as well in the process because you'll be able to think better.

Planning and Preparation
Plan your month, your week and your daily activities. By planning what you want to accomplish, you'll be better able to prepare yourself properly. I hate to start a project, even cooking a meal, only to discover that I don't have a necessary ingredient or tool to complete what I set out to do. Here is another way you can eliminate wasted time and energy by being prepared.

Quality Over Quantity
Choose your purchases with an eye for quality. You'll enjoy your possessions longer and in the long run, this makes them a better buy. Don't be a pack rat. If you haven't used something in a year, look for ways to dispose of it. Keep your life simple.

Reminders Keep You On Task
If I didn't have notes stuck around or a handy timer, I'd forget all kinds of things that are important to remember, just not important enough to lodge meaningfully on my brain. It gets worse the older you get, you know. I put notes on my desk, my computer, my door, my purse, my car, fridge - wherever I'll see them when I need to. Yeah, yeah, I know, it doesn't do anything for the decor, but remember, "form follows function".

Sell - Sell - Sell
You don't make money if you don't sell your service or your product. That's why marketing is so important. Without strong marketing efforts, you can't sell. Be on the constant look out for better ways of presenting your service or product. Always be on the look out for more products to use as incentives, front end sales or back end sales.

Test Everything
Everything you own or do should pass a test. If you haven't used it in 6 months or a year, toss it out of your life. Sell it, give it away or throw it out. Testing is also vitally important for all of your marketing strategies: test your advertising, test your sales pitch, test your prices, test your referral methods and so forth.

Utilize All Your Space
Most of the time we only think about the usefulness of space within our grasp - that space that is eye level or below. But think vertically. How much space do you have from eye level to your ceiling? Could you more effectively make use of that space with cupboards, shelving or decoration? Look up and see how much more organizational space you really have.

Visualization and Conceptualization
The mind does not know the difference between what you emotionally visualize and what you actually do. You can literally teach yourself to type or play a piano through visualization, but only if you utilize all of your senses and emotions. If you regularly spend time visualizing yourself accomplishing great things in situations where you are apprehensive, you will ultimately be able to conquer those situations because your mind "believes" you have done so already.

Written Words Speak Louder
Any teacher worth her/his salt makes the student take notes. If you had purchased an ebook from me, I would have made you take notes by not letting you print the ebook. When you take notes your retention rises dramatically and you will retain what you learn far longer. Written words also convey an unspoken message of finality as they are believed to be non-negotiable. In business, make all of your agreements written to avoid misunderstandings and for the utmost legal protection.

X Means It Is Done
Use a large colored "X" to identify what you have accomplished on your "to do" list. Or if you cross an item off, do it in large colored ink, like with a marker. The feeling of self-satisfaction intensifies the larger it is. Then go celebrate your achievements.

Your Self Worth
Remember to take time for yourself. Everyone needs rest and relaxation, food, companionship, fun, creativity, spiritual input. Be sure to allocate time each day for your own rejuvenation and to maintain relationship with the ones you love.

The Influencers In Your Market

- Marketing to "influencers" is simply smart marketing.
- It increases your return on marketing dollar because the Lifetime Value of an influencer is much higher due to the fact that they can bring you a lot of referrals.
- Who are the influencers in your market?
- Are you giving them special attention?
- Do you have a special marketing program just for them?
- Take some time to create a comprehensive list of the influencers in your market, then develop a special relationship marketing program tailored just for them.
- You'll find that your sales will go up and your marketing costs will go down...and who wouldn't want that?

Strategies for Success

As I write this, the United States economic condition continues to be pretty strained. In the past several years since the September 11 tragedies, Hurricane Katrina, and now the housing and banking crises, it seems that terrible things happen on a very regular basis; then there have and continue to be huge corporate bankruptcies and scandals. Times are very uncertain with the terrorist threat always looming in the background. With Russia invading Georgia (probably after control of their oil pipeline) it becomes clear we may be entering a Resources War on top of everything else.

Strategies for hard times are important to have as a part of your marketing arsenal. Difficult times require us to work harder, to focus our energies on strategies and services that have the greatest potential for success. We need to be flexible and creative, seeking ways to help our clients. Even more than ever, our marketing strategies need to be highly focused on what will most benefit our potential and past clients - not on what we hope to gain personally.

The Economic Climate

You should know there has been an economic recession every ten years since 1780 and there is no reason to believe that will change. As a matter of fact, we may now see the economic cycle swing from one extreme to another even more frequently, or we may see down cycles last longer than usual. There is no doubt that we have entered a more uncertain period than ever before in U.S. history. The USA is now a debtor nation instead of a creditor nation. Before too many more years pass, we will no longer have the largest economy on the planet. China and India will be the largest and this will impact us like never before.

A wise business person will know where they are in relation to these cycles and be prepared with strategies for times of business slowdown. Depending on where you are located, these cycles may be more or less severe than other parts of the country. Regardless of that, we all tend to feel the fluctuations of the economy.

Decorating businesses, no matter what area of specialization, are considered part of the frills of life. Fortunately the staging business is viewed more as a necessity by lots of people. When the economy is down, however, the frills are the first to be cut back or eliminated and the last to recover. You need to know that going in and be prepared for it. Fortunately, this aspect of home decor has millions of prospects, unlike other businesses whose target market may not be as broad.

This is one good reason to consider setting up a credit card merchant account. Don't do it until you have started to get some regular business, but you are going to find prospects that will balk at paying your services by cash or check but who would still be willing to schedule a consultation if they can pay by credit card.

I have my merchant provider services set up on my web site so that people can purchase my products and services with a credit card. It is therefore no problem to offer credit when I am setting up appointments. All you need to have is a form to fill out the particulars of the price and gather the credit card number, expiration date and a signature from your client when you arrive on the appointment. Later you can process it manually over the internet. You can even set up a pay pal account for this which is easier and less expensive than the typical merchant account.

In a tough economy, find things that you can offer clients and prospects that are completely free or that will save them money. These *bonuses* might very well make the difference! Actually, people like bonuses no matter what the economy is. You can collect articles from magazines, the newspaper home and garden sections, reading books -- just about any where. You can give this information to your client for free. They will appreciate you, remember you favorably and, hopefully, pass your name and phone number on to someone else.

Continuing Education

Never stop learning. It's really important for you to continue to grow, both professionally and personally. Look for seminars, classes you can take, books you can read -- grow your mind and your creativity. Keep checking back on my website for new training and tools of the trade that will help you grow and develop and make the whole process much easier. Read my newsletters.

This is how I have been able to develop so many exclusive products. I like exclusivity. It means you're the only one who has it. Exclusive products promote your expertise.

Age doesn't matter. Go back to college. Get away from the TV and dive into a good marketing book. Get up earlier and take that seminar. I always feel that if I can come away from any kind of self-education effort with *one good idea*, then it has been worthwhile.

But don't just be a collector of good ideas. If you don't put them to work for you, they are valueless. So when you get a good idea, no matter what it's source, put it into practice immediately. The more time that goes by from the idea being planted in your mind, the less likely you are to ever use it. So act upon your newly gained knowledge immediately.

The Savings Rule

I hope you agree with me that all of our blessings come from God. I appreciate what He has given to me. I recognize that all wealth and power belong to Him and He wants me to devote a small percentage of what He has given to me back to Him.

As a Christian, I faithfully give a percentage of what I earn to help other people. I know that He has promised to meet my every need and He has. When you give to help others, and do so as abundantly as you can, it will come back to you many times over.

I also recommend that you practice the very strategic and economically sound policy of putting aside 10% of your earnings into a savings plan or some other kind of investment portfolio and let this money start to *work for you.* Don't be someone who is always working for money - create ways for money to work for you. Look in your local Yellow Pages for a professional financial consultant. They will be happy to discuss the issue with you and help you plan for the future.

I highly recommend you read a New York Times Bestseller of recent times called, *Rich Dad, Poor Dad* by Robert T. Kiyosaki. It is easy reading and you will finish it quickly. Kiyosaki lays down a simple mindset that will have the most profound effect on your life and economic future if you follow it. The younger you are when you start, the more benefit it will have for you exponentially. It's an excellent read (just one example of a third party endorsement)!

Becoming a Leading Strategic Force

Building a Six Figure Income and Gaining Even More Profits from Your Business

Huge success doesn't come overnight - not for any business, and certainly not for a staging or redesign business. The best opportunity you have to ignite explosive growth and stimulate profits is to invest your time, effort and capital to turn your business into a leading marketing force in the industry that has a specific strategy.

Winning companies dominate their competitors in two specific, primary ways: better business strategy and brilliant strategic marketing. All you have to sell, really is your talent. That is all that separates you from your competitor, unless you have a design store or products you are selling specifically.

The best way to advance your company to the forefront, then, is through a world-class strategic marketing process that has been tested and refined by the "war rooms" of the most successful marketers on the planet today. Happily this business doesn't have a whole lot of competition, but you're still going to have to market your business smartly, wisely and continuously.

Developing a Super Strategy - The Secret to Winning in Today's Market

Most businesses use a "tactical" marketing game which generally isn't very successful, if at all. If you do the same thing, your results will be as poor as theirs. But if, instead, you reformulate, execute and fully deploy some "super strategies", it can distinctively and preemptively change the rules of the competitive game in staging and give you a very distinct advantage.

A super strategy is the secret to winning wars and it's also the same secret to winning marketing wars. In a war, it's the difference between a stunning victory or a massive defeat. In marketing, it's the difference between failure or mediocrity and phenomenal success.

So to start you out correctly, I'll be pushing you to create a super strategy (remember all these back end products and services I've been telling you about in this manual are part of my strategy for my business, and you need to do the same thing) and focusing your total attention of building your business in that manner. Once you have created this custom strategy to meet your personal goals, you'll be able to marshal all the different marketing concepts into one unified, powerful, focused business building force that makes everything your business does from now on work 100 times better than before!

You'll be able to realistically target markets, client segments, and positioning advantages that you want your business to dominate. This will allow you to literally "own" your market in your area and have the strategic mechanism to fully achieve each goal you set.

A marketing Super Strategy represents the most powerful form of growth hormones you can give to your business today. Nothing else you can do will produce the massive multiplier effect that strategic marketing, as opposed to tactical marketing, will deliver.

WHAT IS THE DIFFERENCE?
A Marketing Super Strategy is the "complete battle plan" -- the fully integrated master-vision and execution plan for your marketing that you formulate and perfect to accomplish the goals for your business. It must be sustainable and continuous. If you were building a home, it would be your blueprint. It's your layout of how everything in your business will fit together like a glove. It's the overall plan and the sum of all the parts of your business, all being headed in one single direction. And it's the only real way you will ever successfully produce the exponential results you are (or at least should be) after for your redesign business.

It is the plan for waging the war itself - it is NOT the multitude of battle plans that will contribute to the war itself. Understand?

The Difference Between Tactics and Strategy

There is a big difference between the strategy and tactics. Understand this and you will be on your way to a six figure income.

I want to examine six critical, strategic ideas that can produce faster growth and higher profits for your business. My purpose is to get you to absolutely realize that investing more time and effort and capital on strategic marketing has tremendous potential to ignite explosive growth for you and give you competitive superiority over other stagers. Here they are:

1. Marketing strategically vs. marketing in a purely tactical way (the way 99% of all business operates) produces a MONSTER difference in results (up to 100 times greater results by marketing strategically)
2. You MUST use strategic marketing to put your business on a growth course for future profits, because without it you are destined to be mediocre, disappointed and out of business
3. How to effectively and optimally use strategic marketing in your business
4. How to overcome the key obstacles and crash the barriers to unleash the full potential of this kind of thinking
5. How to best utilize a Super Strategy
6. How to get a strategy mindset to practically eliminate your competition altogether, or at least render it inconsequential.

YOUR ULTIMATE GOAL
The ultimate goal you've got to pursue is to evolve your design business to thrive in your marketplace. You've got to produce products and services your customer's value more highly than your competitor's. In short, you must be able to **outperform** the competition at every turn.

Six Questions You Must Answer

Let me ask you some penetrating questions:

1. How focused are you and how certain are you of your business-marketing strategy?
2. Are you a prototype of innovative strategic marketing winners in the future or an old fashioned tactical marketing dinosaur or a neophyte beginner?
3. There are an infinite number of choices and challenges strategic marketers must consider in turbulent markets and economies such as we have today. How many different scenarios, factors, threats and alternatives have you actually carefully examined and evaluated lately?
4. Your business and marketing strategy should specify exactly how your business intends to successfully compete in the design market. What does your current strategy (or the lack of one) say about you?
5. Your business and marketing strategy should provide the conceptual "glue" that gives shared meaning to all the separate marketing activities and programs you intend to utilize. How cohesive and strong is the marketing statement your current strategy makes?
6. Your strategy must be straightforward in its intent, direction and integrated action. How clear and focused is yours?

Four Key Factors

Your Marketing Strategy Should Be a Function of Four Key Factors:

1. The arena you compete in
2. The "advantage" or positioning theme that differentiates your business from the competition within that arena
3. Access. What communication, media and distribution channels you employ and deploy to get across your "advantage" or positioning theme
4. Activity. The scope and scale of marketing actions to be systematically and sequentially performed in the media and distribution channels you employ.

These choices are highly interdependent. Alter one and you must revise the other three elements of your overall strategy. Have you ever given thought to any of them already? Have you before realized the necessity of integrating them all together into a seamless united whole? If you really and truly want to be amazingly successful in this business, or any business, then you have some serious thinking to do first.

The best time to do this is now. In the beginning. Don't wait until competition takes over your market to examine and develop new opportunities, approaches, positioning and advantages. You can't wait to examine new products or services or opportunities. And you can't wait until you start losing business to try to build business.

So I hope you can see by now that finding the right growth strategy for you requires a very well thought out strategic marketing plan - one that does not diffuse your resources, opportunities, time or health. You need to choose the best combination of tactics, weave them together into an overall strategy, while minimizing risk, waste and ineffectiveness.

Without a clear, integrated, WRITTEN goal-based Super Strategy and vision for your staging business, your company is likely to be reactive in its current actions, and aimless in pursuing future growth directions or activities. Not only that, but it requires an ability to see the marketing and competitive forces operating in your part of the country - and be able to predict how they will most likely change, react and evolve in response to the competitive threat YOU will bring to the forefront.

By systematically focusing dedicated attention to these issues and continuously searching for new and better ways to strategically gain competitive marketing advantages - the outcome you desire will be fully and quickly achieved.

Provide Value for Your Clients

"There is only one valid definition of a business' purpose: to create a satisfied customer." (Peter Drucker) It is your clients who will ultimately determine what your business is or isn't and how successful and prosperous you thereby become. A masterful marketing strategy is a clear, certain statement of direction, purpose, objectives and outcome your business confidently expects to achieve.

The acid test of your strategic marketing plan is whether or not it will deliver and sustain a decisive competitive advantage for your company. It's really that simple and basic. Remember, I said "sustainable". Therefore, you need to know the answers to the following eight questions:

1. How do YOU currently evaluate marketing tactics like advertising or promotional effectiveness?
2. Does your current marketing approach stress product leadership, service leadership, customer leadership or brand leadership? Or does it stress nothing?
3. Can you clearly define your value proposition?
4. Do you use strategic marketing to continually move your sales up the "value ladder"?
5. How thoroughly have you assessed and utilized your tangible, intangible and knowledge-based marketing assets?
6. How many new products or services have you or will you strategically introduce in the next 18 months?
7. How many new markets or selling systems have you gone after strategically?
8. Have you developed a formalized, written marketing growth strategy?

The Answers are Not Hidden – Look Outside

Master looking outside your business to sense critical changes, trends, threats and opportunities - then thoroughly analyze each of these situations or conditions to develop the best strategic options to pursue. So how do you best do it? First your business needs to build a forward-looking, ultra competitive marketing strategy that effectively specifies EXACTLY how your business intends to successfully compete in the interior redesign industry and staging industry.

Whatever you settle on, it must be all of these: 1) sustainable, 2) preemptive, 3) preeminent. You have to be able to produce a sustainable competitive advantage that you can predict! If you can't do that, it's not a strategy you should be following. You need to arrive at a point where you can predict, with reasonable certainty, what the outcome of your concepts, offers, proposals, etc. will be.

Do you know what the end result is that you want for your business? If you don't know where you want to go, how will you get there? You must know what your final destination is to be. And after you have settled on a destination, ask yourself if it is the best and highest destination you are capable of achieving? Don't sell yourself short.

You'll never be able to achieve your own Super Strategy unless and until you first examine and carefully evaluate the best performing tactical options, opportunities and marketing alternatives "OUT THERE", so you can grasp what kind of strategic visions and goals are truly possible.

Frequently, when you approach the creation of a marketing strategy from this mindset, you dramatically increase your sights on how much more is really possible from the same effort, investment, staff (if any), opportunity, cost and time. Without critical thinking, sequential activities, systematic execution and implementation - little gets accomplished.

You need to be able to accurately predict how your marketing strategies will most likely change, respond and evolve to the new actions you will take. And even further, you need to be able to accurately predict the responses of your competition and the marketplace. Does this sound impossible? Overwhelming? Well, you wouldn't be alone if you felt that way. That's why you have to have a near-obsessive commitment to winning! This is what it takes to make the difference between mediocrity and huge profits.

Not every one has that kind of commitment to winning. I recently invited my sister to revisit my website and take a look at the list of free tips links on my sitemap. She was blown away. Over time, she had no idea that my site had grown so vastly from it's fledgling beginnings. But she doesn't realize that I've only just begun and am still a long way from the place I intend to be. She commented that she would never have the time to read everything I have there now. That's ok. I never intended for any single person to read every single page on the site. It's there for them should they need it, but it was designed for quite a different purpose.

You see, I have a Super Strategy at work and my free tips pages are only one tactical part of that overall strategy. I commit time every month to building that part of my plan, but it is only one part of the strategy. It has it's purpose and place, but it will not, by itself, even begin to accomplish the goals I have set for my business. It is my Super Strategy that will accomplish that.

So the first step in your successful marketing strategy development is to determine the basic strategy you want to successfully mount and the reason why you think it represents the best possible approach for your business objectives.

Truly world-class strategic marketing is only possible when your products, services, markets, current selling systems, competition and market opportunities have been clearly and accurately defined.

To help you recognize a number of critical elements that heavily influence what kind of strategy you should be using, write down the answers to these questions:

1. What is your unique selling proposition going to be and why?
2. What's your front-end acquisition mechanism going to be and why did you choose it?
3. What will your back-end, repurchase offering/series/sequence be and, again why did you choose that combination or order?
4. Do you know what your allowable acquisition cost, incremental profit contribution and cost per lead/ customer or product sale is?
5. What's your repurchase rate, retention rate and attrition rate?
6. What's the need you are either creating or filling and how will/are you doing it better or more appealingly than your competition?
7. How many methods of creative marketing success are you incorporating?
8. How many applications for growing your business are you going to be using and why?
9. How are you building an edge against the competition?
10. What are you doing to establish and sustain credibility and trust?
11. Do you create all your marketing with the end result clearly in mind?
12. Does your marketing have true "flow" and strong value appeal to your prospective customer?
13. Do you know how to effectively evaluate advertising and direct mail?

14. Are you collecting sales copy, sales letters, advertising examples from other industries that have been successful and studying them?
15. Have you implemented a criteria chart that all your ideas must pass before being employed as a tactic?
16. Do you understand the lifetime value of a customer and know how much you can expect to profit from each customer?
17. What system have you implemented that will get your present clients to purchase more from you more often?
18. Do you understand the economics of strategic marketing?

Your business has to create more value in your customer's mind. If you do that successfully, you will experience infinitely greater growth and profitability for your staging business. I am always seeking ways to increase the value of my products and services. This entire treatise on the subject of Super Strategies is just one segment of that process. You see, originally this part of your training was not included in earlier versions. I have added it now to make the whole experience more valuable to you, my readers. I know it's complicated and you may not understand much of it upon first reading it. So you should read it several times and take notes. It will become more clear as you digest it more thoroughly. It will really become clear as you start to implement some of it and test the waters and try it out.

Yes, it's more work than you want to do right now. But it's totally up to you to decide at what level of success you wish to be. And that goes for anything and everything in life. I'm trying to teach you marketing's greatest single contribution to business! **It gives you knowledge of how you can best leverage UP all your opportunities, efforts, assets, capital, people and activities.**

And once you have made your decisions and begun to implement them, it then becomes necessary to set up a system that will help you analyze what you are doing. You will need to continuously evaluate, measure, monitor, quantify and improve every single tactic you put to use. By doing this your overall strategy will be tweaked and tweaked again, until you find the core system that functions optimally. And even after you achieve that, you will want to continually adapt everything you are doing to the constantly changing marketplace and the tactics employed by your competition. So it's a never ending process. But that's what makes it both fun and challenging.

Four Major Strategy Options

There are four major ways a strategy can be built: 1) Product Leadership; 2) Service Leadership; 3) Customer Leadership; and 4) Brand Leadership. Which one will you pick?

Don't let this sound too complex to you. You just need help recognizing all the underlying forces that competitively impact or influence your business performance, profitability and success.

So let's give you some specific things to do:

- You need to cultivate a framework for effectively predicting competitor behavior. So study what your competition is doing. Look at their advertising: websites, yellow page advertising, flyers, brochures, sales pitches, etc.
- You need to better comprehend the vital links between how profit is created, maximized and sustained. How are you getting your qualified prospects to hire you, how are you getting each client to utilize your services to the maximum and getting you a good supply of referrals to sustain your business.

- You need to totally rethink your past ideas on what competition and competing to win really means. Is it always an adversarial thing or could there be some friendly cooperation that benefits both parties?
- You need to be able to better assess the staging industry, understand your competitor's positions, and search for alternative means for filling the needs of your customers.
- You need to choose a competitive position that gives you the greatest advantage - but it needs to be an advantage that you can sustain over the life of your business.
- You need to bring a disciplined, integrated structure to your business if you want to grow it into something superior.
- You need to adopt a far more sophisticated view of competition that surpasses those around you.

What I'm really saying, to put it bluntly, is that you need to become a world-class strategic marketer if you want to make it to the big time. This will not happen overnight. It takes time. It takes willingness to read, study and analyze what other people are doing that has made them successful. It takes hard work.

Your challenge from this day forward must, therefore, become identifying what advantages exist and incorporating as many as possible into the centerpiece of all the strategic marketing you ever do. You need to think differently. Little by little you will start thinking continuously along the lines of how to achieve greater market penetration, product expansion, market expansion, diversification, brand equity and much, much more. You'll start seeing economic uncertainty as a key opportunity, not a detriment. You'll evaluate many more marketing scenarios than you ever expected to do in your life. You will learn.

Best of all, you'll eventually create a battle-tested blueprint approach for taking your products, services and entire business and transforming it all into greater perceived value in your marketplace. That will be great for your clients!

You'll be able to answer questions like these:

- Which markets offer me the best opportunities for most profitable growth?
- What do my target customers really need or want?
- What mix of channels, partners will help me reach and sell to the most desirable group of clients at the lowest marketing and selling costs possible?
- Do I offer the right products/services or solutions - and if not what should I be offering?
- Do I have a compelling value proposition?
- What would make the message even more appealing?

Yeah! It's a learning process. And those that are willing to tackle it will go on to be hugely profitable and wildly successful. And those that want to cringe and run away right now, claim it is too hard and too much work, will no doubt end up failing, or at best be only marginally successful. So at this point, you are faced with a decision. You can do nothing. You can market your design services in a purely tactical way and lose ground every year or operate strictly on a reactive basis and cross your fingers and hope for the best.

Or you can go back and re-read this entire section two more times, taking notes. And after you have done that, you can choose to begin to attack your business strategy with a whole new attitude and direction. If you choose the latter, you will not stop learning here. You will seek to learn as much about marketing as you can from other books and courses, from studying the sales materials you get in the mail that "sell you" on the sender's products and services. You will go online and study the sales letters and marketing strategies of businesses from every conceivable segment, including those in the staging and re-design industries. You will teach yourself to look at the possibilities and then you will put them into practice. The choice is yours.

The Strategy of a Six Figure Business

I've saved this for last because it is the core belief system that drives everything I do, stand for, teach, create. It's the foundation that my consulting, publishing and design business is built upon. It's the one key fundamental I teach above and beyond anything else in every consultation I perform and in every product or service I offer.

I saved it for last so that it will be the last concept you read and hopefully the one you treasure. **This is the single most important segment of this Primer for high income potential.**

"I have a very simple philosophy on life. You shouldn't steal from yourself. If you're going to commit your life to an enterprise, wealth creation, the security and the financial well-being of your family . . . and if other people -- your staff, your team, your employees, your vendors -- are going to commit their lives to you, you owe it to yourself and to everyone else to get the highest and best results. You should never accept a fraction of the yield when with the same effort or less, the same people or fewer, the same time or less, the same capital or less, the same opportunity cost or less, can deliver so much more to you currently and perpetually." -- Jay Abraham (multi-million dollar marketing guru)

This quote is from a man who is president of one of the most successful entities of its kind in the United States. His business is approximately 400% larger than his closest competitor. His company has grown 15 times in the last five years. It is ten times more profitable. It commands an absolute, unequivocal predominance in every area that it has penetrated. His people have more fun, they are more formidable and they are more invincible than anyone you or I have ever met.

This is the foundational pillar of their success.

They strove to have enormous empathy with their clients.

They saw their purpose as leadership. They saw their purpose and their role as being a leader, an authoritative, consultative force in their marketplace. They believed it was essential that they communicate and convey to their prospects and clients that they shared common feelings. In other words, "I feel the way you feel. I understand what your problem is."

They understood there was a distinct difference between giving information and giving advice. They worked hard at letting people know that their role was, "Here's what you should do about a problem, situation or opportunity." Then after that, they supported their solution with a compelling, irrefutable definitive set of facts. They saw their role as helping people focus on issues they had never verbalized.

Their view, which should be yours, was to present views their clients could trust. They saw their role, their function, their purpose, their advantage, their positioning as being a leadership authority -- but also they saw their role as being benevolent, nurturing and loving.

Be the refreshing, distinctive alternative to the mundane and the unfulfilling norm. Don't strive to be main stream because people think that main stream is a commodity. Main stream is not distinctive. Main stream has little value. No one wants to feel like a commodity. Commodities have no purpose. They have no connectivity. Main stream is mediocrity. How can anyone get excited about "rising up" to be mediocre?

Show them the truth as you see it. Help them take the next step. Connect the dots for them, give them a plan, help them take the next step, protect them from making errors, make the steps logical, appropriate, obvious and easy. Listen to them, see what they want even if they can't, and then help them achieve what they can't even put into words.

Try not to be self serving in your efforts to be selfless. It will show. Take your belief system and direct it outwards -- towards the benefit of others. If you can genuinely see your higher cause of purpose on this earth as being to enrich other people's lives, to bring them greater benefits, greater protection, greater advantage, greater financial benefit, greater savings, greater safety, greater productivity -- greater whatever it is -- then you will surely achieve total fulfillment and success cannot help but come your way in time, but the exciting thing is, when you achieve personal fulfillment you already have become successful.

So if you want your business to really soar, have a passionate awareness and commitment to a higher purpose beyond your own self enrichment. Focus on helping other people's lives be better, help other people become more fulfilled, help other people get more out of the process and out of life and home.

Embrace every client's situation with hope and promise. This is my wish for you too -- that you will get so much more out of everything you do. I hope you will allow yourself to get so much more productivity, profitability, connectivity and residual value out of every action, every hour, every dialogue, every contact, every client – remembering that the more you put others ahead of yourself, the more they will be blessed and this will bless you.

If you can communicate those sentiments to your prospects and clients, and if you look at everyone you meet or talk to in that way, you will gain a new and deeper appreciation of them. You will have a lot more respect for them. And you will see those same feelings generated in them.

Remember these simple questions and ask them of yourself often:

1) What problems am I going to help my clients solve?

2) How can I have the most positive impact on the people I'm trying to reach?

3) If I were on the receiving end, why would I want this service?

4) If I were on the receiving end, what's in it for me?

Learn to love your clients. It's the most valuable gift you will ever give them.

In conclusion, I encourage you to constantly seek ways to enrich, protect and enhance as many lives as you can. If you do that, I can guarantee you that you will create value, livelihood and fulfillment for yourself and your life will become quite profound. Take full advantage and give yourself over to your true purpose.

I submit to you that until and unless you understand that you have a higher purpose for being in this business or any business, you can't begin to take advantage of your full potential. Your purpose cannot and should not be to get rich or you will never get there. Your purpose must be to see what you can do for others and what you've already done for them.

Most people fall in love with their product or their company. Instead, fall in love with your client. If you can't, you're in the wrong business or you don't appreciate your business or you don't appreciate your worth. Most people think, "What do I have to say to get people to hire me?" Instead say to your self, "What do I have to give? What benefit do I have to render?" Actually the Bible said it already thousands of years ago: "Do unto others as you would have them do unto you." Become a value creator. The more value you give others, the more value you generate (not for yourself but for your clients). The more contribution you make to the richness of their lives, the more successful you will become and the more bonded you will be to them -- and they to you.

Passion for Your Business and Service

Without passion, it will be exceedingly hard to have a business and next to impossible to build a six figure business. Passion will drive you when nothing else will. Passion will sustain you when the going gets rough. Passion will keep you interested in what you do and how valuable it is for other people to know about your services.

Passion will transfer from you to your prospects. Passion will transfer from you to your clients. Passion will transfer from your clients to the people they know and then that passion will transfer back to you. I wrote earlier about the Law of Attraction. Whatever you put out there in life, life will strive to give to you in like kind. So if you're putting out excitement, appreciation, compliments, positive attitudes, goal focus – life will give you that back.

If you're putting out into the life force words of complaint, if you're playing the blame game, if you have no passion for your work, if you fear to try, if you're negative – life will give you back all of the same thing, giving you even more to complain about, more people and things to blame, less passion, more fear and more negativity.

Building a six or even a seven figure business in home staging is absolutely achievable.

> But many people go through life with a blueprint in their make-up that was created out of the spirit of poverty. That blueprint controls what they think. What they think controls how they feel. How they feel controls what they say. What they say controls how they act. And how they act controls their results.

To change the negative results you have always experienced, you've got to change your blueprint about money and business and about you. Unfortunately I cannot help you with the specifics of that in this manual too, but I'll be writing more on this in subsequent manuscripts. I've certainly given you enough to get your business started and moving in the right direction.

Homeowners need solutions, not strategy. Now go show them what you have to give. Have fun!

Chapter Six

Additional Important Resources

Staging Portfolio Secrets

Creating a powerful portfolio, and more importantly, learning how to use that portfolio in a highly effective and strategic system of marketing and promoting your business is no easy task. It is too involved to include in this manual. That's why this subject has now become another book in its own right. In this manual I'll teach you step by step how to create a powerful biographical sheet that highlights your talents and strengths, and how to incorporate that into your portfolio full of beautiful before and after pictures, then set about getting easy face-to-face meetings with the type of people who can really help you build your business. For details, visit: http://www.stagingportfoliosecrets.com.

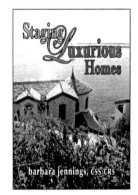

Staging Luxurious Homes

One of the best overall marketing tactics is to concentrate a certain amount of your time and energy courting affluent homeowners and their agents. Why? Because they have the money to purchase your consultation services and staging services. In addition to that, they are very busy people, usually concentrating more on making money than in selling their home, and they are naturally excellent candidates for a home staging service. I've written a one-of-a-kind tutorial that will teach you essentially everything you need to know to tap into this highly prized market and even specialize in staging wealthy homes. http://www.decorate-redecorate.com/staging-luxurious-homes.html

Home Staging for Yourself

The Home Staging for Yourself Checklist Guide is our newest tool for helping you make money on every appointment. You'll always encounter people who want to do the staging themselves or who just refuse to hire professional stagers. With this 80-page Guide, you can fill it out for them so they can follow the instructions and stage their own home. You simply sell them the guide for a higher price than you paid. Since the list is so exhaustive, it will silently urge them to possibly hire you instead. http://www.decorate-redecorate.com/home-staging-for-yourself.html.

Basic Interior Redesign Business

While some of this training will be naturally repeated in the redesign training I offer, I would highly recommend you get both of my ebook/manuals on starting, growing and managing an Interior Redesign business as well as what you have purchased here. You will find many similarities in staging and redesign, however there are some crucial differences you should know. Many strategies and tactics will work for both businesses, but you owe it to yourself to know all about that business as much as this one. This is my basic business training, but I also offer an advanced training as well. To get your copy of **Rearrange It!** visit this link at http://www.decorate-redecorate.com/redecorate.html.

Advanced Redesign

You have just completed the Basic Home Staging training. But it will not likely be enough for some of you who are more enterprising and who really want to take your business to the next level. For you I have written **Advanced ReDesign**. It is 15 powerful chapters on how to take advantage of a number of other critical strategies and tactics to send your business onward and upward. You will not have time to implement all of these dynamite ideas and do them justice. No one does. http://www.decorate-redecorate.com/advanced-redesign.html.

Decor Secrets Revealed Ebook

For top notch training in all of the necessary interior arrangement principles and techniques of professional designers, consider getting my electronic book of 25 chapters devoted just to these specifics. The ebook has over 500 color photos. It is an easy, breezy read and will teach you a lot about furniture and accessory arrangement design. Even if you've already got some design training, I've had full service designers with a 4-year degree tell me they learned more than in their formal classes – or were reminded of concepts they had forgotten about. Please look on this as further investment in your success.

For more details: http://www.decorate-redecorate.com/decor.html.

Arrange Your Stuff

Approaching furniture arrangement concepts from a slightly different angle, my 189 page soft cover (plastic comb binding) workbook of a wide range of sketched rooms, including the before sketch and then followed by anywhere from 1-4 sketches of how the room was and could have been arranged professionally. Lots of tips to help you immediately dissect any room and know how to solve it. Filled with the top and most common furniture arrangement configurations, you should find the answer to most rooms in these pages. Details: http://www.decorate-redecorate.com/arrange-your-stuff.html.

Where There's a Wall – There's a Way

A soft cover book of 128 pages, you'll get 101 ways to dress a naked wall. Originally written in the 1980s, it is still apropos today because the design concepts never go out of style. It's got design tips for creating simple to complex wall groupings and line drawings to stimulate your own creativity. You're going to encounter the need for groupings. In the back of the book are several pages of templates which you could photocopy to help you with your own designs. Details: http://www.decorate-redecorate.com/book.html.

Certification Courses to Consider

The best place to see a quick overview of everything currently available is at this link: **http://www.decorate-redecorate.com/home-staging-redesign.html**. It's a chart and you can easily see all of our "a la carte" components and compare the Silver and Diamond Courses.

Courses have been designed for those unique individuals who are really serious about building a career level business, want everything all at once, and want to save money in the process. It is not a route I recommend for everyone, particularly if you're only interested in supplemental income or you would be too strapped economically. That's why I offer plenty of options in an "a la carte" fashion so you can tailor your training and any additional products you might be interested in to your personal timing and resources.

But for those who can jump into a course, it makes the most sense. Duo certification is guaranteed with a Diamond Course and single certification is guaranteed with a Gold Course.

Diamond Combo Courses

(Standard Course) http://www.decorate-redecorate.com/diamond-redesign-training.html
(Deluxe Course) http://www.decorate-redecorate.com/diamond-home-staging-combo.html
(Ruby Course) http://www.decorate-redecorate.com/diamond-ruby-combo-course.html.

Diamond Standard, Deluxe and Ruby Combo Programs - Our most comprehensive training programs, the Diamond Standard, Deluxe and Ruby Certification Courses give you all of the design training and business training you'll ever need (both basic and advanced), numerous sales aids, some management tools of the trade, double guaranteed certification, custom stationery to effective launch your business, brochure web pages or websites, double business listings in our directories and bonuses, but you get two businesses instead of just one.

Silver Combo Training - Get all of our two businesses plus redesign training in one easy package. This program does **not** include the "tools of the trade" – it is strictly training, but is all of our training ebooks and books for a packaged price for two businesses, not just one. For details: http://www.decorate-redecorate.com//silver-redesign-training.html

Partnering

While most people do not have a partner, we do make it possible to train your partner for a substantially lesser fee (which amounts to the certification fee). We do not certify businesses – we only certify individuals within a business. For more information on adding a partner, call us or visit our checklist page and scroll to the bottom for details. http://www.decorate-redecorate.com/home-staging-redesign.html

Upgrading to a Course

Since you have already purchased this manual (and it is included in all of our courses) you can get credit for your purchase or get a substitute product of equal value instead (except for shipping and handling charges). To upgrade to a course, you must call us at (714) 963-3071 as we will have to calculate a credit or substitution and process your order manually.

Sales Aids and Tools

Editable Home Staging Powerpoint Presentation Slides and Script – Another great tool, this 65-Slide Presentation is great for use before real estate agents. It primarily promotes the services of a home stager, but ends with redesign as well. Comes with a script that you can edit for your own purposes. See **http://www.decorate-redecorate.com/home-enhancement.html**

Interior Redesign Powerpoint Presentation Slides and Script – Don't try to "tell" people what you do – "show" them with our exclusive 60-slide presentation. It comes with a full script which you can tailor to your situation. For use with Windows PC computers, whether or not you have PowerPoint. See **http://www.decorate-redecorate.com/redesign-slides.html**

Musical Slideshow Prospecting CDs – Don't try to "tell" people what you do – "show" them with

 our Before and After Musical Slideshow. It's the perfect way to turn a prospect into a client and makes it so much easier for you to sell the benefits of your services. Available in sets of 3, 6 or 12. Visit **http://www.decorate-redecorate.com/staging-for-sellers.html**

For Interior Redesign Slideshows, visit: **http://www.decorate-redecorate.com/get-clients.html**

Steel Furniture Lifter With Carpet and Hard Floor Sliders – Save your back. Get the furniture lifter that will help you move the heaviest of furniture by using the concept of leverage. We sell the lifter along with two sets of sliders (one for carpeting; one for hard floors). I don't sell them separately because you need both to do the job. I do sell sliders separately because you're going to want to have more than one set on hand to cut down on those back-breaking tasks. For the Lifter Toolbox Set, please visit: **http://www.decorate-redecorate.com/furniture-lifter.html**.

Furniture Sliders for Carpet or Hard Flooring – Don't hurt your back moving heavy furniture. Do it the easy, effortless way with furniture sliders. We have them for both carpeted floors and hard floors. See **http://www.decorate-redecorate.com/furniture-movers-carpet.html** or **http://www.decorate-redecorate.com/furniture-movers-hard-floors.html**

Decorating Organizer/Tote – It's hard enough to go shopping for your decorating projects and keep track of all your swatches and samples. We've got a very professional organizer/tote combination that makes it super easy. And you'll look classy too. This is a super organizing tool and I use mine all the time. See **http://www.decorate-redecorate.com/decorating-shopper.html**

Promotional Postcards – Use our colorful, professionally printed promotional postcards to get the word out about your services. Many styles to choose from. Cards are sold in sets. We have staging cards, redesign cards, staging & redesign cards, variety paks, certification announcement cards and a quick start promo pak. See **http://www.decorate-redecorate.com/postcards.html**

Furniture Arrangement Kit – One of the best overhead furniture arranging kits. You'll get around 1600 furniture decals to apply to special grid paper so you can create a bird's eye view of any room in your home or for a client. The furniture comes in multiple styles and sizes and all decals are reusable. See **http://www.decorate-redecorate.com/furniture-arrangements.html** For an Elevations Furniture Arranging Kit, visit **http://www.decorate-redecorate.com/furniture-elevations.html**

Additional Training Options

Flower Power – Whether you're decorating for a social event for your client or decorating your own home, knowing how to arrange flowers is a specialized talent you would do well to have. While we have some floral arranging training available in Advanced Redesign, you'll get the complete and thorough version in Flower Power. **http://www.floraldesigntraining.com**

Great Parties! Great Homes! – Learn how to decorate for parties and social functions, how to be the perfect hostess and how to be the perfect guest. **http://www.decorate-redecorate.com/planning-parties** Great training for learning how to effectively promote your business and acquire referrals. Since most business in staging and redesign happens through face-to-face relationships, being active socially is a crucial part of building your business.

Pro Art Consulting – I worked the residential market as well as the corporate market. However, in the business world I offered my services as a corporate art consultant, specializing in designing decorative art programs for business facilities. If you want to work with business clients as well, this is a very low risk service to add. Select ebook version or printed version. **http://www.decorate-redecorate.com/work-at-home.html**

Newsletters and Discussion Forum

Decorating Newsletters – Sign up for our free Decorating Tips newsletter that comes out monthly. Send a blank email to **join-ezine@decorating.listserve.us**. You will be asked to confirm by our ListManager, so be sure to confirm and also be sure to white list our website and the server "decorating.listserve.us" at your email account to ensure you get the mail. Otherwise you might have to check your junk mail folder to find it.

Business Building Newsletters – This newsletter is private and only available to those trainees that have purchased redesign/staging training. Write us for information on this if you did not purchase this manual directly from me.

Free Discussion Forum – Be sure to visit our free discussion forum and join. It's a place to share ideas, tips and thoughts and to ask questions. You'll be in a community of home stagers, redesigners and decorators from all over the country. Visit: **http://www.decorate-redecorate.com/smf.** Membership is free to all.

Certification For Those That Want It

Certified Staging or Redesign Specialist – Certification is not necessary for success, but some people really want that extra credibility so we have a private certification process for you. It involves an exam and submission of a portfolio to be judged which makes it one of the most prestigious offered anywhere. You may apply for single or double certification. Application fee. Apply here: **http://www.decorate-redecorate.com/certified-redesigner.html**

Bonus Section

Possible Business Names

The following business names are generally very descriptive and should be good choices. Many of these names are in use already; many are not. If you select a name as shown, you must first apply for a fictitious business name, otherwise known as a DBA (Doing Business As) in your county to make sure the name is not already in use in your part of the country. Check with your County Clerk's office for the registration office nearest you.

If the name is not already in use in your county, you may register the name for your own use. If you are planning to develop a website, you might want to see if the name is already taken as a Dot Com. If it is, then choose another name or change the name slightly so that you can register the domain name to match your business name.

Business names are usually good for about 5 years before they must be renewed. Domain names are renewable annually. If you are using your own name in your business name, you do not need to file a fictitious business name statement.

If you don't see a name here that appeals to you, hopefully you'll find some that will generate ideas for your own creation. Just remember to make your business name as memorable and specific as you can for best results. People should not have to guess at what you do.

_____ Designs on Staging
_____ Staging Group
_____ Staging Team
_____ Staging Ideas
_____ Stagings
_____ Staging Group
_____ Staging Touches
_____ 's Staging Services
Stage A Better Place
Stage A Better Home
A Staged Look
A New Staged View
Affordable Staging
Affordable Staging & Redesign
Affordable Interiors & Staging
Affordable Decorating & Staging
Affordable Redecorating & Staging
Affordable Home Décor & Staging
Accent on Staging

Accent on Staging Arrangement
Accent on Staging & Rearrangement
All About Staging
All About Staging & Design
All About Staging & Redesign
All About Your Home Staging
American Staging
American Staging & Redesign
All American Staging
All American Staging & Redesign
A Staging Intervention
Arrange a Stager
Arrange a Space
Arrange a Home Staging
Stage It Right!
Staging It Right!
Staging Your Home

Staging Your Space
Staging Your Place
Staging Places
Staging Interiors
Artful Staging
Artful Staging & Redesign
Artful Designs & Staging
Artful Redesign & Staging
Artful Spaces & Staging
Artful Places & Staging
Artful Homes & Staging
Artful Interiors & Staging
Stagemospheres!
Bright Staging
Bright Staging & Redesigns
Born Again Staging
Catch the Stage
Centsible Staging
Centsible Décor & Staging
Centsible Design & Staging
Centsible Redesign & Staging

Centsible Designs & Staging
Centsible Redesigns & Staging
City Living Staging
Champagne Chic Staging
Champagne Chic Design & Staging
Champagne Chic Redesign
Charisma Staging
Charisma Home Staging
Chic Staging
Chic Staging & Design
Chic Stagers
Chic Staging Interiors
Chic Home Staging
Center Stage
Cherry Creek Cottage Staging
City Dwellers Staging
City Dwellers Home Staging
Clutter Gone Staging
Clutter Gone Stagers
Country Creation Staging
Country Staging
Country Home Staging
Creations by Staging
Creations by Redesign & Staging
Creative Visual Staging
Creative Finishes Staging
Creative Staging
Creative Home Staging
Creative Interiors & Staging
Creative Arrangements & Staging
Creative Rearrangements & Staging
Creativity on Stage
Cream Staging
Staging on a Dime
Staging Solutions
Staging Rx
Décor Staging Solutions
Staging for You
Decorating & Staging Rx
Dramatic Staging
Elegant Staging
Elegant Home Staging
Elegant Staged Places
Elegant Staged Spaces
Elegant Staged Interiors
Enhanced Home Staging

Enhanced Staging
En'terior Staging & Designs
Staging Expressions!
Staging Your Taste
Staging Your Style
Staging You!
Extraordinary Staging
Extraordinary Staging & Redesign
Extraordinary Interiors & Staging
Extraordinary Home Staging
Extreme Staging
Extreme Staging Makeovers
Extreme Home Staging
Staging Your Nest
First Impressions Staging
Finely Staged Interiors
First Staging Interiors
Fruitful Staging
Stagedteriors
Great Owl Staging
Great Staging Interiors
Great Spaces Staging
Great Home Staging
Home and Garden Staging
Home and Garden Staging & Redesign
Home and Garden Home Staging
Harbour Side Staging
HomeStage
Home Stage Home
Home Stage Professionals
Home Staging Professionals
Staged Sweet It Is!
Haven Staging
Haven Home Staging
House Angels
Illusion Staging
Illusion Home Staging
Illusion Creators
Impact Staging
Impact Home Staging
Impact Staging Interiors
Impressions West Staging
Staging Focus
Inside/Out Staging
Inside/Out Staging & Designs
Inside/Out Staging Spaces
Inside/Out Home Staging

Interior Staging Matters
Interior Staging Specialists
Interior Staging Solutions
Interior Staging Inspirations
Interior Redesign Solutions
Interior Staging Magic
Interiors Plus Staging
Inviting Spaces & Staging
Inviting Places & Staging
Inviting Interiors & Staging
Interior ReArrangements & Staging
Interior Makeovers & Staging
In Your Space Staging
In Your Space Home Staging
In and Out Staging
In and Out Home Staging
Instant Staging
Instant Designs & Staging
Instant Redesign & Staging
Instant Home Staging
Instant Home Makeovers
Interior Max Staging
Interior Depot Staging
Island Home Staging
Less is More Staging
Let's Stage It!
Lifestyle Staging
Lifestyle Home Staging
LifeStyles Staging
Liveable Staging
Living Designs & Staging
Many Leaves Staging
Many Ways Staging
Metropolitan Design & Staging
Metropolitan Redesign & Staging
Metropolitan Designs & Staging
Moore Staged
Marshall Arts Staging
Makeover Deluxe Staging
Me and My House Staging
Move It Around Staging
New Dawn Staging
Oceanside Staging
Oceanside Staging & Designs
Oceanside Staging Interiors

One Day Staging
Organizing with Staging
Organizing Staging
Services
Organizing Your Home
Organizational Staging!
Outside the Box Staging
Porch Lite Staging
Porch Lite Staging &
Redesign
Properly Staged
Property Staging Potential
Property Home Staging
(Your City) Staging
Ready Set Sell
Room Pruning
Room Staging
Radiant Room Staging
Radiant Home Staging
Real Estate & Staging
Staging by _____
Stage It
Stage, Show, Sell
Stage It – Sell It
Stage to Success
Stage for Success
Staged to the Max
Staging for Profit
Stage to Profit
Staged to Show
Staged to Sell
Show and Sell Staging
Stage One
Stage Two
Stage Three
Stage Five Staging
Staging Spaces
Staging to Impress
Staging to Sell Fast
Staging to Sell Quick
Staging to Sell Quickly
Staging Places
Staging Interiors
Staging for You
Stage Now!
Staging With Style
Staging Atmospheres
Staging Concepts
Staging Designs
Staging Interventions
Staging Solutions
Staging Places
Staging Spaces
Staging Interiors
Staging Your Taste
Staging Impressions

Staging Services
Staging Strategies
Staging on a Budget
Staging Sense
Staging Cents
Staging Solutions
Staging Diva
Staging Divas
Staging by Design
Staging for You
Staging Instantly
Staging Touches
Staging Solutions
Staging Interiors
Staging Spaces
Staging Places
Staging Interiors
Staging Your Nest
Staging Interventions
Staging Solutions
Home Staging Solutions
Staging Consultants
Staging Makeovers
Staging Savvy
Staging Works
Staging Just for You
Staged to Sell
Staged for Selling
Staged Around You
Staging Your Nest
Staging Your Place
Staging Your Space
Staging Your Home
Staging Rooms
Staging Up Your Nest
Staging Revival
Staging Refined Spaces
Staging Rearrangements
Serene Staging
Serene Home Staging
Serene Staging &
Redesign
Set the Stage
Setting the Stage
Show Home Staging
Showhome Staging
Showcase Staging
Showcase Home Staging
Signature Staging
Signature Staging &
Redesigns
Signature Home Staging
Signature Interiors &
Staging
Simply Yours Staging
Showcase This House

Smart Staging
Smart Staging & Designs
Smart Home Staging
Smart Interiors & Staging
Smart Spaces & Staging
Smart Places & Staging
Space Lift Staging
Space Lift Staging &
Designs
Space Lift Redesign &
Staging
Stage II Staging
Stage II Home Staging
Stage Right Staging
Stage Right
Stage Left
Staged for Purchase
Staged to Sell
Staging Center
Staging Savvy
Staging Consultants
Staging Deluxe
Staging for Success
Staging for Dollars
Staging for the Ages
Solutions from Staging
Staged Homes That Sell
Serene Staging Spaces
Serene Atmospheres
Shabby Nook Staging
Sunshine Staging Group
Sunshine Home Staging
Sunshine Redesign &
Staging
The Art of Staging
The Joy of Staging
The Staging Duo
The Staging Junkies
The Staging Touch
The Staging Nest
The Staging Instinct
The Staging Studio
The Staging Depot
The Staging Home
The Staged Home
The Creative Staging
Company
Cutting Edge Staging
The Next Level Staging
The Next Stage
Transforming Interiors
Transforming Homes
Transforming Your Home
Transformed Homes
Transformed Interiors
Transitions by Staging

Some Questions and Answers

QUESTION - "Dear Barbara, Since I have just registered my business, the Chamber of Commerce here has just offered me a spot in their Home & Garden Show (held in the Hockey/skating forum) each spring. (I live in a small city & most people here probably haven't heard of Home Staging, Redesigning, etc.) The total is $321 for a 10' x 10' booth including draping, lights & backdrop. (An ad 13 weeks running in our local paper was close to that amount!) It is on Apr. 7-8-9th : 5 hrs. Fri., 8 hrs. Sat., and 6 hrs. Sun. Since I'm not the type to call people looking for business, or leaving flyers, etc. in doors & P.O. boxes, I think this just might work well for me. Having been a teacher I have some skills to help me in setting up an attractive booth. I will be using your disc Rearrange It! and some before/after pictures of my own (both on the computer & hard copies) if I can get a laptop set up (my computer is not a laptop!) I will be reviewing all the info contained in your ebooks, etc. to make the best presentation I can. Now -- can you give me any hints, etc. in this regard? Could I use a couple samples from your books Arrange Your Stuff or Where There's a Wall There's a Way? I would definitely have your name, email address, etc. on these few samples. I know I can't use your materials to teach a class on this -- this is only to whet the appetites of potential clients! With all the help you have & continue to give me and because it is dishonest/ illegal - I have no intention of pretending your work is my work! I had given my presentation to our two Realtors before you came out with the Home Staging discs, etc. so I thought I would have no use for them. Now -- I wouldn't be able to get them on time even if I gave it more thought! (Yes, I know -- Be Prepared!)

ANSWER - It will be largely a waste of time, effort and dollars UNLESS you have built into everything a way to capture their names, addresses, phone numbers and email addresses. Many people who do these types of shows fail to keep the initiative and follow up. They think they'll just sell at the show and when that doesn't happen they are mightily disappointed. Offer a free redesign in a drawing as an incentive or give something away in the drawing that people would consider valuable. But they only get it if they sign up and enter. Give away a special little gift for any referrals someone might give you on the spot. It takes good, strong follow up to turn people into clients as you'll find that many will just be wanting information or just curious. I'm worried about you not being aggressive enough after it's all over.

Bear in mind that many people need to meet you more than once to make a decision to buy or hire you and that the best way to build a consultation business is by word of mouth. Conduct a mini seminar so you're viewed as an expert. Bring in some white folding chairs to speak to a group of 5-10 people gathered once each hour. Place signs out in front of your booth about when the next seminar will take place. You may be able to use the CDs for a small group but not very large if viewing on a laptop monitor. It's one thing to sell something on the spot that they carry away and have right away. It's another thing to sell a future service that is intangible. You also have to find a clever way to draw them into your booth and get them to sit down to watch a presentation or engage them in some way and talk to them with excitement.

Hopefully you'll line up help so that if you're talking to one group other people aren't being neglected. It can be tough to sell in that type of situation. Lots of people just browse the whole show, buying nothing, then return to those that interest them or not at all. I personally don't like to stop and chat. I mostly just want to pick up cards and brochures and move on as my time is limited and my legs start to ache pretty soon. I'm also not sure I would try to sell both types of services from the same booth, but you could of course try it. You have to create a buzz somehow

214

so your display will have to be phenomenal to compete with those around you selling a gadget or decorative pillows or a new swimming pool or whatever. Location in the show is also crucial. You want to find out where your booth will be and who will be around you before making the plunge.

You'll want to have professional business cards and literature to give away, but most importantly you need to collect their info and follow up. Your booth needs to be full and attractive too. People walk right by a booth where it doesn't look like much is going on. It's like passing by a store with scant merchandise. A 10x10 booth is quite small when you think about it and start factoring in some furniture, especially. Just make sure you really plan it out carefully or you just might waste your money. Ask for the demographics too and know what kind of traffic you'll likely get. See if you can get referrals to other booth sponsors so you can talk to people who have been in the show and get their reactions. I have never had a single vendor from a show, even where I signed up, contact me later to try to sell me. That is just plain stupid on their part. You have to work the show too. Try to get set up quick and go around and visit other booths periodically, especially on the first day. Notice which booths are getting lots of interest and the ones that aren't. Try to add more to what you're offering on day 2 and 3 that you glean from others on day one. If you act quickly, you still could get the Home Staging slideshow and our postcards in time.

We now have staging postcards and redesign cards. It's a month away. Put your stamp or label on the back and hand them out for people's goody bags. Hope this helps you.

QUESTION - "Hi Barbara, I am a trainee and I wanted to know if you had that letter that I could send to realtors that talks about a complimentary $50 gift certificate that they give to their clients'. But once their clients call me to come to their house what am I expected to do for $50?. (I'm thinking a basic interview but not to many ideas, because people like to steal your ideas.)

ANSWER - Well, I don't have a letter to give you and it's best that you construct one yourself anyway that suits you. I've found that it's generally better to not worry about how much you give away. You want to make sure that the person feels they got their money's worth. That will be more beneficial to you in the long run anyway. If you have a copy of my Advanced Redesign, there is an 8 page check list of typical tasks a home seller might expect to have to make. Often by giving them an overwhelming list of things they will opt to have you come and do much of it for them. Overwhelming them with suggestions works in your favor, not against you. But there will always be DIY sellers and you won't be able to change that. So don't try. You could, of course, divide up a list into an overview list as opposed to a comprehensive list. You could offer the shorter list for the comp certificate and then mention that a really comprehensive list will entail a full consultation fee of say $200+.

QUESTION - I have studied at home under your "Silver" program. I have been asked twice about being "accredited" as I begin marketing my services. I also note on other's websites they tout themselves on their website as being "accredited". These stagers/redesigners call themselves as such because they completed 3-5 day seminars with XXXXXXXX I am wondering if Barb Jennings allows us as rookies to use her name at our websites to indicate our training? I want to get certified but have no customers as yet. Thoughts?

ANSWER - You cannot use our designation or insignias unless you actually go thru certification with us. There is nothing wrong with you saying that your training is from a company who demands passage of an exam and submission of a portfolio before granting certification status and that you are working to complete your qualifications. As a potential client, I would be curious as to how the person became certified and would be immensely impressed by someone who went to great lengths to prove they had the knowledge and skill prior to obtaining their credentials. Certification does not guarantee anyone's success in the business, but it is especially valuable to build your personal confidence and wind up with a powerful designation that you can market with confidence. But I continue to say that persona is primarily determined by how you carry yourself, your attitude, the manner in which you speak to agents and prospects, your look and professional decorum.

So if you're having problems, you might also want to get some feedback from trusted people on how you're coming across to people to make sure there is nothing in that area that is working against you. You can certainly mention our website and company on your website and link to your listing in our directory. You just can't use the CSS or CRS insignias unless you are officially certified by us and have received a Certificate of Completion from us.

We also never charge any renewal fees for maintaining your designation. And unless one did something illegal, we would never take back a designation once given.

QUESTION -I ordered my print copy of Rearrange It and it should be here soon, however, in a wonderful twist I have my first potential redesigning job and the client has called to inquire of my services. I was focusing on the staging part so this is a great, but unexpected surprise and I am a bit in a quandary about the fee issue. I want to give her a discounted rate as she knows I am new to this and I would like to request before/after pictures as well as the referral you recommend (not that that has anything to do with a discounted rate) in the Home Staging for Profit. I am wondering if I should charge a consultation fee and then take my graph paper and ideas home and come up with a plan, or do I just charge a flat room rate (for physically moving etc) which would include the consultation and is that done right there on the spot? I am excited and anxious to get my new training manual so I am armed with the info I need for this aspect of my business! Also, do you recommend bringing the same 'tools' for the redesigning job as I would for the staging job? i.e. measuring tape, dig. camera, invoice, furniture mover discs...any other important things that you might think would be great. I am putting together my 'case' with essentials. I thank you in advance for all information and help and appreciate your constant guidance and presence!

ANSWER -I offer my clients a half day (4 hours) or full day (8 hours). I don't like hourly. Set your fee according to what you feel your time and expertise are worth. I take: measuring tape, invoice, steel furniture lifter, plenty of sliders, two cameras (wide angle and zoom), a good fan deck in case I'm asked color questions. I never go out the door without a commitment and agreement to the fee, but new people are in a different mindset than me. I don't do consults only but some people find that a good way to move them to a half day or full day service. For me it's a waste of time. But do what works.

I never measure and come back. I don't bother to measure unless I'm hired. What for? Try to be available to work right then and there, not going back home to do drawings. Not necessary and a waste of time. Work it out right there. In the book you'll see the most common arrangement configurations. One should work. Take book with you and leave in car. If you get stuck, sneak out for a peek and get ideas. It's not a complicated service. Don't make it so.

QUESTION - I am in need of help as to how to get my business "off the ground." We seem to have problems getting clients. At first we had several but now not even phone calls. At Christmas we had a holiday decorating job at a new bank that literally fell into our laps. We were invited to the Open House and thought this was a great connection. We also ran an ad in a Christian magazine that goes out all over the state and only got one client from that. In March there was an article in home staging XXXXXX Magazine that featured our business. We felt sure that this would give us a big boost. We have passed out information sheets in a prominent neighborhood, handed out tons of business cards and have our name and contact information on the back of our cars. We have contacted a few real estate companies also. What can we do? We have only been in business about six months. Any suggestions would be appreciated. Thanks for your help.

ANSWER - You are doing all of the right things, but perhaps not the best things. Marketing a business, is a never-ending process, and some methods work better than others. Many methods are short lived (press releases are an example). You get the exposure, and hopefully some instant business, but then it dies off. So you have to take the actual press release and use it. Send a copy of your release or magazine article to every person on your list. This gets your name back in front of them. Most people have to hear about your business and services repeatedly before they respond or start talking about you to others.

Second, I notice that the signature of your email has to do with a missionary union rather than your business. Perhaps you want to keep that, but if you want to build your business and use email for contacting and maintain contact, you should put a tagline and the name of your website as your signature, not something else. Third, you are in a consultation/people business. Because of that, you must recognize that the best way to get business is "face to face". It appears you are relying mostly on print and media exposure.

Consultants usually find it easier to garner business by building relationships. Have you called any person on your list, who seems to know many people and invited that person to lunch? Are you doing any entertaining? Are you holding any mini-seminars where you are viewed as the "expert"? Are you staying in touch with the real estate companies?

A real estate broker in my church began sending me greeting cards on a routine basis. I had not indicated any interest at all in refinancing my loan. I sit near him at church, but didn't know him at all. But I kept getting his cards. On the back of the envelope, he affixed a label which says, "OH, BY THE WAY, I'm never too busy for your referrals." Finally, months and months later, I decided to look into the matter. Guess who I called to refinance my loan?

Fourth, look beyond the obvious people: homeowners and agents. The loan broker I just wrote about set me up with his financial consultant for some advice and future business. Have you contacted loan brokers, title companies, home appraisers, landscapers, and the like to build relationships so they can refer you to their clients and vice versa? Did you purchase a copy of "Staging Luxurious Homes" yet. There is an extensive list in that manual of all sorts of organizations you can join and hook up with other professionals and upscale client prospects and build that kind of face-to-face contact I wrote about earlier. Just a thought. I hope this helps. Never give up!! Join the Better Business Bureau, a local press club, and a networking group. Do volunteer work. Meet people and form friendships. Business will come.

QUESTION - I am also finished with my info for my website. My services page is giving me some problems. I have only been able to pull up a few websites locally to see what they may be charging but no pricing is listed. I have also been on competitors sample websites to see what others were doing and maybe 1/3 listed pricing. What do you recommend, listing or not and, of course, I don't know how to estimate staging jobs yet. Help!!!!

ANSWER - This is a tough one to answer. On the one hand, when a person visits a site (at least with me), I like to find all the information I'm looking for right there. I don't want to have to call anyone. I get in the routine that the internet is a private place to look around and that if I want to buy something, all the details are there for me and I shouldn't have to call anyone first. That's kind of annoying and I avoid it.

There is also the question you have to ask yourself: Do I want someone making a decision about me based solely on the strength of my web copy? If so, then I better write great copy. If not, then I better try to motivate them to contact me. But even when they contact you by phone, and the invariable question is, Why much do you charge?, you can lose them at that point because it is a whole lot easier to say "no" or "maybe" over the phone than it is to say it in person.

On the other hand, if you post your pricing on the web, you're not bothered by people who aren't really interested in your help and who are just time wasters.

So my suggestion is to consider having a range of low to high, with explanation, and urge them to call you with their questions. If you get a call or email, then they already have an inkling of the costs involved and moving forward is easier than if the person has absolutely no knowledge of what they might need to pay out. You'll have to test different approaches, different pricing, etc. just like all new business owners. What works for one might not be good for you, and vice versa.

QUESTION - I have a question for you regarding ordering, as I am getting ready to order 'Decor Secrets Revealed' as well as 'Rearrange It' and then I know you recommend getting the Consultation Checklist Guides from the Home Staging for Yourself so I was thinking since I have an upcoming Staging consultation job (yep! already, however it is an acquaintance realtor who I am going to do a 'freebee' for since it is my 1st official job and she knows it and realizes I am a bit green and she's the only one that will know that!) I thought that perhaps the guidelines would be good to have...do you think so & if I read right, they come as a booklet so is there a way to sort of business personalize them at all?

I am a little nervous and overwhelmed and still trying to figure out what exactly to bring to my first consult, since I don't have any 'official' materials and would like to know if you were going to say in a nutshell what I would need to take along to this first consultation what would that be?

I just want to say again how much I am enjoying your training approach and material so far and I am so excited to get into it further. I just want to make sure I am ordering what is right for me as I am going to focus on the Staging as well as the Redesign aspect. I am feeling a bit like I need to hurry and at least get a website name up so that I have a website email address to put on my business cards etc. I have done the license end and gone as far as inquired about my insurance, I wanted to do a few jobs before I actually put the money out on that. What do you think? I know you can give advice necessarily but I just thought I'd see what your input was on it.

I don't want to take anymore of your time, I realize how busy you are and am thankful to have you on the helping end of my Home Staging questions/dilemmas.

ANSWER - Thanks for the great feedback on the newsletter. Always happy when people feel it is worthwhile. The checklist is available as an 80-page booklet and so, so easy to use in your consultations. It eliminates the need to take notes or to create some plan afterwards. Really helps you do the consultation portion, whether or not you do the full service or not.

Take with you:

- Measuring tape
- Business card
- Digital Camera
- Check List from Home Staging for Profit Manual or Advanced Redesign Manual (assuming you have one or both)

218

- Blank Invoice Form

Worry about the other stuff only if you get hired to do all the labor needed.

QUESTION - I have a question for you. Does your company have any before and after shots that could be used for brochures? We are in the midst of setting up our brochures with a marketing company and are looking for some great shots. Any ideas will be helpful.

ANSWER - Our pictures are not available for use by others. You can purchase pictures, called "stock photos". A Google search will bring up sites that sell images but unfortunately you won't likely find before and after photos. Those you kind of have to earn yourself by doing the work. My advice, though you didn't ask for it, is to hold off on the brochure for now or construct it so you have some good images, just not before and after. You can also create your own by taking shots of rooms in your home, friends, relatives. No one will ever know they are not actual client rooms. Get the room how you want it, take shots from every angle, then either take everything out of the room and shoot that or put it back in a typical manner and shoot that.

QUESTION - I bought the book Rearrange It and want to know if I can still qualify for the certification. I know I must send in pictures of rooms that I have completed. I already have four rooms to be done in the next 2 weeks. Please let me know what else I have to do to be certified.

ANSWER - You can apply any time. I would, however, strongly recommend you take our design training as well, as so many questions on the exam have to do with design. I would recommend these two: Decor Secrets Revealed (ebook) and Where There's a Wall (softcover). Here is summary of what's involved in certification: http://www.decorate-redecorate.com/certified-redesigner.html

---

QUESTION - Hi Barbara, I have a question regarding how to charge for air travel. My client whose pictures you featured in your newsletter this month wants to fly me to Texas to look at a house she just leased. She wants me to see it before she moves so I can tell her what to take and where the movers should put everything. It's a 4-story house so that's why she wants to know where to tell the movers to place the furniture. She is paying for a plane ticket for me to fly in and out the same day. I'm just not sure how to charge for this service and travel time. Also, I'm just wondering if this is really necessary and instead I could go through her current house to tell her what to take and what to leave. But then she wouldn't know exactly what floor of the new home to place the furniture and I would probably lose a larger fee. The other question is – I am a flight attendant who can travel for free but it's space available and would take much longer to get there because my airline doesn't go non-stop. I could also get reduced fares on another airline that does go non-stop. I feel like I'm being deceptive if I don't let her know or if she finds out. Should I just let her know that I am a flight attendant, not to tell her I will fly on my own, but just to be honest? She will also want me to come back after she's moved in so if she knows I can fly for less, I think it would be more attractive to her. I have found that people say a lot when they are excited about something and then it never happens.

ANSWER - As for travel, tack on your normal full day fee, and add a cushion amount to the daily rate because you're going to be working, no doubt, for far more than 8 hours, including travel. You have to account for possible delays and so forth. This woman appears to have plenty of money, so not to be concerned. As for sharing that you're a flight attendant, that's tricky. On the one hand, you'd like to save her some money, but on the other hand, to divulge that you're a flight attendant might diminish her perceived value of you and your expertise. Any person willing to fly you there for a day is not hard up for money and you're not going to get or lose a future job based on what you could save her by getting the ticket yourself. Besides, with having to go and come back stand by, you could incur delays which you'd want to get paid for, so it's kind of a toss up from that respect. However, I also try to do what I feel is in the best interest of the client and that's what I advise you to do. Give her the option and let her make the decision. Your conscience will be clear and she'll know you're the kind of person that has her best interest at heart. That will go farther for you in the long run than any possible diminished respect at not being "full time" in the business. Tell her you're phasing out of the airline business but keeping your foot in the door for the free travel perks. That will offset any possible negative, and we don't know if there would be a negative at all. If you build in enough cushion to cover you for delays and such, then you're paid no matter what.

QUESTION - Hi Barbara, I'm just finishing up the book, which I have really enjoyed and most assuredly benefited from. I do, however, share a concern that my insurance agent discussed with me today. Have you ever heard of liabilities/claims, etc. made by sellers that their home was not sold faster or for a better price; claims repeatedly marketed in the home staging industry?

ANSWER - You have to address that on the front end, in writing. What you promise is that "most" homes have experienced the benefit but that you cannot guarantee, nor could any stager guarantee that the home would in fact sell faster or for more money. You talk in generalities and percentages. Your attorney should be able to craft an agreement that protects you on this issue. If you deal with the issue in advance, you should not have to be concerned about this issue. Of course, you should always have a client sign or initial that they understand you cannot predict the future.

QUESTION - I am going to locate all of my stuff. Should I just start reading and then give you guys a call when I am done? Or is there a test? How do I get certified?

ANSWER - If you are a Gold or Diamond trainee, certification is guaranteed (we'll work with you if you need extra help). Just let us know when you purchased the program and we'll send you the appropriate exam. If you're not a Gold or Diamond trainee, and did not pay the fee to be processed, you must first pay the application fee and then we'll send you the exam (staging or redesign) or you can purchase the double certification and get both. Here is what you should study: Decor Secrets Revealed, Where There's a Wall There's a Way, Rearrange It, Home Staging for Profit, Arrange Your Stuff. If you study these you'll pass the exam easily, no matter which one you take. Besides it's an honor system exam and an "open book" exam with no time limits. Then you'll need to prepare and submit a portfolio.

QUESTION - I got a call from a gal that wants to put her vacant house on the market in April, and she'd like a quote from me as far as staging it is concerned. I'm fortunate to have inherited a LOT of extra (classic/traditional) furniture and would probably only need to add a few pieces to my inventory to get the job done; if, in fact, that's the way I should handle it. The home is a 2-story and has a dining room set in it and nothing else. The house was on the market for 90 days this past fall, and, since I have my real estate license, I can check out the photos online to get a good idea of what I'm up against before I even see the house. I figured I'd make a list of what I have that I'd likely use, tour the house, figure out what else I'd need to either find/buy or rent, get a quote from a local mover to capture that expense; and then "run the numbers". The homeowner's wanting a ballpark figure from me as to cost, but I'm thinking I need an idea of what she'd feel is within her budget, before I move very far forward at my end. I also need to better understand just how much staging she wants done. I've seen homes that were done VERY minimally and others where every single room was staged just like a display. My thought at this point is that I really need to ask her a LOT more questions to better define her requirement. I also figured I could make a few calls to figure out what others are charging for this sort of thing in the area. Lastly, because I'm just starting out, this would be a great start for my 'before and after' portfolio. That said, I'm not sure how much I should look to make in terms of actual profit, if anything at this point. Any ideas for me?

ANSWER - First, never do anything this size for free. I advocate a few freebies in redesign when you're starting out, but not in staging, particularly for a vacant home. It's just too complicated and you'll hate the project if you're not making some money on it.

Yes, you need to ask more questions on the front end. I like your research plan you have outlined. As for budget, I'd come straight out and say, "What's your budget?" If she says she doesn't have one, then that's usually not true. Everyone knows what they feel they can spend; they just might not want to tell you.

You then say, "I know it's difficult for you, but I need to get a general idea of what you feel comfortable spending to do it right. I'll give you 3 plans to choose from, but it's extremely helpful to me to get your feedback. I want to be extremely sensitive to your wants and needs. I'm sure you must have a range in mind of what you feel comfortable spending."

Then be silent. Wait for an answer. Wait. Wait. You'll pick up cues from her at this point, even if she doesn't give you an actual figure. So then you tell her that you need to jointly agree on a budget and that you will work very hard to bring the whole project in under budget, but you've got to know what level of service she feels she needs and can afford. Wait for an answer.

When (and only when) you feel you've gotten her to commit herself as far as numbers go do you proceed with your own numbers. Then give her your "pre-set" plans to choose from. When you have "pre-set" plans on paper, people have respect for you as a professional and don't feel like they are going to be charged any more than anyone else would be charged.

It's kind of like going into a store. Would you rather shop at a store where everything has a price tag or would you rather shop at a store where nothing is priced and the clerk looks you over first before telling you how much an item sells for?

I, for one, would rather shop at a store where everything is priced already and I'll walk out of stores where I feel I'm being put in a "negotiating" situation over price. It's one of the reasons I hate to go car shopping and usually opt for the non-negotiating dealerships, once I've done my research and know what the car is roughly valued at before hand.

Now that's an over simplification, I know, but whenever possible I think it best to have some pre-set plans and policies that you adhere to and that you convey to your client prospects. It's company policy, you see.

Experts will tell you to set your prices according to: 1) what you feel your time, expertise and energy are worth; 2) what the "so-called going rate in your area is"; 3) what you feel the "market" will bear; 4) the overall complexities of what is "normal". But I say: Go with #1.

Look at my own online business. I have Bronze, Silver, Gold and Diamond levels and consumers can choose the level they want. I outline very carefully what is included in each level. My pre-set 9*pricing moves up and down. When you are new it seems overwhelming. And you'll make mistakes and get hurt a little on pricing, perhaps. But as you do more, you'll be able to hone in on the level of pricing that works best in your area – based on YOUR worth, not someone else's.

PRICE LEVELS

Develop 3 levels of service. Basic, Designer, Deluxe. Calculate the amount of time you think each level will involve, by the day, not the hour (that will drive you crazy). Apply your daily rate. Then add a little extra time as a cushion and allow a rate for that.

Then calculate all the "out of pocket" costs, like rental fees, etc. and price these separately, including a fee for the use of your private furnishings. So you have let's say:

BASIC   DESIGNER   DELUXE PLAN $XXXXX
PLAN $XXXXX   PLAN $XXXXX

Spell out what is included in each plan. Then separately itemize a range for rental fees, etc. $XXXXX.XX - $XXXXX.XX. Explain what this fee is for and what it does and does not include, and that it is only an estimate, and may move up or down depending on the needs of the project.

She can then easily choose the Plan she wants, knowing that some costs will be extra and that those cannot be pre-calculated. What ever she chooses, stay within the budget. People will usually focus and lock in on the lowest figure in a range, so make sure you have adequately covered yourself on the minimum figure.

Contact Information and Referrals

Barbara Jennings
Decorate-Redecorate.com
Box 2632, Costa Mesa, CA 92628-2632

Just as I have been teaching you to ask for referrals and testimonials, I myself would appreciate any testimonials and referrals you might share with me. Please write me and tell me what part of this manual has benefited you the most. If you are confused by any part, please let me know that too as I will send you a personal response and try to clarify any section that is confusing to you.

And please tell your friends about Decorate-Redecorate.com and about the free discussion forum. I'm never too busy for your kind referrals.

If you find any errors in this manual or any links that do not work, I would appreciate it if you would take a minute and write me at **support3@barbarajennings.com**. We've tried to catch the errors, but try as we may some pesky ones just get by us anyway. Periodically we have to change our email address due to an abundance of spam mail, so if the above one doesn't work, please visit our "About Us" page for the current contact links. You'll find that page at **http://www.decorate-redecorate.com/about.html**.

If you found this manual to be helpful to you, whether you're just starting out or whether you already have a staging business of your own, please write me and share your experiences. And don't forget to join my free discussion forum at: http://www.decorate-redecorate.com/smf.

God bless you and may you prosper mightily.

Other Helpful Resources

Resources you might find helpful:

The Art of Display by Katherine Sorrell

A Passion for Collecting by Caroline Clifton-Mogg

Rich Dad, Poor Dad by Robert Kiyosaki

Getting Everything Out of All You've Got by Jay Abraham

How to Win Friends and Influence People by Dale Carnegie

Accounting for Dummies by John A. Tracy, CPA

Creating Web Pages with HTML by Patrick Carey

Consultative Selling by Mack Hanan

Small Time Operator by Bernard Kamaroff

How to Set Your Fees and Get Them by Kate Kelly

Guerrilla Marketing - Secrets for Making Big Profits from Your Small Business by Conrad Levinson

Conceptual Selling by Robert B. Miller and Stephen E. Heiman

Passion for Excellence by Thomas J. Peters and Nancy Austin

In Search of Excellence by Thomas J. Peters

Honest Business and *Marketing Without Advertising* by Michael Phillips and Salli Rasberry

Running a One-person Business by Claude Whitmyer, Salli Rasberry and Michael Phillips

FrontPageWorld.Com - Pre-designed Web Sites

Wordtracker.Com - Key Words and Phrases Search Tools

PlanetOcean.Com - Tips on optimizing your web site

Bonuses and Sample Forms

Disclaimer

This manual is sold with the understanding that the publisher and author are not engaged in rendering legal, insurance, tax, marketing or other professional advice or services. All attempts have been made to give accurate information as it has pertained to the author's own experience and background. If legal advice or other expert assistance is desired, the services of a competent attorney, CPA, insurance agent or other professional person should be sought.

Neither the author nor the publisher can be held accountable for errors or omissions, nor similarities to other business books or training programs. Some of the information regarding actual clients has been altered because of privacy issues. Any resemblance to actual persons or businesses is, therefore, purely coincidental. Standard business practices, marketing techniques and management philosophies, common to all consultants and other types of businesses, have been discussed and presented. The author and publisher further accept no responsibility for inaccurate or misleading information, nor for omissions of any kind, particularly with regard to training using hazardous materials or tools.

All readers of this manual are forewarned to use discretion and take all security and safety measures possible, paying close attention to all instructions given by various manufacturers for their own products.

These forms are free for your personal usage in your business as a re-designer, home stager or consultant, but are not to be used for training purposes or resale under any condition.

Estimate

CLIENT NAME _____ DATE _____

ADDRESS _____ TIME _____

CITY _____ STATE ____ ZIIP ____ NEAREST CROSS STREETS _____

DIRECTIONS TO HOME _____

QTY	SERVICES PERFORMED/PRODUCTS RECEIVED	REGULAR PRICE	SPECIAL PRICE

Invoice

CLIENT NAME   DATE

ADDRESS   INVOICE NO.   TIME

CITY   STATE   ZIIP   NEAREST CROSS STREETS

DIRECTIONS TO HOME

QTY	SERVICES PERFORMED/PRODUCTS RECEIVED	REGULAR PRICE	SPECIAL PRICE

Subtotal
Sales Tax
Delivery
Total

Control Form

CLIENT NAME _____ _____ DATE

ADDRESS _____ SIDEMARK

CITY _____ STATE ____ ZIIP ____ NEAREST CROSS STREETS

□ Redesign Services
□ Paint/Color Consultation
□ Home Staging
□ Holiday Decorating
□ Exterior Holiday Decorating
□ Home Shopping Services
□ Relocation/Move-In Services
□ Blended/Downsized Services

□ Public Speaking/Workshops
□ Floral Arrangements
□ Artificial Plants
□ Live Plants
□ Custom Framed Art
□ Custom Throw Pillows
□ Custom Area Rug
□ Custom Candles

□ Reorganization
□ Exchange Program
□ Refinish Furniture
□ Reupholster y
□ Restoration Services
□ Other_____
□ Other_____
□ Other_____

RETAIL SALES	SALES TAX	SHIPPING	DELIVERY/INSTALL	TOTAL SALE
$	$	$	$	$

Vendor/Suppliers/Labor Used

NAME OF SUPPLIER	WHOLESALE AMT	FREIGHT/OTHER	CK NO.	AMT PD	BALANCE DUE
_____	$	$	#	$	$
_____	$	$	#	$	$
_____	$	$	#	$	$
_____	$	$	#	$	$
_____	$	$	#	$	$
_____	$	$	#	$	$
_____	$	$	#	$	$
_____	$	$	#	$	$

Due Date_____ Delivered On _____ Invoice No. _____

Deposit Rec'd_____ Amount $_____ Balance Due $_____

Project Completed □

NOTES_____
_____
_____
_____

Independent Contractor Agreement

Agreement is made this _____ day of _____, _____(year).

The following outlines our agreement:

_____

_____

_____

_____

You have been retained by _____,
as an independent contractor for the project of

_____

_____

_____
You will be responsible for successfully completing said project according to specifications stated below.

The project is to be completed by _____.

The cost to complete will not exceed $_____.

You will invoice us for your services rendered at the end of each week □ or month □.

We will not deduct or withhold any taxes, FICA or other deductions. As an independent contractor, you will not be entitled to any fringe benefits, such as unemployment insurance, medical insurance, pension plans, worker's compensation insurance, or other such benefits that would be offered to regular employees.

During this project you may be in contact with or directly working with proprietary information which is important to our company and its competitive position. All information must be treated with strict confidence and may not be used at any time or in any manner in work you may do with others in our industry.

Please submit information regarding:

Worker's Compensation Insurance Policy for Employees (Name of Company, Phone and Policy No.)

_____

Liability Insurance Policy (Name of Company, Phone and Policy No.)

_____

Signatures:

Independent Contractor_____
Date_____

Company Representative_____
Date_____

Change Work Order

Hirer: _____

Contractor: _____

Contract Date_____

1)   The Hirer authorizes and the Contractor agrees to make the following work changes to the above dated contract:

_____

_____

_____

_____

_____

_____

_____

_____

_____

_____

_____

_____

_____

_____

_____

_____

_____

2)   The agreed additional charge for the above change(s) is:
$_____.

Dated: _____

_____
Hirer

_____
Contractor

Authorization to Return Goods

Date_____To_____

      Please allow this letter to acknowledge that we shall accept certain return goods for credit. The terms for return are:

1.   The aggregate cost value of the goods subject to return shall not exceed $_____.

2.   We shall deduct _____% of the cost price as handling charges to process the return goods, crediting your account.

3.   All return good shall be in re-salable condition and represent goods we either currently stock or can return to our supplier for credit. We reserve the right to reject non-conforming goods.

4.   Return goods must be invoiced and are subject to inspection and return approval before shipment to us.

5.   If good are shipped via common carrier, you shall be responsible for all freight costs and risk of loss in transit. Goods shall not be considered accepted for return until we have received, inspected and approved said goods at our place of business.

6.   Our agreement to accept returns for credit is expressly conditional upon your agreement to pay any remaining balance due on the following terms:

_____
_____
_____
_____
_____

You understand this return privilege is extended only to resolve your account balance and is not necessarily standing policy. Thank you for your cooperation in this matter.

                             Very truly yours,

_____
Company Representative

_____
Company   Address

_____
City   State   Zip

Consulting Services Agreement

The parties to this agreement are as follows

_____
Consultant

_____
Client

The Consultant will consult with and advise Client in the following matters:

FEES & EXPENSES:

The consultant's fee for the above services is $_____ based upon an estimated duration of _____.

A retainer (if any) of $_____ is immediately due and payable.

Future payments will be made upon completion of this assignment or as stipulated below:

_____

_____

Expenses will be reimbursed upon receipt of the invoice.

Signed this _____ day of _____, _____(year).

_____

Consultant Signature   Client Signature

_____
Date

Conditional Sale Agreement

The undersigned Purchaser hereby purchases from

_____

_____
(Seller)

the following goods and/or services:

_____
_____
_____
_____

Sales Price
    $_____

Sales Tax (if any)
    $_____

Finance Charge (if any)
    $_____

Insurance (if any)
    $_____

Shipping/Freight/Delivery/Installation
    $_____

Other Charges (if any)
    $_____

Total Purchase Price
    $_____

    Down Payment $_____

    Other Credits $_____

Total Credits
    $_____

Remaining Balance
    $_____

    Annual Interest Rate _____%

The amount financed (if any) shall be payable in _____ installments of $_____ each, commencing _____ from date hereof.

Seller shall retain title to goods until payment of the full purchase price, subject to allocation of payments and release of security interest as required by law. The undersigned agrees to safely keep the goods, free from other liens and encumbrances at the below address, and not remove goods without consent of Seller.

Purchaser agrees to execute all financing statements as may be required of Seller to perfect this conditional sales agreement.

At the election of Seller, the Purchaser shall keep goods adequately insured, naming Seller loss-payee.

The full balance shall become due on default; with the undersigned paying all reasonable attorneys fees and costs of collection. Upon default, Seller shall have the right to retake the goods, hold and dispose of same and collect expenses, together with any deficiency due from Purchaser, but subject to the Purchaser's right to redeem pursuant to law and the Uniform Commercial Code.

THIS IS A CONDITIONAL SALE AGREEMENT.

Accepted:

_____   _____
Seller   Purchaser

_____
Address

_____
City   State   Zip

Release of Mechanic's Lien

FOR GOOD CONSIDERATION, the undersigned contractor or subcontractor having furnished materials and/or labor for repairs, additions or construction at the premises known as

_____,

standing in the name of

_____

do hereby release all liens, or rights to file liens against said property for material and/or services or labor provided to this date, with it acknowledged however, that this discharge of lien shall not necessarily constitute a release or discharge of any claim for sums now or herein after due for said materials and/or services, if existing.

This release shall be binding upon and inure to the benefit of the parties, their successors, assigns and personal representatives.

Signed this _____ day of _____, _____ (year).

In the presence of:

_____   _____
Witness   Company Name

_____   _____
Address   Contractor/Subcontractor

_____   _____
City, State, Zip   Address

                                                     _____
                                                     City, State, Zip

Moving Check List for Seller

One Month Before Moving

Pick up a Change-of-Address Kit from the Post Office and fill out and give or send to: www.VisitRelocationCentral.com, as well as:

- Friends and Family
- Banks
- Insurance companies
- Credit card companies
- Magazines and newspapers - cancel local newspaper delivery
- Doctors, dentists and other providers - transfer drug prescriptions
- Past employer - for W2 forms

Make Lists of what is to be moved and what is to stay:

- Take a look around the house. Start to think about what you don't want to take with you.
- Use up perishable foods
- Sell, donate or hold a garage sale for unwanted items
- Large appliances?
- Outside furniture?

For full service moves:

- Get written estimates from several moving companies
- Will the movers pack for you?
- What items won't they move?
- Get appraisals of high-value items in case of future claims

For do-it-yourself moves, make arrangements for truck rental and moving help, and buy packing supplies:

- Boxes
- Packing and masking tape
- Markers
- Newspapers
- Twine
- Start packing boxes. Mark boxes clearly as to contents and room to be placed in.

Mark "Open First" clearly on boxes containing important items to be unpacked first:

- Dishes
- Pots and pans
- Alarm clock
- Bedding
- Special toys
- Towels
- Light bulbs
- Plates
- Tools - hammer, pliers, wrench

Phone and make arrangements for picking up your important records:

- Birth
- Doctor
- Dentist
- Legal
- Optician, optometrist
- School - make sure your records have the school's imprinted seal
- Veterinarian

Things to do concerning your new residence:

- Inquire about your new state's auto licensing procedure and auto insurance rates.
- Check with your insurance company about transferring coverage to your new home.
- Arrange to have a sitter watch your children at their house on moving day.
- Contact your child's new school and notify them of your upcoming move.
- Contact the Chamber of Commerce of your new town. Request a relocation package.

Two Weeks Before Moving

Pack your vital documents in one place:

- Passports
- Military records
- Mortgage records
- Marriage license
- Birth certificates
- Vehicle titles
- Stock certificates

- Insurance papers
- Bank records
- School records
- Medical records
- Tax records
- Business legal records

Make arrangements to disconnect your utilities and to connect them at your new residence. Get refunds for any deposits made. Have meters read. Give new address for them to send their final bill.

- Cable - return box if necessary
- Electric
- Gas

- Internet access
- Telephone
- Water

One Week Before Moving

Take hazardous materials to your local hazardous material disposal facility, such as:

- Lawn mower gas
- Snow blower gas
- Paint
- Aerosol cans

Plan what goes in the car with you:

- A car tune up might be a good idea, depending on the distance of the move.
- Toys and games for kids
- Special breakable items or collections
- Important documents and records
- Change of clothes and toiletries for your first day
- Vacuum cleaner - if you want to clean right away
- Toilet paper
- First aid kit
- Food kit with bottled water, cereal, bananas

Special Arrangements:

- Make travel arrangements for your pets and plants.
- Purchase moving insurance if you have valuable antiques and collections.
- Arrange to have a sitter watch your children at their house on moving day.
- Make arrangements for cleaning.

Close out your bank accounts:

- Checking
- Savings
- Safe Deposit Box
- Start a new bank account in your new town.
- Transfer account from current bank?

The Day Before Moving

- Defrost, clean and air out your refrigerator.
- Clean your stove.
- Pay the moving company by credit card. If there is any problem, you can enlist the credit card company's help in resolving a payment dispute if you feel you are entitled to one.
- Purchase traveler's checks for other possible expenses.
- Pack your former town's phone book for future correspondence.
- Get a simple breakfast ready for the morning of the move.
- Pick up ice and beverages for moving day.
- Take down curtains and curtain rods.
- Get a good night's sleep!

Moving Day

- Strip your beds.
- Moving company - will they disassemble?
- Show movers around. Make sure your possessions to be moved are inventoried with them.
- Write "subject to further inspection for concealed loss or damage" on contract when you sign to protect yourself should you find damage while unpacking.
- Get all keys together. Put in a safe spot.
- Make sure moving van driver has correct address, phone number and directions. Confirm delivery date with him.

- Check all rooms one last time. Remember closets and cupboards, basement and garage! Make sure all windows and doors are locked.
- Check the exterior of the house for water hoses and gardening tools.

More Moving Tips to Reduce Stress

- Save receipts, as moving expenses can be tax-deductible
- Return items like library books or rented videos
- Retrieve important items you may have lent out
- Back up computer files onto disk before packing away your system
- Arrange for the transfer of medical and dental records
- Pack a cooler with drinks and snacks for the trip
- Hire professional packers -- or be your own pro.
- When you pack, you open up the hidden places. Packing up the attic, basement or a messy kitchen drawer, will force confrontation with a part of the self that has not been visited for years. Often "I have" means saying "I am."
- Professional packers do not make judgments. They do not sort through your closets, sighing over the pants that won't fit anymore. They pack everything.
- People often say, "I wish we had taken that lamp (or bookcase or chair) with us. I could really use it now."
- Unless you are on a really tight budget, err on the side of taking too much. There will probably be a Goodwill or a Salvation Army in your new city.
- If you pack your own household, follow the example of the pros.
- Pack everything. Pack fast. And don't make judgments.
- Pack an emotional first aid kit.
- When you undertake a voyage into the unknown, you pack sun block, Band-Aids, and insect repellent, as well as the basic medications for unexpected encounters with local food and water. Prepare an emotional first aid kit to deal with stresses you are likely to encounter.
- Coping phrases to repeat when feeling frazzled: 'Let go and relax." "I can deal with this." "I face the future with confidence."
- Tapes of meditation and visualization to help you calm down when you have a bout of anxiety.
- A book or a tape of yoga exercises or some physical activity you enjoy.
- Favorite photos of friends, family, places and pets.
- Phone numbers of friends and family who can be called when you really need to talk to a familiar voice: someone to laugh with; someone who will listen; someone who just moved a year ago and can offer good advice
- Honor your new home.
- As you unpack, play your favorite music and enjoy your favorite foods.
- Arrange one room -or one corner of the room-to look familiar.
- Some people create a ritual of settling in to make the new house their own.
- The top deck is your creativity, your connection with air and sunlight.
- Creative activity will unfreeze your mental processes. Write a journal entry or a novel, paint a picture or a sketch, stitch a quilt, make a piece of jewelry.
- The lower deck is your connection to the physical. Exercise gives you confidence and energy. Don't be surprised if you feel less homesick after a long walk, a good run or a challenging aerobics class.
- Make new friends by doing what you love.
- Fill your life with activities that will be creative and fulfilling. When you nurture yourself, you communicate strength and confidence to others. If you are seen as vulnerable and needy, you will attract negative people and negative experiences.

- Remember what you promised yourself you'd do "after we've moved." You may have promised yourself you'd get a dog or take opera lessons. Don't wait.
- By doing this while you're in transition you'll have more energy and vitality rather than if you wait until you're "settled."
- Be your own best camp counselor.
- Camp counselors, boarding school directors and drill sergeants know: If you fill the time, newcomers won't have time to be homesick. Set up time to explore your new city. Create a demanding schedule and stick to it. Map out your itinerary for the first few weeks before you move so you'll begin to set a structure to your days. By staying busy you'll give yourself a chance to acclimate to your new home more quickly.
- Celebrate everyday life.
- Think small.
- A walk around the lake.
- A perfect cup of coffee in a nearby coffee shop.
- A friendly face at the local hardware store.
- Listen for the moments when you say, "I could get used to this..."
- Ask The Big Move Question: Can I still be who I am after I move?
- Moving often interrupts identity. The secret to a successful move depends on how you answer the question, "Can I still be me?" To answer this question, write ten "I am" statements about yourself -- anything from "I am a mother" to "I am a dog-owner" to "I am friendly and outgoing." Before you move, ask yourself, "How will this list change after I move?" After you move, ask, "How has the list changed? Am I pleasantly surprised?"
- Embark on an adventure. Believe it or not, many people love to move and describe their relocation as a great adventure! I like to compare moving to time travel. After the moving van has been loaded, you go to sleep in a bare room. The next morning, you wake up to a world of exciting possibilities.
- No matter what happens, you will find at least one pocket of joy in your new life. Everyone I've interviewed said, "Even when I was happy to move, there was always something I hated to leave behind. And even when I dreaded moving, there was always something wonderful that I had never expected."

A Warning and Word of Advice

Some stagers and re-designers ask their clients to leave the home before doing a project. They like the idea of bringing them back later for some kind of "unveiling ceremony". I think this is quite foolish for a couple of reasons.

1) Any time you're in someone's home all by yourself, you open yourself up to possible litigation and accusations of theft or breakage or other things you're not guilty of doing. In a society where people are quick to sue, this is an unnecessary risk you should weigh carefully.
2) When your client is not there, participating in the process or at least available for questions and answers, you are eliminating a great time of bonding that could be taking place were the client in the home during the staging or redesign. So I would ask you, "Why would you not want to take every opportunity to bond with your client that you get?" Bonding and making and nurturing a friendship is one of the most important aspects to getting a great testimonial and follow-up referrals that you can have. It seems rather foolish to me to ask the client to leave for any reason.

Example of Room Feature List

Room_____

Measurements of Room

_____

This Room's Outstanding Features Include:

- _____
- _____
- _____
- _____
- _____
- _____
- _____
- _____
- _____
- _____
- _____
- _____
- _____
- _____
- _____

Box Content List

Room_____

- From Location
    - Upstairs
    - Downstairs
    - Attic
    - Basement
    - Garage
    - Front Yard
    - Back Yard
    - Side Yards

Contents of Box:

- _____
- _____
- _____
- _____
- _____
- _____
- _____
- _____
- _____
- _____
- _____
- _____
- _____
- _____
- _____
- _____
- _____
- _____

Open House Check List

Exterior

- Pick up and store all toys and lawn tools.
- Pick up and store all pet gear.
- Remove all vehicles from curb and anything else that obstructs view.
- Sweep or hose down driveway and walkways.
- Use leaf blower to give tidy look.
- Clear away debris from pool or hot tub.
- _____
- _____
- _____

Interior

- Empty all wastebaskets.
- Pick up dirty clothes and place in hamper near washing machine.
- Clear all counters, desks, table tops and store papers away.
- Remove any hazards, such as throw rugs, extension cords, small toys.
- Store away all personal items found in bathrooms.
- Clear away all children's toys and straighten beds and room.
- Vacuum, sweep and dust all rooms.
- Sterilize counters, bathtubs, showers, sinks.
- Wipe off all tables and put chairs under tables and desks.
- Arrange fresh floral arrangements in every room.
- Make sure all rugs are cleaned and properly placed.
- Open all shades, curtains, drapes (unless you need to detract from something outside).
- Open some windows to freshen the rooms.
- Turn all lights on in every room.
- Turn soft music on.
- Add fragrance oils in bathrooms and kitchen.
- Add the fragrance of fresh baking.
- _____
- _____

Last Minute Home Enhancement

- Place linens and flower arrangements on table.
- Arrange a book, game or hobby project on the table.
- Turn off all televisions.
- Arrange guest towels in bathrooms and kitchen.
- Put thermostat or air conditioner at a comfortable level.
- Re-check every room for cleanliness and orderliness.
- Leave home and take your pets with you.
- _____
- _____

Moving Sale Tips

- Choose a weekend date for most traffic.
- Thoroughly clean all items for sale.
- Create feeling of outdoor "fair", not a garage sale.
- Tie colorful balloons to a tree, mailbox or back of chairs.
- Play light energetic music.
- Dress all helpers in the same color t-shirts or matching hats or aprons.
- Be early in your preparations. Shoppers tend to ignore the start times. Be sure the garage sale is properly promoted.
- Make and display large, easy to read signs for neighborhood.
- Avoid hand lettered signs.
- Use stencils or a computer to produce signs of quality. Professional looking signs will pull in weekend drivers.
- Place sequence of 3-4 signs on main street in both directions.
- Place additional signs or arrows on side streets.
- Price items based on what you would be willing to pay if you were a buyer.
- Condition is a key factor in pricing. Visit other garage sales to get comparisons and a feeling for what works and what doesn't.
- Leave ample space around all sections for easy browsing.
- Label areas such as: Antiques, House wares, Sporting Goods, Clothing, Toys, Linens, Special Bargains
- Tri-fold clothes for tables; hang on hangers for others.
- Make sure all clothing is labeled for sizes.
- Tie linens together in sets with colorful ribbons.
- Use plastic zip-lock bags to display small items.
- Don't over display tables. If too many items on a table, they will look like junk and sell for less.
- Attach description with dates and pertinent information on antiques and collectibles.
- Watch out for people arriving in a group of two or more. Some may be decoys to distract you while others pocket items without paying for them.
- Put tablecloths on tables; put area rugs or vinyl tarps on cement.
- Use bright colored sale stickers that are easily found.
- Write descriptions and uses out and attach to unusual items.
- Check tables and other areas periodically throughout the day to make sure displays look attractive.
- As inventory at the front of the driveway sells, replace it with other merchandise. This helps attract the "drive by" customers and encourages them to stop and look.
- Place sun umbrella in outdoor table to provide shade when needed.
- Be sure to lock the house. Don't let buyers have opportunity to enter your home or your garage. Block off access and peering eyes to contents in the garage.
- Wear a belted fanny pack around your waist with plenty of change. Do not have a change box on a table.
- Place some folding chairs at the check out tables and other places for you, your helpers or customers to sit.
- To easily test electrical appliances, have a power cord handy.
- Keep extra marker and price stickers in your fanny pack to replace lost stickers and for end of the day markdowns.

- Prepare snacks and meals in advance for yourself and helpers.
- Place like kinds together: clothes on hangers on rack, dishes and accessories on tables, furniture all in one section.
- Place several calculators around for easy processing.
- Have plenty of bags of various sizes.
- Have plenty of newspapers on hand for wrapping and bagging.
- Have plenty of scotch tape on hand.
- If you don't have much help, have a wrapping table next to the checkout so people can wrap things themselves.
- Be prepared to bargain. Many people assume negotiation is part of the process.
- Remember the goal is to sell out, if possible.
- Remain open, enthusiastic and cheery.
- Consider offering light refreshments, such as lemonade in paper cups.
- Have a "kids only" section.
- Toward end of day, offer extra discounts for multiple purchases.
- Discount all prices by 50% in the last hour. Make a sign to display just for final hour.
- Donate what doesn't sell. Don't keep it.

Place classified ads for most cost-effective method of advertising. Use the words "Moving Sale" rather than "Garage Sale". Don't list phone number. Give ample descriptions of the type of merchandise for sale: dining table, silver, sewing machine, twin beds, quality house wares, children's clothes, games, books, tools, lawn furniture, camping equipment and much, much more! Free lemonade. Give address, start and end times, and nearest cross streets.

Expect some people to arrive BEFORE your stated start time. Be prepared early.

Sample Features and Benefits Handout

Welcome To
1738 E. Elm Street
Any Town, Any State
$###,###
This is an outstanding family home in Any Community
Suburbs
Located 15 Minutes from Downtown and 10 Minutes from
Major Mall
Located in Nationally Acclaimed AnyName School District
Nestled in Prime "AnyName" Neighborhood

A floor plan that ushers in the outdoors
while facilitating a great family interaction
incorporated with casual living atmosphere.

FEATURES (example)

- **A Large Family Oriented Backyard for Plenty of Family Fun and Entertaining** - Two sets of patio doors make access to the back yard easy. An oversized cement block is a fabulous place to enjoy a gazebo or a game of basketball (hoop included) or badminton. Beautiful planter along the perimeter creates plenty of opportunity for layered floral arrangements. Mature perennial plants. Professionally designed landscape.
- **Spacious Gourmet Kitchen with New Ceramic Tile Floor and Counters** - Enjoy cooking for your family in this luscious, open kitchen. 1 Built-in Microwave. Dishwasher, disposal, compactor. Convection Oven. Plenty of storage for all your fine cookware. Cooking island, rollouts.
- **Master Suite with Freestanding Fireplace on Marble Inset** - Snuggle in bed and read your favorite book while enjoying a warm, toasty fire. Walk-in closets. New marble vanity, newly restored sunken bathtub. Double wide floor to ceiling mirrors.
- **Walnut Paneled Family Room** - Beautiful walnut paneling. Brick fireplace. Large double wide patio doors. Plenty of shelves to display all your beautiful accessories. (Possible Den/Office)
- **New Wall to Wall Carpeting Throughout**
- **New Counter Tops in Kitchen and Bathrooms**

Neighborhood Life Style Sheet

Offer to provide a neighborhood life-style sheet that seller can make copies of for buyers to pick up.

Features to Include:

- **Neighborhood Information** - List number and ages of children on the street, include summary of adult occupations and interests, neighborhood associations, neighborhood watch programs.
- **School and Daycare Information** - Write about quality of schools. Get information from school district. If they have brochures, pick up some copies to leave out. List public and private schools: preschool, elementary, middle and high school. List community colleges and 4-year colleges and universities. Include information on school bus pickups.
- **Babysitters** - Include a list of local babysitters if you have them.
- **Recreational Information** - Include list of parks, sports clubs, recreational clubs, community playhouse theaters, movie theaters, museums, libraries.
- **Local Retailers** - List your favorite stores in the area: grocery stores, department stores, dry cleaners, shoe repairs, video stores, hairdressers, restaurants (fast food and sit-down), children's stores.
- **Access to Freeways**. State the directions to and average time of travel to freeways.
- **Utilities** - List contact information for electricity, gas, water/trash and give the average costs for the home.
- **Personal Letter** - Include a description of living there and how the town or city has changed and improved. Emphasize the quietness, any favorable weather assets, length of time neighbors have lived there, special opportunities not available elsewhere and so forth. Share some of your best memories living in the home.

Nifty System for Generating Referrals

When you enter the consulting field, and you are a staging or redesign consultant, you will quickly realize the value of getting referrals from your clients, your prospects, people you know, family, friends, co-workers, other trades people, and so forth. Referrals are very powerful and help to grow your business and sustain your business.

But getting referrals doesn't happen automatically. You've got to take a pro-active approach and put systems into place that help you generate them. Here is one of the best systems you can utilize. It's a system of sending out regular greeting cards to people you want to stay in touch with.

I recently decided to award the refinance of my home to a mortgage broker who consistently sent me greeting cards. His approach was very, very low key. Since it wasn't by email or phone, I never got upset when I received his periodic greeting cards. What he was doing was reminding me, ever so gently, and every so often that he was still in business and ready to help me if I needed him. So after getting his cards a few times, and when the timing was right, I contacted him to handle the processing of my loan application.

If you will capture the power of sending out greeting cards to the people you want to do business with and people you want to refer business to you, you will go a very long way in building, growing and sustaining your business for the long term. There are services that will do most of the work for you such as www.sendoutcards.com. Would appreciate it if you would put me down as the referring party who sent you.

Typical Package Deals You Might Rent for Projects

24 Pieces

- 1 Sofa
- 1 Love Seat
- 1 Cocktail Table
- 2 End Tables
- 2 Lamps
- 1 Centerpiece
- 2 Framed Art
- 1 Dining Table & 4 Chairs
- 1 Dresser & Mirror
- 2 Night Stands
- 2 Lamps
- 1 Headboard
- 1 Queen Bed
- 1 Ficus Silk Plant (6')
- 1 Twin Bed
- 1 Twin Headboard
- 1 Twin Nightstand
- 1 Lamp
- 1 Table Plant

18 Pieces

- 1 Sofa
- 1 Chair
- 1 Cocktail Table
- 2 End Tables
- 2 Lamps
- 1 Centerpiece
- 1 Dining Table & 4 Chairs
- 1 Dresser & Mirror
- 1 Night Stand
- 1 Lamp
- 1 Headboard
- 1 Queen Bed
- 1 6' Tree
- 1 table plant
- 1 floor lamp
- 1 console table

13 Pieces

- 1 Sofa
- 1 Chair
- 1 Cocktail Table
- 2 End Tables
- 2 Lamps
- 1 Dining Table & 4 Chairs
- 1 Dresser & Mirror
- 1 Night Stand
- 1 Lamp
- 1 Headboard
- 1 Full Bed

Typical Terms and Conditions

The following sample agreement is merely that: a sample. I do not provide it with any kind of guarantee or warranty of protection for either the home stager, the seller nor any agent. I provide it merely as a loose guideline only. If you're drawing up a contract for a home owner to sign, where you will rent the furnishings, you should hire a reputable attorney to construct one for you to make sure you are fully protected in your state, province or country.

- _____permits the Hirer to hire the Goods for a minimum specified period until such time as the hiring is determined as hereinafter provided. The Hirer shall be a mere bailee of the Goods and no property in them shall pass to the Hirer.
  - An inventory of the furnishings will be provided by _____ for the Hirer or his/her representative at the time of installation. (b) The Hirer shall ensure that there is adequate and suitable goods vehicle parking close to the delivery address and that the property is suitable for the goods required without any dismantling or alteration to the goods or the property. (c) The Hirer is responsible for ensuring that adequate adjacent services are provided for any electrical appliances and for the commissioning of such equipment.
  - The Hirer shall during the continuance of the hiring keep the Goods in good and substantial repair and condition - reasonable wear and tear only expected - and keep the Goods at the address where installed by _____. (b) No goods shall be removed from the above declared hire location unless written authority is given by _____.
- Hirer shall during the continuance of the hiring pay to _____, without previous demand, the agreed charges by monthly standing order or other direct credit. Initial payment to be made prior to installation. A transport charge providing for one delivery and one collection is included.
- The Hirer shall not during the continuance of the hiring sell or offer for sale, loan, rental, sub-let, or otherwise assign the possession of the Goods.
- The Hirer shall protect the Goods against any distress, execution or seizure and shall indemnify _____ against all losses, cost, charges, damages and expense incurred by reason or in respect thereof.
- The Hirer shall not interfere with, adapt or alter the Goods in any way.
- The Goods are to be insured - without excess - by the Hirer during the period of hire for perils including loss or damage by accidental fire, lightning, explosion, storm, flood, escape of water from any tank, pipe or apparatus, impact and theft. The Hirer shall keep _____ indemnified against all loss and damage incurred to or by the Goods howsoever caused.
- The Hirer shall pay to _____ all expenses incurred by or on behalf of _____ in ascertaining the whereabouts of or repossessing the Goods and of any legal proceedings taken by or on behalf of _____ to enforce the provisions of this agreement.
- The Hirer shall at all reasonable times on prior written notice to the Hirer's address permit _____, its servant and agents to have access to the Goods for the purposes of inspection or repair.
- The Hirer may determine the hiring at any time by giving seven working days notice in writing of the preferred collection date to _____ and on the expiry of such notice _____ shall remove the Goods without hindrance and refund the Hirer the balance of any complete months rent paid in respect of any period after the date of termination, the minimum hire charge excepted.
- _____ may determine the hiring at any time by giving one month's notice in writing to the Hirer's address and at any time without notice (a) upon the Hirer making default in the punctual payment of the hire charge, (b) on the making of a receiving order in the bankruptcy against the Hirer the calling of a meeting of his creditor or his executing any assignment for their benefit, (c) upon the Hirer going into liquidation whether voluntary or compulsory except for the purpose of reconstruction or amalgamation or suffering a receiver to be appointed of any of its assets, (d) upon any execution being levied upon the Hirer and not satisfied within seven days. In any such case _____ may retake possession of the Goods and for this purpose may enter upon the premises where the Goods are installed and such determination by _____ shall not affect the right to recover damages for any breach of this agreement before such determination.
- Any notice required or permitted to be given by _____ to the Hirer hereunder shall be validly given if served personally on the Hirer or posted by recorded delivery service addressed to or left at the Hirer's last known address and shall if sent by post be conclusively deemed to have been received by the Hirer 48 hours after the time of posting.
- The expression "The Goods" includes all additions, replacements and renewals thereof and all accessories, components, and addition thereto.
- Any time or other indulgences granted by _____ to the Hirer shall not affect the enforcement of the strict rights of _____ hereunder.
- The Hirer shall pay in advance the security deposit advised by _____. This security deposit will be refunded or credited following the return of the hired items at the conclusion or termination of the hire period provided the Goods are in good and substantial repair and condition—reasonable wear and tear only, as determined by _____, excepted.
- The Hirer agrees that he or his representative will inspect all the Goods on delivery and accept them in new or nearly new condition.
- The Hirer is responsible for any statutory requirements applicable to the goods (eg Television License).
- The above terms and conditions are enforceable under the laws of the United States.

Things to Do List

_____
_____
_____
_____
_____
_____
_____
_____
_____
_____
_____
_____
_____

Phone Calls to Make

_____
_____
_____
_____
_____
_____
_____
_____
_____
_____
_____
_____

Staging Props to Purchase

_____
_____
_____
_____
_____
_____
_____
_____
_____
_____
_____

Vendors to Acquire

_____
_____
_____
_____
_____
_____
_____
_____
_____
_____
_____

Cleaning Products to Acquire

_____
_____
_____
_____
_____
_____
_____
_____
_____
_____
_____
_____
_____

Tools to Acquire

_____
_____
_____
_____
_____
_____
_____
_____
_____
_____

21-Step Business Set Up Check List

☐ Choose Business Name and Domain Name

☐ File Fictitious Business Name Statement

☐ Place Legal Notice of Fictitious Business Name

☐ Open Business Bank Account

☐ Apply for Resale License

☐ Acquire Business License

☐ Create Press Release

☐ Make Business Cards

☐ Create Contact Lists

☐ Get Business Phone and Business Email Address

☐ Create Website (Diamond and Gold trainees get one we'll set up – just submit content)

☐ Join Professional Associations for Networking

☐ Get "Staging Portfolio Secrets" to create a strong portfolio and use it for success

☐ Get "Staging Luxurious Homes" to Market to Affluent, Wealthy homeowners and agents

☐ Get a Supply of 5-10 "Home Staging for Yourself" Checklist Booklets to make consults easy

☐ Call or send promotional cards to all your prospects

☐ Follow up with phone calls to all prospects

☐ Study all training ebooks and/or manuals thoroughly

☐ Redesign or stage your own home, taking before and after pictures

☐ Redesign or stage a couple homes for friends for portfolio

☐ Send out press releases

More Photo Examples

Before

After

Fill just the most glaring gaps and leave the rest of the room simply appointed when staging a kitchen.

Interior Redesign, some times called "one day decorating" or other such terminology, is a closely aligned business you can also run. While the goals are different, many of the processes are

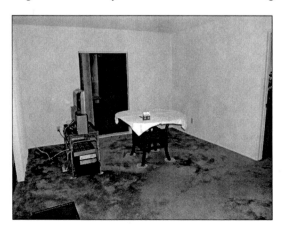

exactly the same. I also teach interior redesign as a business. Here you can see a small apartment that was redesigned after being freshly painted (yes, there is even a market for services in apartments, condos and townhome renters and owners). It doesn't matter if the space is large or small, nor whether the furnishings are new or old. As an interior re-designer, you can help make anyone's dwelling look fabulous just by arranging what they already have in the space.

This bedroom doesn't show very well because it lacks a few finishing touches to make it really come alive. Whether the home is to be staged or redesigned, you can make a significant difference when you know what to do. I haven't dealt with the entire design subject in this manual because it is much too vast a subject to do justice here. But you can see that little changes can have a powerful effect. You just have to know how to achieve them.

The main thing to remember when staging, is that you're trying always to highlight the assets of the home: its architecture, its view, its spaciousness, and its variables. Unlike interior redesign, you'll be looking for a "pared down" look, one that is attractive, but one that doesn't exude too much personality which can become distracting from the home itself. On the other hand, not having enough furniture in a room can have the opposite effect and make the home feel too sterile. So a talented stager knows when enough is enough, using what is already available or adding to the space what is appropriate, attractive and in the right scale.

You may run across homes that have already been staged by a real estate agent who really doesn't understand how to provide such a service or who doesn't have the time or means to do it properly. If the property still stays on the market for a long time, you should approach the agent about lending a hand to make the property present itself in a more enhancing manner.

In this example, the home had been staged by the agent. By re-purposing this bedroom into a nursery, the stager was able to easily suggest another use for a room in an area where many grandparents live and entertain grandchildren.

The scale of the furniture in this room was off. Yes, it makes the room look larger, but also makes the room feel awkward and undesirable. See how much better the room looks after the scale of the furniture has been changed by the professional stager.

Just because a room appears to be a bedroom, doesn't mean it must be staged as a bedroom. Here a different usage is suggested to buyers as the room is turned from a bedroom into a home office. If the view is nice, leave the drapes open. If not, close the drapes.

Unsolicited Testimonials

"Well, if someone needs "proof" that this stuff works...it happened here folks! Barbara, as I mentioned the "whooper house" had been on the market 9 months and needed to sell in 5 weeks or the owner was going to loose her new house that is being built. . . . Saturday afternoon an outside realtor unexpectedly called to see the house. Her clients were relatively sure they were going to put a bid on another house but were willing to look at one more house. The house wowed them and they wrote up a contract that afternoon on this house...!!!! UNBELIEVABLE. Well, being a good realtor, Rosemary, held the open house today, as scheduled, and the owner received another offer!!!! UNBELIEVABLE! Just wanted to share, Candi Hutchison"

***

"Hi Barbara, my client at first just wanted me to stage the main living areas but once we got started, she decided to do the entire house which came out really nice. . . . I got an email from the photographer today that did the tour for the realtor and he wanted my name and information for another realtor who he thinks really needs my help for a 3 1/2 million dollar home!!!
I'm just really excited about this and hope it opens up doors to other projects. Thanks to you for your training and all your very informative manuals which I refer to quite often! - Sharyn Hutchinson"

***

"I had a color consult this week that was a gift certificate that was won at a function I attended. . . . She was sooo happy by the time I left. . . . But most of all I want you to know I could not have done it without my training. You see I have the eye, and the talent however this client is very analytical just by virtue of what she does. She wanted me to explain certain things because she has no talent in this area of decor. She has lovely taste but you know what I mean. The fact that I was able to address issues and explain them in a very professional manner was worth every penny I spent and all the hours of reading. THANK YOU THANK YOU THANK YOU!!!! I will continue to use all my books as reference guides and use them over and over again. GOD BLESS YOU. Happy wishes, Audrey Schechner"

***

"I would like to begin by telling you how much I have enjoyed my Diamond Deluxe Course. Every aspect of the course was above and beyond what I expected. . . . The agents representing the sellers told us we showed the home so much better than the owners. - Marlane Adams"

***

"I was working with one home, and when I was looking to rent furniture the person at the place of my choosing asked where I was getting my certification from. After I mentioned your name and program, she said that she has worked with 2 other individuals from your program. And, she thought very highly of the work being done by these people. Just thought you'd like to know that! - Debi Wheatley"

***

" Thank you for this delightful course. I am enjoying all the materials . . . Even though I have a Home Economics degree and have worked in the home improvement industry for 17 years, I still needed something to help me with my confidence. With my husband's encouragement I decided that what I needed was a course and a certification. I'm very glad I chose yours because I believe that my philosophy of home design is similar to yours. . . . Pam Elkins"

Printed in the United States
215073BV00001B/5/P